W9-ACE-719

Endorsements for

Daring to Ask for More

When Elisha was invited to ask of God what he would, Elisha dared to request a double portion of the Spirit. Pleased with his holy audacity, God granted Elisha's bold petition. God longs for us to pray large, much larger than we do. In *Daring to Ask for More,* Melody Mason has shone the light of God's Word on the path to true revival—*Holy Spirit–inspired, daring, audacious prayer.* I know this book will be a tremendous blessing to many.

Doug Batchelor, President and Speaker, Amazing Facts

If prayer is "the key in the hand of faith to unlock heaven's storehouse" as *Steps to Christ* declares, then Melody Mason's new book is long overdue. *Daring to Ask for More* is precisely God's strategic appeal to this generation living on the edge of eternity—more of the Holy Spirit, much more; more of the character of Christ, much more; more of self-sacrificing love, much more; more of courageous witness, much more. *Daring to Ask for More* indeed! May our hearts be stirred up as never before to seek God through prayer as never before, while there is still time.

Dwight K. Nelson, Senior Pastor,
Pioneer Memorial Church, Andrews University

"So I sought for a man among them who would make a wall, and stand in the gap before Me on behalf of the land" (Ezekiel 22:30, NKJV). Melody Mason, a true intercessor, stands in the gap. She not only writes about prayer, *she prays!* Her faith-filled ministry of prayer and this book, in particular, have made a major impact on my life personally and on the ministry of ASAP Ministries. I believe this book is what every church member, leader, and ministry needs to powerfully move them forward towards greater results of kingdom growth for His glory.

Julia O'Carey, Director, ASAP Ministries

Daring to Ask for More will expand your faith while giving you a down-to-earth practical approach to prayer based on God's Word. At the same time, it will help you to recognize the dangers of counterfeit forms of prayer so you can avoid being swept away by deception in these last days. If you struggle with your prayer life or just want to learn how to go deeper with God on a more intimate level, you have chosen an excellent book to help you reach this goal.

Ivor Myers, Pastor, Author, and President,
Power of the Lamb and ARME Ministries

Deep in our hearts is a desire to walk daily and closely with our God. It is this trusting relationship that forms the foundation for a deepening prayer life—one that dares to ask our Father for more! If you were blessed by Melody's booklet *Praying for Rain,* you will also be inspired and encouraged by this new full book on prayer.

Bob Folkenberg Jr., President,
Chinese Union Mission of Seventh-day Adventist

I have read many books on the subject of prayer, but none touched my heart like this one, so much so that I couldn't put it down! It is inspirational as well as practical and instructional. It exudes "prayer power" that will change your life. It has helped me so much in my prayer life to go deeper and beyond the basics. And it's been thrilling to realize that I can truly dare to ask God for more!

Alice Scarbrough, Arkansas-Louisiana Conference Prayer Ministries

Daring to Ask for More offers fresh insights to answered prayer, success in ministry, and a closer walk with God. This book will encourage you to seek a deeper walk of faith and give you practical tools to help you in the process. *Daring to Ask for More* also gives keys to help us recognize some of the counterfeit revivals sweeping modern-day Christianity as well as how we can avoid them and make sure we are on the right side in this final great-controversy battle.

Melody Mason is a true woman of faith, and she knows what she's talking about when it comes to prayer. Our division has been richly blessed by her prayer ministry. If you talk with Melody, you will find that her enthusiasm and passion for prayer are contagious.

A richer prayer life will bring positive change in our lives—our faith will grow, and our happiness will increase. I am delighted to offer my endorsement for this book, and pray that it will help you to draw nearer to our Savior and Friend, Jesus Christ.

Paul S. Ratsara, President,
Southern Africa-Indian Ocean Division of Seventh-day Adventist

Ellen White wrote, "There is power for us if we will have it. There is grace for us if we will appreciate it. The Holy Spirit is waiting our demand if we will only demand it with that intensity of purpose which is proportionate to the value of the object we seek." How valuable is the Holy Spirit? That isn't the question, is it? Rather, how valuable is the Holy Spirit to us? The answer to that question is measured by the intensity of purpose we invest in prayer. Melody Mason's new book, *Daring to Ask for More,* is driving me to my knees. My needs are so great and my resources so few, what self-righteousness it is to pray so little. Thank you for that push!

Frank Fournier, President, ASI

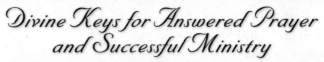

MELODY MASON

Divine Keys for Answered Prayer
and Successful Ministry

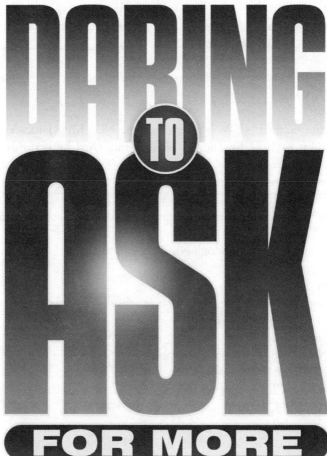

DARING

TO

ASK

FOR MORE

Pacific Press®
Publishing Association

Nampa, Idaho | Oshawa, Ontario, Canada
www.pacificpress.com

Cover design by Gerald Lee Monks
Cover design resources from dreamstime.com
Inside design by Kristin Hansen-Mellish

Copyright © 2014 by Pacific Press® Publishing Association
Printed in the United States of America
All Rights Reserved

The author assumes full responsibility for the accuracy of all facts and quotations as cited in this book.

Unless otherwise noted, Bible texts are taken from the King James Version (KJV).

Scripture marked NKJV is taken from the New King James Version®. Copyright © 1982 by Thomas Nelson, Inc. Used by permission. All rights reserved.

You can obtain additional copies of this book by calling toll-free 1-800-765-6955 or by visiting http://www.adventistbookcenter.com.

Library of Congress Cataloging-in-Publication Data:

Mason, Melody, 1976-
  Daring to ask for more: divine keys for answered prayer and successful ministry / Melody Mason.
    pages cm
  ISBN 13: 978-0-8163-5624-9 (pbk.)
  ISBN 10: 0-8163-5624-6 (pbk.)
  1. Prayer—Christianity. I. Title.
  BV210.3.M373 2014
  248.3'2—dc23

                              2014025002

August 2014

Dedicated

To all those who hunger and thirst for *more* faith, *more* power in prayer, *more* personal victory in daily life, and most of all, *more* of our precious Savior!
Jesus will answer your cries. Keep daring to ask for more!

Blessed are they which do hunger and thirst after righteousness: for they shall be filled.
—Matthew 5:6

Acknowledgments

Pastors and other leaders, there's a message here for you!
Don't skip this!

*I*t is only because of God's providential leading and divine blessing that I have the great joy and privilege of serving Him in full-time ministry today. I say *privilege* because it's not an honor I deserved or earned. I hold no degrees in ministry, nor do I have a radical testimony about being rescued from the epitome of darkness. I'm simply an ordinary Seventh-day Adventist girl born in the dry desert of Ezekiel 37, upon whom God has miraculously breathed and brought to life, *and now put to work*!

Because of this undeserved honor, first and foremost I want to praise **God, my Creator and King,** for His abundant blessings on this project throughout these past months. My prayer is that He will take my feeble efforts and multiply them many thousandfold—for His kingdom glory. I consider myself a pencil in His hand, and my prayer is that He (not the pencil) will receive all the honor and praise for any benefit received through these pages.

I praise God that He's also brought some key people alongside me on this journey. Without their encouragement, mentorship, and support, this book would never have been written. While I can't mention all the names of those who have influenced and inspired me in this writing journey, I'd like to take time to acknowledge a few.

I want to say thank you to **Pastor Paul Ratsara,** who has become my friend, adopted father, and mentor in prayer ministry. Pastor Ratsara, I still remember the day we met at the General Conference. Not long after, you insisted that our prayer team come and work with the Southern Africa-Indian Ocean Division. Since then, I've had the privilege of working with you multiple times in ministry, both in your own Division and at other church leadership events. As you know, your talks, sermons, and personal influence have been the chief inspiration behind this massive writing project. Thank you for humbly allowing me to take these messages and share them with the world. Thank you for believing in me and encouraging me to keep writing, even when I felt inadequate for the task. Thank you for your example in prayer. I'll never forget what you told me about God giving you some of your greatest blessings in answer to long nights of wrestling in prayer, and that the secret to successful ministry is learning to *stay connected to Jesus—daily*! May we all learn from your testimony. Most of all, thank you for challenging me to keep moving forward and keep daring to ask for more by faith. May the Lord receive all glory for every aspect of this project, and may we *remain faithful until He comes to take us home*!

I also want to thank **Elder Ted Wilson and the many pastors, administrators, and ministry professionals** in all levels of leadership throughout our world church, for what you are doing for the Lord. As I've worked more closely with many of you these past few years, my respect for you has deepened as I've come to recognize that *being a pastor or other church leader in this day and age is not easy*! Sadly, the vast majority of us laity in the church not only take what you all do for granted (both in our local congregations and in the higher levels of leadership), but also often make your job more complicated by our murmuring and complaining, just as the children of Israel did for Moses and Aaron. For this I want to sincerely apologize. I want to hold up your arms in prayer—a prayer pleading that God will give you the grace and strength you need to do the work that lies before you at this critical time in earth's history. It is because of *you all* and for *your sake* that I've been compelled to write this book. I write it not only so you will be encouraged and inspired to go deeper in prayer personally (as prayer is "the key in the hand of faith" for every need), but also so that many others will be motivated to join me in holding up *your* arms in prayer. While this work may be a feeble attempt to challenge all of us to deeper prayer, know that it comes from a heart of love and prayer for all—that God's church may stand strong in these final days.

I want to say thank you to my parents, **David and Sylvia Mason,** for their unceasing intercessory prayers for me and for my brothers Homer and Daniel. Mom and Dad, thanks for all those prayers! I'm sure it's because of your prayers that each of us still love the Lord today. We've seen many miracles over the years, but I'm sure that only in eternity will we truly understand how significant your prayers have been in our lives. And yes, Mom, you can cry happy tears now. *My writing marathon is finally over!*

God has blessed me with many other key people who have helped me become who I am today.

I think of **Brian and Karen Holland,** staff at Oklahoma Academy, who gave me a home away from home during my college years and became my second family. Not only did they help me gain a solid spiritual foundation as a young Seventh-day Adventist, but they loved me, mentored me, and held on to me during my struggles in *the spiritual wilderness.* Thank you for your persistent love and prayers!

I think of **Jerry and Yvonne Eller** (along with their children), whose friendship, encouragement, generosity, prayers, and support—even before I was born—have undoubtedly helped mold me into the person of prayer I am today. I love all of you and look forward to eternity together!

I think of my childhood best friends **Valerie Crosier** and **Heather (Cook) Vixie,** who have walked consistently by my side through many adventurous years, encouraging me, praying for me, and supporting my many ministry projects—even when it meant I couldn't hang out with them as much as before. I love you girls dearly and am thankful for your friendship!

I think of my academy roommate **Gabriela (Rusch) Pawlucki,** who modeled daily devotions to me, and in so doing made a profound difference in my prayer life during my teen years. Thank you, Gabe, for living out genuine Christianity!

I think of **Pastor Jerry and Janet Page** and the amazing inspiration they've been in my life, mentoring me in prayer ministry even while busy leaders in the Central California Conference. It is because of this special couple that I started working with prayer ministry at the General Conference and started doing prayer ministry full time. Truly, God is using them to lead our world church into deeper prayer! Praise the Lord! You both have made a huge impact in my life! Thank you, thank you, thank you, from the bottom of my heart!

I can't forget my many prayer partners who have prayed for me, have prayed for this project, and have supported me in various ways behind the scenes during these months of writing:

Pastor Ivor Myers, Dave and Nina, Calvin, Dawn, Kim, and my many other ARME teammates, thanks for the inspiration you've been in my life during this writing process. I couldn't have better partners in ministry. Together we have learned that united prayer really does work. As a result, my life will never be the same. I love you all!

Eric and Leslie Ludy—Thank you for challenging me to keep *daring to ask for more* in my walk with God, and for encouraging me to keep moving forward towards the Promised Land. Thank you also for allowing me to share some of the inspiration in this book that you've shared with me as well as with many others.

Anne Curnow—Thank you for the hours you've spent on this project editing and critiquing! You were the first one to help me with it, and your help has been amazing!

Luis and Tracie Alonso—Thank you so much for following the Lord's convictions, as God has used you to encourage me at crucial times during this writing project.

Alice Scarbrough—Thank you for believing in me and for your encouragement from beginning to end. You've been a blessing, cheerleader, and true friend!

Marian Parson—Thanks for inviting me to become part of the official ARK-LA Conference Prayer Ministries. I've *loved* working with you and the Conference this past year.

Raluca (Stefan) Ril—Thanks for your friendship, and especially for your partnership in prayer—even across the ocean. I rejoice in how the Lord has worked in answer to *our first ten days of prayer* and how He's been using you to impact lives all over Europe.

Chelsey Mittleider—Thanks for always encouraging me in my writing, and for connecting me with a great editor named Steven Winn. It was a *divine providence* on all sides and I praise the Lord for how He's worked through you in this process.

Steven S. Winn—Thanks for taking this project on as my final official editor, initially by faith, simply because you were passionate about the message! Thanks also for your patience and *ever-thankful spirit* along this journey. Just so you know, I will always be the one *most thankful*!

Julia O'Carey—Thanks for being a true friend and prayer partner, even praying with me through the night at critical times this past year while I was writing!

Melissa Miranda—Thanks for inspiring our ARME Ministries team to make prayer a priority! If that hadn't happened, I definitely wouldn't be writing this book today.

Martin and Liana Kim—Thank you both for your friendship and inspiration in prayer, and for constantly encouraging our team to humble ourselves and to *keep going deeper* in prayer.

Joseph and Puteri Astran—Your passion for the Lord, and God's dramatic answers to so many of your prayers in your young adult groups this past year, are amazing! I didn't get to share your testimony in this book, but it will be shared in the future. I love you both!

Teri and Elise Salvador—You are my fellow mom-and-daughter prayer partners rescued from Laodicean Christianity! Your dedication to prayer and willingness to go all out for God has been inspiring. Elise, although you were only fourteen years old when you led prayer at the General Conference with our prayer team that first time—none of the leaders had a clue you were so young—you did it with grace and boldness. I know the Lord has amazing plans for your future!

My **Marshall and Clinton Seventh-day Adventist church families**—Even though I'm gone most of the time in ministry travels, thanks for cheering me on, for praying for me, and for being anxious to get reports when I return.

My **Witts Springs Bible Study friends**—How can I thank you enough for your prayers and support this past year? You've all been a great encouragement and blessing!

My **Bangla Hope family,** especially the **Waids, Shati, Litton, Uncle Gary,** and my girls **Melanie and Savanna**—Thank you all for your prayers across the ocean! Even though I can't be in Bangladesh as much as I would like, know that you are always close to my heart.

And finally, my **Praying for Rain Prayer Partners**—Truly God is hearing and answering our prayers for our church. Let's keep praying! The *rain* will come!

Table of Contents

Part III—Understanding the Battle Over Prayer

Foreword

*O*ne of our greatest encouragements and joys in life these days is witnessing how the Lord is raising up a worldwide movement of young adults on fire for Jesus! Everywhere we travel, we discover young people who are longing to know God personally as never before, young people who are studying His inspired writings to learn what truth is, who are praying with intensity and power, and young people who are obeying Jesus in service in any way that He asks! Because of this, we believe that the last promised Elijah movement is upon us! (See Malachi 4:5, 6.)

Melody Mason is a young friend leading out in this movement! Through her prayer ministry, Melody has been used by God to touch and minister to many of us who work for the General Conference these last few years. She has also ministered to leaders and laity alike throughout the worldwide church. Additionally, she has gathered groups of young adults to come together each year for weeks at a time to bathe the Annual Council[1] in prayer, lifting us all up by name to the Lord. What a blessing!

We first met Melody some years ago as a young nurse asking for prayer as she was still seeking to find God's real calling for her life. We believe that God calls us (each of us who have had a little more time walking with the Lord) to joyfully pray for and mentor our young friends. Because of this, Janet began praying for and mentoring Melody when we were working in the Central California Conference. What a joy it has been to see Melody grow into a profoundly deep Christian disciple who now helps lead a dynamic ministry, has become an author, and serves as a major prayer leader and intercessor for our church in these last days.

In addition to her prayer ministry, Melody has also helped the General Conference's Revival and Reformation initiatives by helping write two mini-handbooks for our major initiatives in united prayer and Bible study. Her first booklet, *Praying for Rain: A Mini-Handbook for United Prayer,* has proven valuable around the world in helping people learn how to pray together unitedly. In fact, there are already nearly half a million copies in print and has been translated into seventeen different languages so far for this booklet alone. Only in eternity will we truly see what God has done because of the many united prayers that His people have been inspired to pray in these last days of earth's history.

We believe that we are fast approaching the time of the final crisis! It is time to intensify our focus on the Lord's call for deeper consecration and heart-searching, wrestling prayer. In fact, in the biblical book of Joel, we are instructed to gather the remnant people, to pray, to fast, and to repent, and as we do this, we are promised that the Lord will do wonders among us, leading to the last great latter rain! Remember, the first Day of Pentecost came after the early disciples met in the upper room doing what Christ had called them to do. Now it is time for us to seek this heart experience again ahead of the final outpouring before Christ returns!

Ellen White said it like this,

> *A revival of true godliness among us is the greatest and most urgent of all our needs. To seek this should be our first work.* There must be earnest effort to obtain the blessing of the Lord, not because God is not willing to bestow His blessing upon us, but because we are unprepared to receive it. Our heavenly Father is more willing to give His Holy Spirit to them that ask Him, than are earthly parents to give good gifts to their children. *But it is our work, by confession, humiliation, repentance, and earnest prayer, to*

fulfill the conditions upon which God has promised to grant us His blessing. A revival need be expected only in answer to prayer.

I tell you that there must be a thorough revival among us. There must be a converted ministry. There must be confessions, repentance, and conversions. Many who are preaching the Word need the transforming grace of Christ in their hearts. They should let nothing stand in the way of their making thorough work before it shall be forever too late.[2]

In another place, Ellen White writes, "More prayer and less talk is what God desires, and this would make His people a tower of strength."[3] What needed words of inspiration!

If you recognize your need for a closer walk with Christ, a walk that includes *more prayer and less talk,* you've come to the right place. This book you hold in your hands will not only challenge you to pray as you've never prayed before, but it will also give you extremely practical tools and specific pointers on how to develop the spiritual discipleship needed as we prepare for Christ's soon coming. This is the *thorough heart revival* we need. We need the authentic Acts upper-room experience, not sometime in the future, but here and now—*today*! Jesus has been waiting a long time to come. He's waiting for our response to His urgent call to get ready to meet Him.

Read this book, follow its counsels, and the power and joy of the Lord will be your strength as you move forward in faith, *daring to ask for more*!

Jerry and Janet Page
General Conference Ministerial Association[4]

Preface

*I*f I told you there was a divine key to success in life and ministry, would you go after it? If I told you that this key is more valuable than all the resources at the disposal of magistrates and kings, would you desire it? What if I told you that this key would open up a whole new world of life and endless possibilities? Would you listen?

Amazingly, this divine key is already in our hands. Indeed, it's been in our hands from the very beginning. The problem is, while we talk a lot about it, most of us haven't yet discovered its true power. To illustrate what I mean, let me tell you the story of an ancient king.

Alexander the Great was a mighty conqueror and king, and although he lived long before the time of Christ (around 300 B.C.), his reputation still lives on today. As history tells us, he conquered all of the "then known world." In fact, it is told, that when he reached Asia, he realized there were no more countries to conquer, and he actually wept.

Besides being a great conqueror, he was also a compassionate ruler. Every year he set aside one day that he called "compassionate day."

As the story goes, on this special day of the year, he randomly selected different people across his kingdom whom he allowed to come and make special requests. They could ask for whatever they wanted or needed. And he would grant their requests. Most people asked for food, clothes, money for medicine, and so on. However, one year, there was a man who *dared to ask for more*! Speaking through the king's spokesman, this man shared his request.

"Can you please tell the king that I want a large palace? And I want . . ." But before he could continue, the king's spokesman interrupted him with irritation. "What impertinence! Don't you see all these people asking for food and medicine? How dare you to think that you can ask the king for a palace!"

But the man continued earnestly, "I want the palace to include a large banquet hall where I can host a celebration, because I have lots of friends. And I want the palace to be well furnished, and I want a special meal prepared." But the spokesman stopped him again, as he was getting more angry.

"I will *not* ask the king for this! This is the most outrageous thing I've ever heard!"

At this point, King Alexander saw the commotion. "What does the man desire?" he inquired of his spokesman.

The spokesman reluctantly turned toward the king and came forward, whispering in low tones that only the king could hear. "King, I'm afraid to tell you this. I can't believe how unreasonable this man is, and I know you will be upset. But he's asking for *a palace*. Not only does he have the audacity to ask for a palace, but he's asking that you'd make a large banquet hall in this palace, because he evidently has lots of friends. And he wants the whole thing to be fully furnished and supplied with food. I'm so sorry. I know this is such an unreasonable request, and I tried to get him to ask for something more reasonable, but he persisted."

King Alexander paused for a moment, then with a large smile on his face, he turned toward the petitioner and enthusiastically replied, "Request granted!"

The spokesman looked at the king in astonishment. "How can you grant such an outrageous request?" he asked in shock.

The king replied, smiling, "You see, all these people are asking for food, for medicine, and for mundane things. They think that's the only thing I can give. But they don't need a king to give them these things. Anyone with extra resources could do these things for them. But this man . . . THIS MAN . . . He's the first man that's really made me feel like the king I am. *For only I can grant such a request!*"

The Bible tells us, "Now unto him that is able to do *exceeding abundantly above* all that we ask or think, according to the power that worketh in us" (Ephesians 3:20; emphasis added). Why do we so often settle for superficial blessings when we serve the King of the universe? Why do we settle for living life three inches below the water-line, barely surviving spiritually, when God is longing to give us so much more?

We are living in the last days of earth's history, and if the gospel is going to go to all the world and Jesus is going to return, things can't continue as they have been any longer. We need a much deeper spiritual experience than we have yet imagined possible. We need a much deeper prayer life. We need a much deeper faith in God's Word. The reality is that we have settled for being *spiritual dwarfs* when God is calling us, modern-day Israel, to become *spiritual giants* standing in the gap, interceding for the lost.

Unfortunately, Satan knows the power that there is in God's Word. He knows the power that there is when we pray. In fact, he knows better than most Christians the *unlimited spiritual possibilities* that are within our grasp if we look to God in faith. Because of this, *he will do anything he can to keep us from genuine faith-filled prayer*! At the sound of fervent prayer, we are told, "Satan's whole host trembles."[1] They tremble because they know they will suffer loss.

Because of Satan's hatred for God's Word and true earnest prayer, he's created a maze of deceptions to counter God's work, and he's been all too successful. I will take some time in this book to talk about some of these subtle deceptions creeping into modern-day Christianity and how we can avoid them. I will also talk about what it means to have true faith, and how we can become so firmly grounded in God's Word that no storms can blow us over; and how we can pray with bold confidence knowing that God is hearing and will answer our prayers.

My fervent prayer is that this book will launch you on the most incredible journey you've ever taken—into the endless frontier of spiritual possibilities that God has waiting for you. I encourage you to keep your Bible near so you can look up the verses I reference. His Word will be our foundation, launching pad, and the fuel with which we move forward in successful prayer and ministry. As I'm sure you will soon discover, God is just longing to pour out His Spirit and just longing to do so much more in your life than you've ever imagined possible for His glory. And the key that opens the door to all these possibilities is within your grasp! It is prayer, faith-filled earnest prayer, for we are told, *"Prayer and faith will do what no power on earth can accomplish."*[2]

So with Bible in hand, let the journey upon our knees begin—the journey of faith—as we humbly and audaciously *dare to ask God for more*!

Part I

The Power and Privilege of Prayer

Chapter 1

The Sky Is Not the Limit

Increasing Our Capacity to Believe

> *For my thoughts are not your thoughts, neither are your ways my ways, saith the LORD. For as the heavens are higher than the earth, so are my ways higher than your ways, and my thoughts than your thoughts.*
> —Isaiah 55:8, 9

When I was a kid, one of my favorite things to do was to camp out under the stars with my cousins. I didn't want to sleep in a tent because I loved looking at the stars, and I still love looking at them today.

When I look up at the twinkling stars in the night sky, I can't help but be amazed at the expansive universe that stretches out far beyond the ability of the human eye to see. I know that I am not alone in wonder and awe, for I'm sure that countless generations throughout history have also looked up seeking to understand the vastness of the starry cosmos. Our solar system is just a pinpoint in the Milky Way Galaxy, which is a cosmic ocean dotted with an estimated four hundred billion stars. And the universe beyond sparkles with billions more galaxies![1]

Truly the heavens *do declare* the glory of God and the firmament *does show* His handiwork! To show the majesty of God, the prophet Isaiah gives us a glimpse of who God is in comparison with who we are: " 'For as the heavens are higher than the earth, so are My ways higher than your ways, and My thoughts than your thoughts' " (Isaiah 55:9, NKJV).

But just how far are the heavens above the earth? Have you ever stopped to think about it? While God's power cannot be measured by human standards, let's pause here a moment. As we know, the basic unit of measurement in the universe is a light-year. To understand the significance of a light-year, let's do some simple mathematical calculation.

Scientific research has shown that light travels at an amazing speed of 186,000 miles per second, which, according to NASA, is so fast that in the time it takes to snap your fingers, light can circle the earth over seven times.[2] That's pretty fast, but we are just getting started!

In one minute, light travels a little over 11 million miles. If we multiply that by 1,440 (the number of minutes in 24 hours), we find that in one day light will travel a little over 16 billion miles. If we multiply this by 365 days, we find that in a year light travels a whopping 5.9 trillion miles. And that, dear friends, is just *one* light-year!

According to scientific calculations, the outer edge of the observable universe is estimated at forty-six to forty-seven billion light-years[3] away—a distance so vast that we can't even begin to comprehend it. But even the best human calculations don't come close to accurately measuring God's expansive universe, much less His immeasurably vast love. Inspiration tells us, "The mightiest intellects of earth cannot comprehend God. Men may be ever searching, ever learning, and still there is an infinity beyond."[4]

When Abraham began his journey of faith, not knowing where he was going and questioning whether he would ever have a son, God took him outside his tent one night and asked him if he could number the stars. "Look now toward heaven, and tell the stars, if thou be able to number them: and he said unto him, So shall thy seed be" (Genesis 15:5). Abraham could only shake his head in awe and wonder, just as we do today. And yet the Bible tells us that God not only knows the number of the stars, He also calls them all by name (Psalm 147:4).

While Abraham couldn't comprehend God's promise, he believed His Word. As a result, "Therefore sprang there even of one, and him as good as dead, so many as the stars of the sky in multitude, and as the sand which is by the sea shore innumerable" (Hebrews 11:12). Amazingly, God is still fulfilling His promise to Abraham today.

As we begin to understand the magnificent God we serve, we might echo the cry of King David: "When I consider thy heavens, the work of thy fingers, the moon and the stars, which thou hast ordained; What is man, that thou art mindful of him? and the son of man, that thou visitest him?" (Psalm 8:3, 4).

Hard as it is to comprehend, our God, who stretched out the heavens by His great power, is mindful of us. He is not only mindful, but He has also created us and commissioned us with a holy calling! We are to be co-laborers with Him. We are to be a light to the Gentiles, to open the eyes of the blind, and to set free those locked in darkness (Isaiah 42:5–7).

Nothing honors God quite as much as when we have faith for the completion of His work, faith that sees far beyond our own ability and grasps His infinite resources—for we are told that nothing is too hard for Him (Jeremiah 32:17). Inspiration assures us, "The power at God's command is limitless."[5]

Limitless? Do we comprehend what this means? When it comes to God, the sky is not the limit; the universe is not the limit. *There are no limits*—except for the limit of our faith! "We have too little faith. We limit the Holy One of Israel. We should be grateful that God condescends to use any of us as his instruments. For every earnest prayer put up in faith for anything, answers will be returned. They may not come just as we have expected; but they will come—not perhaps as we have desired, but at the very time when we most need them."[6] If we truly realized how big our God is, we would have a lot more faith to move forward in His work. We would also have a lot more faith when we pray.

Let me share the testimony of a humble man named Golden. This ongoing modern-day miracle story has inspired and challenged me as no other.

The impossible becomes possible

Golden Lapani grew up as a practicing Muslim in Malawi, Africa.

After becoming sick and being sent home to die, he was preparing for the end when he had three dreams. In each one he saw Jesus and was told distinctly, "If you want to be healed, become a Christian."

So he began studying the Bible and not long after became a Seventh-day Adventist Christian. Not only was he healed, but the gospel changed his life! He began to preach enthusiastically about Christ wherever he went and many were converted. This wasn't an easy task, for his former friends, feeling that he had apostatized, tried to kill him multiple times. But God always delivered him. Deciding to serve God full time, he left his career as a biology teacher and took up farming so he could dedicate more time to preaching.

Back in Malawi, working and preaching as a layperson, he brought at least eight thousand people to Christ, 50 percent of these coming from the Muslim background. In another area, he had similar blessings. Many considered the area to be impossible to evangelize, as there were only eighty Seventh-day Adventist Christians and there had been no new baptisms in quite some time. Undaunted, he began to pray and work.

After preaching the gospel for about five weeks, almost three thousand were baptized. In less than two months, miracle after miracle began to happen! In the last twenty-seven years, Golden has led many thousands to Christ.

In the powerful book *Christian Service,* Ellen White writes, "The Lord Jesus is our efficiency in all things; His Spirit is to be our inspiration; and as we place ourselves in His hands, to be channels of light, our means of doing good will *never be exhausted.* We may draw upon His fulness, and receive of that *grace which has no limit.*

"When we give ourselves wholly to God, and in our work follow His directions, He makes *Himself* responsible for its accomplishment."[7]

What a faith-boosting promise—to know that when we are living in the will of God, we have access to resources that will *never be exhausted,* and to the grace *which has no limit*! But not only that, *He Himself* will be responsible to see His work accomplished. He doesn't delegate here! Do we truly recognize the gifts we've been given for the accomplishment of God's work today?

Golden is a living testimony to God's glorious grace, *which has no limit*. Those of us in the West may say, "Well, that's Africa! Doesn't the gospel work always spread like wildfire there no matter who is working?" Not necessarily! Some of these areas where Golden has worked are difficult regions where they haven't seen church growth in years. Furthermore, Golden doesn't rush people to the baptismal pool. He allows only those to be baptized who are grounded in the truth because he wants the conversions to be lasting.

According to him, the secret of his success is simple. It is Bible study, fasting, and much prayer! He often wakes up long before dawn to pray, and sometimes he prays for seven hours a day!

Think of all the programs, training materials, multimedia presentations, and other evangelistic resources we often feel are necessary to win souls to Christ. Yet we still fall short in accomplishing what one man accomplishes with only prayer, childlike faith, and trust in the Word! Training materials and resources are good; if we have them, we should use them. But we cannot trust in them for success. "The laws of Christ's kingdom are so simple, so compact, and yet so complete, that any man-made additions will create confusion. And the more simple our plans or work in God's service, the more we shall accomplish."[8]

God is not in the business of mastering methods. He wants to be the Master of men and women. When He has once captured the heart, the sky cannot limit what He will do through the life of even *one fully consecrated person*. "There is no limit to the usefulness of the one who, putting self aside, makes room for the working of the Holy Spirit upon his heart, and lives a life wholly consecrated to God."[9]

We may not all be called to be preachers or evangelists, but *all of us are called* to share the good news of the gospel. God is waiting for His people to recognize their spiritual need and wake up to the possibilities so He can do something—something much greater than what happened at Pentecost, something much greater than what happened with our early Advent pioneers, and something much greater than what we see happening today. The Bible tells us, "With men it is impossible, but not with God: for with God all things are possible" (Mark 10:27).

Are we ready? Are we praying? Are we really in earnest to receive the power of the Holy Spirit that will enable us to complete His work?

According to our capacity to believe

We are told in the book *The Desire of Ages:* "Only to those who wait humbly upon God, who watch for His guidance and grace, is the Spirit given. The power of God awaits their demand and reception. This promised blessing, claimed by faith, brings all other blessings in its train. It is given according to the riches of the grace of Christ, and He is ready to supply every soul *according to the capacity to receive*."[10] This is the secret to receiving the oil of the Holy Spirit in answer to prayer. It is given according to our capacity to *receive*. It is also given according to our capacity to *believe*! "If thou canst believe, all things are possible to him that believeth" (Mark 9:23).

We don't understand the great God we serve because we have grown complacent and satisfied as Christians. We have grown content with superficial Bible study, superficial devotions, and superficial prayer. We've grown content with a superficial relationship with the King of kings. As a result, we are satisfied when we receive superficial answers and superficial blessings.

God wants to reveal Himself to us, He wants to do more, but He can't, because we don't believe Him for more! Ellen White laments, "Just so long as the church is satisfied with small things will it fail of receiving the great things of God."[11] Instead of being content where we are spiritually, let's start asking Him for *more* in prayer! Let's start believing Him for *more* by faith! Let's start searching *for Him more* in His Word! As we will discover in the Bible, *the sky is not the limit* to who our God is or what He can do.

So let's move forward on this incredible journey of faith! Let's start *daring to ask God for more*!

Chapter 2

The Great Paradigm Shift

Learning to Pray Like Men and Women of Old

> *Thus saith the LORD, Stand ye in the ways, and see, and ask for the old paths, where is the good way, and walk therein, and ye shall find rest for your souls.*
>
> *—Jeremiah 6:16*

Throughout the Bible we find amazing story after amazing story of answered prayer. The Bible is so full of astounding miracles that it's no wonder many modern-day scholars and intellectuals scoff in disbelief. When have we seen manna falling from heaven or encountered a talking donkey? When have we wrestled with an angel, seen an ax head floating to the surface of a stream, or watched the dead raised to life? Since when have God's servants been swept away in chariots of fire?

If we take time to read through the record of prayers found in the Bible, we will find an amazing pattern. When God's people prayed, He almost always answered with a Yes. Only a handful of times did He say

No. In the church today, it seems that God saying Yes is the exception and not the rule. If God says Yes to a prayer, we get so excited that we keep repeating it for weeks and months because it is so rare and special. If God answered Yes so often in Bible times, what has changed today?

A big part of the problem today is that we approach God's Word with doubt. We may be thinking, *We can't take these Bible stories too seriously because that was Bible times, and today is different. God couldn't possibly work the same today.* So we edit Scripture and filter it through our modern-day thinking. But has God changed? No, of course not! He does not change. His Word is still just as true today as when these amazing events occurred. He was a God who answered prayer in Bible times, and He is still the same God today!

The Bible clearly states that we serve a God who hears our prayers. This should give us great confidence in prayer. However, all too often, we still don't believe. And this is a problem because having confidence that God really does hear and answer prayer is vital to our spiritual success today. One of my favorite verses comes from 1 John 5:14, 15: "And this is the confidence that we have in him, that, if we ask any thing according to his will, he heareth us: And if we know that he hear us, whatsoever we ask, we know that we have the petitions that we desired of him."

In this verse, we find a key to answered prayer: *praying according to God's will.* But what does this really mean? Referring to this passage, Ellen White writes, ". . . We must ask for the things that He has promised, and whatever we receive must be used in doing His will. The conditions met, the promise [of answered prayer] is unequivocal."[1]

When you read the Bible, you soon discover a pattern. God is love. He is after the salvation of souls. He is after the establishment and building up of His eternal kingdom, where no more sin or sorrow will be seen. He's not interested in coddling our flesh or prospering us so we can hoard salvation for ourselves. This would be contradictory to His benevolent nature. But if we are praying according to His will and for His glory, that the work can go forward and that more souls can be saved, we can pray boldly and with confidence, even in the face of human impossibilities.

This is pretty simple! However, let's examine this concept a little further.

A new look at "if-it-be-Your-will" prayers

It's common practice for us to end our prayers with, "And we ask all these things according to Your will. Amen." This is as it should be because we cannot demand God to do anything. We must always pray in humble submission to His will. "Let men pray that they may be divested of self, and may be in harmony with heaven. Let them pray, 'Not my will, but thine, O God, be done.' Let men bear in mind that God's ways are not their ways, nor His thoughts their thoughts."[2]

However, could it be that we don't fully understand what God desires to teach us through His invitation, "Pray according to My will, and My answer will be Yes"? Could it be that "If it be Your will" has become only a tagline that we throw on the end of our prayers just to be safe if things don't turn out the way we hope?

The Bible records Joshua's prayer when he commanded the sun to stand still: "Sun, stand thou still upon Gibeon; and thou, Moon, in the valley of Ajalon" (Joshua 10:12). Wouldn't it have been wise to end his bold prayer with, "If it be Your will, O God"? That way he would have been protected if the sun did not obey. But for some reason, he did not pray this way.

When Joshua prayed that the sun would stand still, he already knew that this was according to God's will because God had promised him that his enemies would be overthrown. However, the key here is that he had spent significant time seeking the will of God prior to making that bold request. Then, instead of sitting back in calm complacency, waiting for God to deliver, he went to work, and as he worked, he prayed. "He [Joshua] did all that human energy could do, and then he cried in faith for divine aid. The secret of success is the union of divine power with human effort. The man who commanded, 'Sun, stand thou still upon Gibeon; and thou, Moon, in the valley of Ajalon,' is the man who for hours lay prostrate upon the earth in prayer at Gilgal. Men of prayer are men of power."[3]

To pray with Joshua's bold confidence, we must know the will of

God. And the only way to know the will of God is by learning to know *Him personally through His Word.*

This is not about impulsiveness in prayer but rather about being rooted biblically upon a solid foundation. This means we are praying in alignment with God's will as revealed in His Word.

Ellen White tells us,

> The man who is working according to God's plan will pray, "Let it be known this day in my work for suffering humanity that there is a God in Israel, and that I am thy servant. Let it be seen that I am working, not according to my own impulse and wisdom, but according to thy word."
>
> When man places himself in this attitude, and realizes that he is working out God's plan, and that God is working out His plan through him, he is in possession of divine power, which knows nothing of defeat. All the power of counteragencies is of no more account than the chaff of the threshing floor.[4]

E. M. Bounds, well-known for his inspirational life of prayer and for practicing what he preached, made prayer a priority in his life from 4:00 A.M. to 7:00 A.M. for many years. "As breathing is a physical reality to us so prayer was a reality for Bounds."[5] He authored numerous books on prayer that have blessed and impacted thousands. He writes:

> Much time spent with God is the secret of all successful praying. Prayer which is felt as a mighty force is the mediate or immediate product of much time spent with God. Our short prayers owe their point and efficiency to the long ones that have preceded them. The short prevailing prayer cannot be prayed by one who has not prevailed with God in a mightier struggle of long continuance. Jacob's victory of faith could not have been gained without that all-night wrestling. God's acquaintance is not made by pop calls. God does not bestow His gifts on the casual

or hasty comers and goers. Much time with God alone is the secret of knowing Him and of influence with Him. He yields to the persistency of a faith that knows Him. He bestows His richest gifts upon those who declare their desire for and appreciation of those gifts by the constancy as well as earnestness of their importunity.[6]

Do we have that bold confidence and persistency of faith gained from knowing God personally as did Joshua and others? Is this the pattern of our prayer life? If not, we should pray that God would take us deeper.

The great paradigm shift

A paradigm is the basic assumptions, ways of thinking, and methodology of a group. As Adventists, we hold a certain paradigm when it comes to faith, the gospel, biblical doctrines, evangelism, and lifestyle—and we base all these on the Word of God. But has our biblical paradigm become warped by the culture in which we live today?

We have lost much of the power that believers in ages past experienced simply because our paradigm has shifted away from our biblical foundation toward the doubt and skepticism embraced by much of modern society. Thus, if our lives and ministries are going to change for the better, we desperately need a "great paradigm shift" in our spiritual walk and faith.

Insanity has been defined as continuing to do the same thing and expecting to receive different results. If we want to see different results, if we want to see the kingdoms of this world shaken as in the days of Pentecost, if we want the latter rain to soak our lives and ministries, if we want to see the gospel go to all the world so we can go home, *something* has to change about the way we are living and doing ministry. That something is *us*—how we live *and how we pray!*

The modern church recognizes that something needs to change. However, the changes it advocates are not all supported by God's Word. The answers we desperately need are not found in the latest and greatest innovative techniques, in programs, or in some new type of mystical prayer. No, the answers we need are found in the examples of the men and women of old. The Bible tells us, "Thus saith the LORD, Stand ye in the ways, and see, and ask for the old paths, where is the good way, and walk therein, and ye shall find rest for your souls" (Jeremiah 6:16).

We've only begun to uncover what made the prayers of God's people during Bible times so powerful. We will continue to study this topic further in the next chapter. But let us pause right here today, going to our knees and asking that God would give us a new paradigm in prayer—*His* paradigm. Let's ask that He would make us men and women of faith who pray with boldness and confidence according to His will *because we've taken time to learn His will.* Let's pray that kingdoms will be shaken for His glory.

We may be seasoned prayer warriors or only babes in the faith, but let us all *dare to ask for more.*

Chapter 3

Walking With God in Prayer

What It Means to Be a Friend

> *And the scripture was fulfilled which saith, Abraham believed God,*
> *and it was imputed unto him for righteousness:*
> *and he was called the Friend of God.*
>
> —James 2:23

M y friend Valerie and I have been best friends since we were about seven years old. Not only did we grow up having fun together, but in our adult years we've lived together, traveled together, done missions together, cried our hearts out together, and more. We've come to know each other pretty well. When Valerie looks at me, I can often guess what she is thinking. And the same is true when I look at her.

Now distance separates us, but our friendship remains strong. We talk often, sometimes daily, and of course, no introductions are necessary. We recognize each other's voice instantly, and right away we begin to share what is on our hearts, picking up right where we left off from the last conversation. When we struggle, we share each other's pain, and when we rejoice, we share the joy. We've been friends through thick and thin for many years now, and I'm not worried that Valerie is going to dump my friendship if I say or do something wrong.

This is how our relationship with God should be. He wants to abide with us through His Spirit. He wants to be part of our daily lives! If we truly know Him, no introduction is necessary when we pray. He recognizes our voice instantly and we recognize His. And we begin right away to share our hearts with Him, picking up right where we left off. If we are upset, we share this with Him. If we have a disagreement with Him over something, we talk it out. If we are sad, we cry on His shoulder. There's no danger that God is going to leave us and walk away!

Just like best friends, we can be so close to God that we can read His eyes as we go throughout our day. Psalm 32:8 says, "I will instruct thee and teach thee in the way which thou shalt go: I will guide thee with mine eye." When we are at the store, we might pick up something we shouldn't buy. We are not on our knees in prayer at that moment, but since we've been spending daily time in His Word, we will at once see His eyes of disapproval: "Don't buy that. You don't need that!" Or seeing someone in need, His eyes will tell us, "Yes! She needs a word of encouragement! Go and talk with her."

God is not some genie in the sky to whom we give our heavenly shopping list or whom we call only in an emergency. He is to be our Friend who walks with us and talks with us day by day. And no matter where we are or what we are doing, our hearts should constantly be turning to Him.

In the book *Steps to Christ,* we are told, "Prayer is the opening of the heart to God as to a friend. Not that it is necessary in order to make known to God what we are, but in order to enable us to receive Him. Prayer does not bring God down to us, but brings us up to Him."[1]

Not only can we communicate with God as we would a friend, but the more we communicate with Him, the more He will begin to share His own heart with us, as well.

If we keep the Lord ever before us, allowing our hearts to

go out in thanksgiving and praise to Him, we shall have a continual freshness in our religious life. Our prayers will take the form of a conversation with God as we would talk with a friend. He will speak His mysteries to us personally. Often there will come to us a sweet joyful sense of the presence of Jesus. Often our hearts will burn within us as He draws nigh to commune with us as He did with Enoch. When this is in truth the experience of the Christian, there is seen in his life a simplicity, a humility, meekness, and lowliness of heart, that show to all with whom he associates that he has been with Jesus and learned of Him.[2]

We need more of this fresh simplicity in our walk with God. When we are struggling or in difficulty, rather than consulting our human best friends, we should *first* go running to God with our burdens. He is truly the best Friend we could ever have!

What it means to be a friend of God

It is one thing to say that God is our Friend. But it's quite another for Him to say that we are *His*! If we are *His* friend, it means that He knows we love Him and that He can trust us with His heart.

This is how it was with Abraham. Abraham didn't have just a quiet, private relationship with God. He was known throughout his country as being a friend of God's. The Bible records this as a legacy of Abraham's life: "And the scripture was fulfilled which saith, Abraham believed God, and it was imputed unto him for righteousness: and he was called the Friend of God" (James 2:23). For me, *that* title outshines all other ministry titles.

God and Abraham were so close that God allowed him to reason with Him regarding His plans. Consider their conversation recorded in Genesis 18:20–33 about the pending destruction of Sodom and Gomorrah. Have you ever wondered what would have happened if Abraham had continued pressing God further than he did? Would God have spared the cities for only *one or two* righteous people? Maybe Sodom and Gomorrah's door of probation would have stayed ajar a little longer because of the importunity of God's friend Abraham.

Abraham is not the only person who had such a close relationship with God that he could reason with Him. Moses walked and talked with God daily. Exodus 33:11 records, "The LORD spake unto Moses face to face, as a man speaketh unto his friend."

One day while they were speaking, God got very angry because down in the valley the children of Israel had made themselves a golden calf to worship. After all that God had done for them, after all the times He had delivered them, after He'd opened the waters before them and miraculously fed them with manna, they still doubted that He was able to lead them to the Promised Land. Then they turned to another god.

In building the golden calf, the Israelites annulled their covenant with God. Their sin forfeited His favor. He told Moses, "Now therefore let me alone, that my wrath may wax hot against them, and that I may consume them: and I will make of thee a great nation" (Exodus 32:10).

Moses objected and began to plead with God. "God, this doesn't sound like You! Are You going to exterminate Your people after all You've done to bring them this far? Your enemies will say, 'Ah, this God, He brought His people out from Egypt, yet instead of blessing them mightily, He destroyed them.' God, it will cause Your enemies to misunderstand who You are. This *can't* be the best plan. Please don't do this!"[3] Astonishingly, Moses capped off his objection to the Almighty's plan by asking Him to repent! "Turn from thy fierce wrath, and repent of this evil against thy people" (verse 12). And how did God respond to His friend's audacious request? "And the LORD repented of the evil which he thought to do unto his people" (verse 14).

Consider what is written about this story in the book *Patriarchs and Prophets*:

> If God had purposed to destroy Israel, who could plead
> for them? How few but would have left the sinners to their
> fate! How few but would have gladly exchanged a lot of
> toil and burden and sacrifice, repaid with ingratitude and
> murmuring, for a position of ease and honor, when it was

God Himself that offered the release.

But Moses discerned ground for hope where there appeared only discouragement and wrath. The words of God, "Let Me alone," he understood not to forbid but to encourage intercession, implying that nothing but the prayers of Moses could save Israel, but that if thus entreated, God would spare His people.[4]

This story is an example, not of God being angry and Moses being bold enough to talk God out of His anger and change His mind, but of God inviting Moses to intercede for Israel so that He could act. Justice called for the destruction of the Israelites. Only the prayers of an intercessor could provide a way for God's mercy to spare them. God knew He could trust Moses with the task, and so as a friend He told Moses what He was going to do. And Moses, as God's friend who knew who He was, responded to the invitation.

God wants to have this kind of relationship with us today. He's looking for intercessors like Abraham and Moses who will stand in the gap for His people so that He doesn't have to destroy the land. God is looking for people who will desire to know Him so intimately that He can call them His friends and trust them with His heart and invite them to pray for things He desires to see accomplished. Are we willing to be this kind of friend to God?

Most of our prayers these days, rather than being pleas for the deliverance of God's people or for the salvation of the lost nations, are quite narrow and self-centered. Much of our praying is little more than spiritual "chitter-chatter." Here is how author Eric Ludy describes "chitter-chatter" praying:

> Spiritual sounding chitter chatter tends to be self-centric in its banter, begging for comforts to be protected, deadlines to be met, surgeon's hands to be guided, tests to be passed, and food to be blessed. It's always about us. And, whereas there is nothing wrong with praying about our own personal needs, prayer—real-life historic prayer—is

otherworldly and built upon the notion of a *forgotten self.* . . .

Bona fide, heaven-inspired prayer—the kind that moves mountains and calms storms—is not something the modern church is used to.[5]

Of course, God cares about the details of our lives. He wants us to talk to Him about these things just as we would with a best friend. But He doesn't want us to stop there.

Thousands outside our doorstep haven't had the privilege of knowing Christ as we have. Millions more around the world are starving for the gift of salvation. While we debate doctrines and hold long committee meetings to discuss how to help our churches grow, believers in countries such as Iran and North Korea are being martyred for their faith. Do we know? Do we pray about these things? Do we even care?

When we remain self-focused in our prayers, it's evident that we don't truly understand God's heart; we don't see His tears of sorrow for the suffering and lost. When we understand His heart for those in darkness, we will become partners with Him in service. We will cry when He cries, and we will pray for *His* burdens, not just our own. We will truly be *His friend.* And it is here that we begin to touch the border of the *endless frontier of possibilities* in the life of faith! It is here, as a friend of God, that we begin to learn to pray the historic, world-changing prayers as the men and women of old so often prayed.

Praying by inspiration of the Holy Spirit

As we read the amazing stories of answered prayer throughout Scripture, the most striking are those of impossible victories won, of territory taken, of people set free from darkness and slavery, and of God's work going forward with strength and power. This was God's main desire in Bible times, and it is still His desire today. Thus, one of the most important keys to receiving answered prayer like the men and women of old is learning to pray in accordance with God's desires.

We find God's desires revealed first and foremost in His Word. It is through His Word that He reveals Himself to us, it is through His Word that He speaks to us, and it is His Word that gives foundation to our prayers. It is only by being rooted in His Word that we are safe, and it is only when we are rooted in the Word that the Holy Spirit can truly teach us how to pray.

Inspiration tells us, "If we will draw nigh to God, He will draw nigh to us, and His glory will go before us. He will indite[6] our petitions, teaching us to ask for the very things that He has pledged Himself to bestow on us."[7]

All too often we have selfishly prayed for things that are not according to the will of God. Rather than praying what the Holy Spirit would have us pray, we've prayed according to our flesh. As James 4:3 says, "Ye ask, and receive not, because ye ask amiss, that ye may consume it upon your lusts."

Thankfully, "Likewise the Spirit also helpeth our infirmities: for we know not what we should pray for as we ought: but the Spirit itself maketh intercession for us with groanings which cannot be uttered. And he that searcheth the hearts knoweth what is the mind of the Spirit, because he maketh intercession for the saints according to the will of God" (Romans 8:26, 27). When we pray with sincerity of heart, even if our request is in error, God will transform our selfish prayers for our best good and for His glory. And in the long run, *this is what we really want.*

More than just transforming our prayers between earth and heaven, we want Him to transform *us* and to teach us how to pray. We want His desires to become our desires and our desires to become His. And this is possible! "If we will consent, God can and will so identify us with Himself, so mold our thoughts and aims, that when obeying His will, we are only carrying out the impulse of our own minds. Then we shall not desire to carry out unchristian desires; we shall be filled with an earnest determination to do the will of God."[8]

This is the beauty of learning to pray by inspiration of the Holy Spirit. Because of the blood of Christ, whose righteous prayers cover our own, we can have confidence that our prayers are reaching the throne room of heaven, for He has told us, "And whatsoever ye shall ask in my name, that will I do, that the Father may be glorified in the Son. If ye shall ask any thing in my name, I will do it" (John 14:13, 14).

While many profess to believe in prayer, it is only the man or woman who has a personal relationship with Christ who will go into the private prayer closet, where no one sees, and shut the door—wrestling with the tenacity of Jacob, Joshua, Esther, and Moses, saying, "I will not let go until You bless me. I'm willing to wrestle through the night if that's what it takes. I know You care about souls. You've asked me to care. I'm not going to stop praying until You work!"

These men and women can wrestle and pray passionately because they know God's heart personally and have come to trust His Word implicitly and unwaveringly. Because they know Him personally, the Holy Spirit inspires their prayers.

Knowing God personally

Many believers today know only the God of their parents or the God of their church. Therefore, they just go through the motions day after day, following the examples of those around them but never really coming to know God as a Friend for themselves. Yes, we believe that God is the God of the church and that He should be the God of our family, as well. But first and foremost, He must be *our* God.

Dear friend, do you know the God of Abraham, Isaac, and Jacob personally? Is He *your* God today? Are you trusting in His blood to wash away your sins or are you hoping to be saved by someone else's faith? We will not be saved because our parents walked with God. We will not be saved as family units. We will not be saved because our names are listed on the church membership records, nor because we've held positions of leadership in ministry. None of these things will count if we haven't chosen *individually* to give God our hearts. "Lord, take my heart; for I cannot give it," we must pray. "It is Thy property. Keep it pure, for I cannot keep it for Thee. Save me in spite of myself, my weak, unchristlike self. Mold me, fashion me, raise me into a pure and holy atmosphere, where the rich current of Thy love can flow through my soul."[9]

This prayer of surrender does not stop after we have surrendered once. It must continue day after day. "It is not only at the beginning of the Christian life that this renunciation of self is to be made. At every advance step heavenward it is to be renewed. All our good works are dependent on a power outside of ourselves. Therefore there needs to be a continual reaching out of the heart after God, a continual, earnest, heartbreaking confession of sin and humbling of the soul before Him. Only by constant renunciation of self and dependence on Christ can we walk safely."[10]

Let's set aside our self-focused agenda and seek *Him* first today—that His will may be accomplished and His name glorified in our lives. Let's dare to walk, live, and pray differently—for He truly is our personal Savior and Friend. Let's give Him our hearts. Then, like the men and women of old, we can move forward, making bold requests as we dare to ask for more. For we aren't talking to just anyone; we are talking to the King—the King who is also our Father and very best Friend!

Chapter 4

From Laodicea to
Life More Abundant

My Story: Moving Toward the Promised Land

> *I am come that they might have life, and that they might have it
> more abundantly.*
>
> —*John 10:10*

*G*rowing up, I envied the spiritual enthusiasm, passion, and
success I saw in the lives of those who converted from
unbelief into Christianity. As I read their stories, I would
ask myself, "Why can't we be so excited about God and about truth?"

Doug Batchelor was once lost without purpose. While growing up
with everything that money could buy and experimenting with all kinds
of things along the way, it wasn't until he ended up in a mountain cave
that he discovered the biblical truths that set him on fire. Now he leads
a ministry that touches millions.

David Asscherick was a skateboarding punk rocker who cared

nothing about God. After reading the book *The Great Controversy*, his life forever changed as he recognized that God designed him for a distinct purpose. Now he puts all his energy and strength into passionately preaching the gospel and has impacted countless people for the Lord.

Cheri Peters was once a despair-filled drug addict on the streets of Southern California. After discovering the love of God, she went from the streets to the television studio where she now spends her days sharing the power of the gospel and helping others find healing and restoration through her own television program airing on Three Angels Broadcasting Network.

Ivor Myers was a hip-hop recording artist on the verge of making millions when God called him out of the music industry to share the gospel. Now, as a pastor and internationally sought-after speaker, God is using him to impact the lives of people around the world. It's because of his inspiration in the initiative Operation Global Rain that we now have the yearly Ten Days of Prayer[1] for the worldwide church. What a difference this has made for so many!

One of my favorite testimonies comes from my friend and mentor in ministry, Pastor Paul Ratsara. Pastor Ratsara grew up as a pagan idol worshiper in Madagascar. He and his family lived under the constant stress of trying to appease the spirits of their dead ancestors, and he was being trained in the science of witchcraft when God rescued him from darkness. Not only did God save him spiritually and lead him into service as an Adventist minister, but He also saved his physical life countless times. Many of his amazing adventures, including being poisoned by jealous relatives and being shot at by military rebels, are recorded in the book *Kidnapped!*[2]

Pastor Ratsara, now serving as the president of the Southern Africa-Indian Ocean Division, recognizes what we've been given in the gospel and why being a Seventh-day Adventist is significant today. As a result, his faith and enthusiasm in ministry has impacted thousands throughout the world church. It is because of his direct influence and encouragement that I'm writing this book today. Stories like his and others inspire me as nothing else. They make me want to be more faithful by pointing me to the incredible God we serve.

In contrast to the testimonies mentioned here, my testimony may seem very dull. I didn't grow up on the stage, rocking out, living in a cave, or doing drugs. I didn't have to worry about appeasing the spirits of my dead ancestors, nor did I have jealous relatives trying to poison me. Rather than spending the early years of my life dodging bullets or escaping what seemed like certain death, I was raised in the lukewarm Seventh-day Adventist Church of the modern West; rich and increased with goods and thinking we had need of nothing when in actuality, we were poor, blind, and naked.

While my Adventist roots reach back close to five generations, because of the spiritual apathy that I saw in the church during my young years, being a Seventh-day Adventist wasn't that attractive to me. Oh, I believed the doctrines, kept the Sabbath, and loved our daily family worships when my father would read the Bible to us, but I didn't really enjoy attending church. However, I didn't give up on the church, for something deep in my heart told me that God desired *more* for His people, and *more* for me.

Thanks to the prayers of my parents, who steadfastly held on to their faith, I was convicted to give my heart to Christ at a young age, and from then on I knew that God was calling me to work for Him. But it wasn't until my high school years, away at a little school called Oklahoma Academy, that I really became excited about being a Seventh-day Adventist Christian. There it was that prayer became much more real and personal to me, and there it was that I began to develop a solid foundation for my faith.

As a result of my increasing desire to serve the Lord, throughout high school and into college, I got involved in anything and everything that I thought would grow my spiritual walk. I was active in young adult groups, volunteered in multiple ministries, got involved in leading Scripture memory programs, wrote articles, and fell in love with missions, traveling here and there around the world. I loved adventure, and as a result, not long after high school, I attended Bible College in Norway, and even spent a few months teaching school as a student missionary in the jungles of South America.

Through my college years, my relationship with God continued to grow, and I moved forward, tackling life and my studies with enthusiasm and passion. I studied nursing at Southern Adventist University, and although the program was extremely challenging (and I lost almost a month of classes due to sickness from pushing myself so hard), God still blessed and I ended up graduating summa cum laude—with highest honors.

After graduation, I began to work not far from my family as a registered nurse. Whenever opportunity arose, I continued traveling and doing mission work. I held evangelism meetings in Kenya, did medical work in Egypt, taught English to elementary students in South Korea, and the list went on. While I was sincerely seeking to serve the Lord, through a series of difficult circumstances that really tested my faith, God slowly began to open my eyes to my need of a *much deeper experience* with Him.

In January 2007, I was providentially led to attend a small discipleship retreat with about fifteen other young adults. The focus was simply on getting to know Christ through His Word, and we shared a powerful weekend. In addition to studying the Bible all day, we spent our evenings praying together. We prayed long into the night for loved ones, for spiritual victory, for deeper understanding of God's Word, and most importantly, for the outpouring of the Holy Spirit in our lives. One of my personal prayer requests was for God to give me a deeper understanding and appreciation of the Cross. This may seem strange, as I'd been a Christian my whole life, but my heart had always felt numb to what Christ had done on Calvary. It didn't touch me personally! As the Bible study and intense prayer continued over the weekend, my faith slowly grew and I began to fall in love with my Savior as never before.

Returning home, I continued to immerse myself in God's Word and to spend more and more time in fervent prayer. It was at this point that I really began earnestly daring to ask God for more spiritually. But it wasn't until the following year that God really began to work. First, He had to show me how desperately I needed Him.

Discovering the power of the gospel

After my plans for a mission trip to Peru fell through, my friend

Paul, a Loma Linda University School of Dentistry student, asked if I'd be interested in accompanying the Loma Linda medical team on a mission trip to Bangladesh. It was a last-minute offer as they were leaving in two weeks, but they needed more nurses, and I was a nurse. Always up for adventure, I eagerly jumped on board.

Two weeks later, I found myself with my teammates in an overcrowded van bouncing through the hot and dusty streets of Dhaka, the capital of Bangladesh—a country of over 170 million, and a country I knew little about.

Although I'd traveled in numerous Third World countries, the suffering I witnessed on this trip shook me to the core. That first day, as I looked out into the hopeless eyes of the masses, and as I viewed the despair everywhere, my heart longed to do something—but what? Even after my friends and I sacrificed a few meals so that we could share more food with the hungry (the cost for one of our American meals could feed thirty on the streets), we recognized that the reality was still *as if we had done nothing*. What could one or two do to help an entire city and country locked in poverty, hunger, and despair?

The next morning as I was having my personal devotions, God spoke to my heart and for the first time I truly saw my desperate need of the Cross.

You see, I'd always been a good kid. I'd been raised in a conservative Adventist home where we didn't do the "bad" things people in the world did. I never drank, I never smoked, I never did drugs. Oh sure, I had made mistakes and there were a few small sins with which I constantly struggled—but nothing like the sins of most people! (Or so I thought at the time!)

But suddenly God showed me my true heart condition. It was filthy, just like those streets of Dhaka. I was full of pride in my accomplishments and *perceived* goodness. I felt better than others because my sins didn't seem that bad, and besides, I had come from many generations of Seventh-day Adventists. (My great-great-grandmother had even been a friend of Ellen White!) Furthermore, I had often congratulated myself on my skills and abilities and on the fact that I was sought after as a spiritual leader by both young and old. I had dedicated my life to service for the Lord (and I was sincere in doing so), but suddenly, I realized that much of my mission work overseas had been more to feed my own selfish desires for adventure than for Him. I had human compassion, but it wasn't *His compassion.* Rather than *really* caring about the salvation of the lost, I cared more about the pictures I would take home with me to show my friends.

Of course, there were times that I felt my hopeless condition. There were times that my sins would overwhelm me, and I would fall down crying in despair at Jesus' feet, wondering if He could even save me. At these times, I would surrender and His peace would fill me. But the personal significance of the Cross was always vague and distant. Continually, without realizing it, I would pick myself up and go back to the security of my self-righteousness and good works until I'd fall again. Because of this, my spiritual journey was often up and down.

Inspiration tells us, "The thought that the righteousness of Christ is imputed to us, not because of any merit on our part, but as a free gift from God, is a precious thought. The enemy of God and man [the devil] is not willing that this truth should be clearly presented; for he knows that if the people receive it fully, his power will be broken. If he can control minds so that doubt and unbelief and darkness shall compose the experience of those who claim to be the children of God, he can overcome them with temptation."[3]

Finally, that morning there in Bangladesh, I recognized the reality that there was no way I could ever make myself acceptable to God. I saw that attempting to change my heart by my own efforts was just as impossible as trying to feed and reach the hopeless millions in the city of Dhaka! Yes, I could attempt to help a few people, just as I could also attempt to change a few things in my heart and attempt to live a holy life. But no matter how much effort I put forth, I realized that I would still always fall short because *the reality was that I was a sinner in need of a Savior.* "But we are all as an unclean thing, and all *our righteousnesses are as filthy rags;* and we all do fade as a leaf; and our iniquities, like the wind, have taken us away" (Isaiah 64:6; emphasis added).

Thankfully, once God opens our eyes to our true heart condition, He offers us hope. "Come now, and let us reason together, saith the LORD:

though your sins be as scarlet, they shall be as white as snow; though they be red like crimson, they shall be as wool" (Isaiah 1:18).

While I sat with my Bible contemplating these passages with the sounds of honking horns, squawking chickens, and crying babies rising from the street below, all noise faded away as I beheld my Savior's love for me as never before. Tears began to course down my cheeks as the significance of what Christ had accomplished for *me personally* on Calvary sunk into my mind.

When I realized what He'd already done for me on Calvary, a work that only a supernatural God could do, and how desperately lost and filthy I was without His robe of righteousness—a gift I could never earn—my heart was broken with a gratitude and love that I could not express. I wept and wept that morning as I told Him over and over again through choking sobs, "Thank You, thank You, thank You for reaching down to save *even me*." As I cried, a strange yet wonderful joy and peace, such as I've never experienced before, overwhelmed my soul. It wasn't until that day that the power and beauty of the gospel touched me so dramatically that I was forever changed.

Ellen White writes in one of my favorite books, *The Desire of Ages,* "The proud heart strives to earn salvation; but both our title to heaven and our fitness for it are found in the righteousness of Christ. The Lord can do nothing toward the recovery of man until, convinced of his own weakness, and stripped of all self-sufficiency, he yields himself to the control of God."[4]

While the majority of Christians today have heard the gospel story many times, just like I had, many still don't understand its full significance. While we preach the gospel, we deny its power. While we try to share it, our lives remain unchanged by it.

Hudson Taylor, an early pioneer missionary to the interior of China, spent many years working in service to the Lord before he realized the personal significance of the gospel. Discouraged with the weight of sin and his constant shortcomings, he longed for peace, but saw only darkness. At times, he wondered if it was even possible that Christ could save him.

One day, the truth of the gospel came home to him, and he grasped the fullness of what Christ came to bring *him*. In a letter to his sister, he describes his awakening experience and its effect upon his life:

> " 'But how to get faith strengthened? Not by striving after faith, but by resting on the Faithful One.' . . .
>
> ". . . 'I have striven in vain to rest in Him. I'll strive no more. For has He not promised to abide with me—never to leave me, never to fail me?' . . .
>
> "The sweetest part, if one may speak of one part being sweeter than another, is the rest which full identification with Christ brings. I am no longer anxious about anything, as I realize this; for He, I know, is able to carry out His will, and His will is mine. It makes no matter where He places me, or how. . . . For in the easiest positions He must give me His grace, and in the most difficult His grace is sufficient."[5]

Witnesses to Hudson Taylor's transformed life later added their own testimonies. " 'He was an object lesson in quietness. He drew from the Bank of Heaven every farthing of his daily income—"My peace I give unto you." Whatever did not agitate the Savior, or ruffle His spirit was not to agitate him. . . . He knew nothing of rush or hurry, of quivering nerves or vexation of spirit. He knew there was a peace passing all understanding, and that he could not do without.' "[6]

Like Hudson Taylor, I wish I'd grasped the power of the gospel sooner, instead of waiting so many years after I had given my life to Christ. But so often, when we've been raised in the church with the Treasure right before us, we don't even recognize what God has really done for us—what He's saved us from, or what He's given us strength to become.

Moving toward the Promised Land

It has been only a few years since I began this amazing new journey, and of course, each day is a growing process. I still have my struggles just as everyone does—and sometimes I fall. I've discovered I have many more sins now than I ever thought possible! But I've also discovered that God can give victory if I keep holding on to Him.

Walking with the Lord each day and experiencing the joy of a personal relationship with Him has become my greatest privilege. Not only is He my Savior and King, Confidant and Friend, but He has become my true *heavenly Love*!

I think I'm probably busier serving the Lord now than I ever was before. But things have changed. My priorities are different! I realize God has given me only a few brief years to work for Him. Rather than being on a quest to see the world, I'm on a quest to see souls brought into the kingdom—whether at home or abroad. I want to see lives changed for eternity. Rather than going to church for what I can get out of the experience, I go to be a blessing and to give. Rather than consulting my changing emotions as I did in earlier years, I've learned to base my faith on God's unchanging Word. Rather than priding myself on my abilities and spiritual accomplishments, I now recognize my true weakness and lean on His strength.

The adventure of serving the Lord has only gotten more amazing. Although I've walked away from the security of a stable job to work in full-time ministry, I don't suffer from stress about paying my bills or about what the future will hold. Like Hudson Taylor, I recognize that in the easiest positions He must give me grace, and in the most difficult circumstances His grace is always sufficient.

While I now consider myself a missionary wherever I am, Bangladesh truly captured my heart on that first visit. I've been back multiple times already and am looking at going again soon. The country is still one of the saddest and most difficult places I've ever visited; however, the people draw me, especially the children.

On that first trip, I fell in love with an orphanage about eight hours north of Dhaka, near India's border. When I first visited Bangla Hope, American Seventh-day Adventist founders Dave and Beverly Waid[7] were caring for 68 children. That number has risen to 133 and continues to grow. Of course, the number of children under their care is only a drop in the bucket compared to a country of needy millions. But one life at a time, they are making a difference for eternity, and I've learned that this is what God is asking us to do—to keep touching one life at a time.

Just like those children at Bangla Hope, we, too, are orphans whom God has rescued from a life of sin. But He didn't rescue us so we could keep His blessings to ourselves. He rescued us so we can help reach others. Some of us He's rescued from the sins of Egypt to help deliver those still stuck in Egypt. Some of us He's rescued from the Laodicea of wilderness spirituality so we can rescue other Laodiceans. Ultimately though, His purpose for all of us is to take us to the Promised Land.

Far too many Christians today, while proud of the fact that they've moved out of worldly Egypt, have gotten stuck in the wilderness and have gone no further. They've raised their families and churches in the wilderness, built their ministries in the wilderness, and thus their faith has been dry and fruitless, just like the culture of the barren wilderness around them.

But God didn't call us out of the Egypt of spiritual bondage to have us pitch camp in the wilderness of spiritual mediocrity. He didn't bring us miraculously through the Red Sea to watch us have fun building sand castles in the desert wasteland. His intent is to take us on to the land flowing with milk and honey. This was His plan for Israel, and it's His plan for us today. Let's stop dawdling in the spiritual wilderness of Laodicean complacency or self-righteousness when God is ready to take us to Canaan! Yes, it will require moving camp and stepping out of our comfort zones, but if God has more for us spiritually, why would we be content with less?

I'd like to close this chapter with a hymn that really sums up what God has done in my own experience. As I've been daring to ask for more, not only have I tasted and seen that God is good here and now, but God has given me amazing glimpses of the *Promised Land of possibilities,* and He can do the same for you.

> *Once it was the blessing, now it is the Lord;*
> *Once it was the feeling, now it is His Word;*
> *Once His gifts I wanted, now the Giver own;*
> *Once I sought for healing, now Himself alone.*

Once 'twas painful trying, now 'tis perfect trust;
Once a half salvation, now the uttermost;
Once 'twas ceaseless holding, now He holds me fast;
Once 'twas constant drifting, now my anchor's cast.

Once 'twas busy planning, now 'tis trustful prayer;
Once 'twas anxious caring, now He has the care;
Once 'twas what I wanted, now what Jesus says;
Once 'twas constant asking, now 'tis ceaseless praise.

Once it was my working, His it hence shall be;
Once I tried to use Him, now He uses me;
Once the power I wanted, now the Mighty One;
Once for self I labored, now for Him alone. . . .[8]

Chapter 5

From the Secret Place of Prayer

The Power of Personal Consecration

> *But thou, when thou prayest, enter into thy closet, and when thou hast shut thy door, pray to thy Father which is in secret; and thy Father which seeth in secret shall reward thee openly.*
>
> —*Matthew 6:6*

I once heard a preacher say that our most recent answered prayers are a testimony of God's near presence. If we aren't having daily answered prayers, then we probably aren't daily in His presence. I don't know that this is sound theology, but with this thought in mind, let me share about "Praying Hyde."

John Hyde, also known as "Praying Hyde," was a missionary to India in the early 1900s and had such an all-consuming burden for the salvation of souls that he would not stop praying until God brought another soul, and then another, to the truth. At one time, he was convicted that he needed to pray for at least one soul a day for the following year. It was an extraordinary prayer challenge, and some even mocked his goal, saying it was unreasonable and presumptuous. However, he had peace from God and so he pressed forward in prayer—and God answered.

It certainly wasn't easy praying through those many long nights and fasting in agony through those long days, but he persisted and God gave him the victory. At the end of that year, more than four hundred souls had come to know Christ directly through his efforts.

Reflecting on this first year, his friend E. G. Carré wrote, "Was he satisfied [after seeing one soul a day come to Christ]? Far from it. How could he possibly be so long as his Lord was not? How could our Lord be satisfied, so long as one single sheep was yet outside His fold?"[1]

The next year, Hyde pleaded with the Lord for greater blessings. This time he asked for *two* souls a day! God answered again, and over eight hundred souls were converted! Still not satisfied, his burden and cry for souls growing heavier and heavier, and knowing that Christ deserves the lives of those He died to save, the following year he again laid hold on God with a holy desperation, pleading for *four* souls a day. It took weeks of praying, weeks of weeping, weeks of wrestling with the Lord before he once again had the confident assurance that God had heard and would answer. And God did!

"John Hyde seemed to always be hearing the Good Shepherd's voice saying, 'Other sheep I have—other sheep I have.' No matter if He won the one a day or two a day or four a day, He had an unsatisfied longing, an undying passion for lost souls."[2]

The supernatural success that followed John Hyde's prayers did not come without a price. And it's a price probably few of us would be willing to pay. Because of the intense prayer burden and agony for souls that he carried, and because of the great taxation exerted upon his body spending days and nights and sometimes weeks in prayer, his heart literally moved from one side of his chest to the other. After a few years of intense wrestling in prayer, while he was still young, he died of a heart condition—a broken heart for the lost.

How often our own fervency pales in comparison with disciples like this. And yet, how his testimony can inspire us to *dare to ask God for more*.

One of my favorite quotes from the Spirit of Prophecy says, "It is the privilege of every Christian not only to look for but to hasten the coming of our Lord Jesus Christ (2 Peter 3:12, margin). Were all who profess His name bearing fruit to His glory, how quickly the whole world would be sown with the seed of the gospel. Quickly the last great harvest would be ripened, and Christ would come to gather the precious grain."[3]

I share the story of "Praying Hyde" because his testimony has challenged me in my own prayer life as no other. I may not be winning my thousands to Christ, as many evangelists and other leaders are. And I certainly don't feel I'm at the point where I could confidently ask God for one soul a day. However, awhile back God *did* impress me that I could ask for at least *one answered prayer a day*. And since I started journaling and keeping accurate records almost two years ago now, there *has not been one day* when I haven't received at least one answer to prayer. Some days I receive four or five answers, and one day this past week I received seven!

From watching God restore broken relationships on the brink of divorce, to seeing Him bring specific lost souls into the truth, to experiencing spiritual and physical healing, to seeing impossible obstacles before me vanish, to having specific needs met when the only One who knew my need was God, to having free gravel dumped on my driveway (yes, God even cares about gravel!), to receiving wisdom and amazingly opening doors in ministry—the answers just go on and on and on. Obviously, I don't have space to share about all the miracles here and now. But as I've seen God answering my prayers every day, sometimes in big ways, and sometimes in small ways, but always in a *significant way,* my faith has been growing and growing.

I believe with all my heart that God is just longing for us to expect more, pray for more, and ask for more in faith. And it all starts with personal consecration in that private prayer closet. We can't dream too big if we are living and working according to His will. It's not about our talents or capabilities anyway. *It's about His! It is for the accomplishment of His purposes that we pray!*

Inspiration reminds us, "You need not go to the ends of the earth for wisdom, for God is near. It is not the capabilities you now possess or ever will have that will give you success. It is that which the Lord can do for you. We need to have far less confidence in what man can do and far more confidence in what God can do for every believing soul. He longs to have you reach after Him by faith. He longs to have you expect great things from Him."[4]

Although praying with others can be a powerful blessing, praying alone in our secret prayer closet is a special privilege that can never be replaced by praying together. Knowing Christ personally and knowing how to wrestle alone is paramount to our spiritual success, both personally and corporately.

From the secret place of prayer

Ellen White, throughout many of her books, has a number of things to say regarding the importance of secret prayer. She writes, ". . . Above all we must not neglect secret prayer, for this is the life of the soul. It is impossible for the soul to flourish while prayer is neglected. Family or public prayer alone is not sufficient. In solitude let the soul be laid open to the inspecting eye of God."[5]

Probably one of the most well-known Christian Reformers from the last five hundred years is Martin Luther, the leader of what became known as the Protestant Reformation. Strengthened by his study of the Word and many hours spent in prayer, he counteracted the errors and false teachings of papal Rome, which had held multitudes of believers in darkness for centuries. Standing only upon the pure truths of God's Word and empowered through the blessing of the Holy Spirit, he made an impact that shook the entire Christian world and is still shaking it today. He chose to stand against what seemed impossible odds, and the papal leaders wanted to send him to the stake (just as they had many others before him), yet he remained steadfast, unmoved by the powers of darkness set to destroy him. Others, seeing his unflinching courage and convicted by the biblical truths that he taught, took their stand alongside him.

What was his secret? How could he stand so courageously against the most influential and powerful religious system in the world and yet not be ruffled? The answer was prayer. His strength came from *the secret place of prayer.*

Consider the following testimony of Martin Luther and his firm belief in the power of prayer—*not the power of force*—to bring victory:

> When powerful foes were uniting to overthrow the reformed faith, and thousands of swords seemed about to be unsheathed against it, Luther wrote: "Satan is putting forth his fury; ungodly pontiffs are conspiring; and we are threatened with war. Exhort the people to contend valiantly before the throne of the Lord, by faith and prayer, so that our enemies, vanquished by the Spirit of God, may be constrained to peace. Our chief want, our chief labor, is prayer; let the people know that they are now exposed to the edge of the sword and to the rage of Satan, and let them pray. . . .
>
> ". . . We shall do more by our prayers than all our enemies by their boastings."[6]

Although human circumstances may have looked bleak and foreboding, Martin Luther knew he served a God not limited or controlled by the plans of evil men, and God rewarded his faith. From the secret place of prayer came the power that literally shook the world in the Great Reformation.

Of Martin Luther it is written that during the times of greatest struggle:

> [He] "did not pass a day without devoting three hours at least to prayer, and they were hours selected from those the most favorable to study." In the privacy of his chamber he was heard to pour out his soul before God in words "full of adoration, fear, and hope, as when one speaks to a friend." "I know that Thou art our Father and our God," he said, "and that Thou wilt scatter the persecutors of Thy children; for Thou art Thyself endangered with us. All this matter is Thine, and it is only by Thy constraint that we have put our hands to it. Defend us, then, O Father!"[7]

And what was God's answer to this great crisis? Inspiration answers, "God did listen to the cries of His servants. He gave to princes and ministers grace and courage to maintain the truth against the rulers of the darkness of this world. . . . The Protestant Reformers had built on Christ, and the gates of hell could not prevail against them."[8]

Prayer, the greatest gift!

In the book *In Heavenly Places,* we are assured, "An appeal to Heaven by the humblest saint is more to be dreaded by Satan than the decrees of cabinets or the mandates of kings."[9]

Do we realize what this means? Through the divine privilege of prayer, God has given us a power for influence that even worldly kings and authorities do not possess! This is hard to comprehend. Yet again and again we are urged, "Ask, and it shall be given you; seek, and ye shall find" (Matthew 7:7). "Ye have not, because ye ask not" (James 4:2). "Hitherto have ye asked nothing in my name: ask, and ye shall receive, that your joy may be full" (John 16:24). "We may expect large things, even the deep movings of the Spirit of God, if we have faith in His promises."[10]

God is the same yesterday, today, and tomorrow. He hasn't changed. He is just waiting to prove Himself strong on our behalf. But He doesn't open heaven's storehouse of blessings on the careless or the hasty comers and goers. He's looking for the sincere of heart; He's looking for personal consecration and for those who are looking upward and longing for more of Him. He's looking for those who are seeking to know Him *personally.*

Sadly, there are certain prayers that will likely never be answered in our lives today—the prayers we never dare to pray. There is a deeper walk with the Lord we may never experience this side of heaven; it is that which we are too feeble and weak of faith to seek.

God tells us, as if trying to help us understand the *unlimited possibilities before us,* "Call upon Me and I will answer you and show you mighty things which you know not. I can do so much more than you've even thought or dreamed! The sky is not the limit in My realm! But you need to ask! You need to believe! And most of all, *you need to seek Me!*"[11] Will we have faith in His promises? Will we seek for more of Him? Will we stand upon His Word no matter the storms that surround us?

God is looking for humble men and women who will spend time on their knees in the secret place, wrestling through the night if need be, to see His truth proclaimed and souls brought into the kingdom. He's looking for men and women who will stand upon His Word in faith and pray until the breaking of the day. Will we be these men and women?

Chapter 6

If My People Will Pray

The Power of a Praying Congregation

> *If my people, which are called by my name, shall humble themselves, and pray, and seek my face, and turn from their wicked ways; then will I hear from heaven, and will forgive their sin, and will heal their land.*
>
> —*2 Chronicles 7:14*

While public prayer cannot replace secret prayer, neither can private prayer replace the power of a congregation in prayer. The two should work hand in hand!

In his book *Adventism's Greatest Need*, Pastor Ron Clouzet relates how he saw corporate prayer powerfully impact an entire congregation that he had just begun to pastor. I love his testimony because it shows how the work in our own personal "prayer closet" can grow into a much larger work that can affect a whole church—and more!

Although the sanctuary of his new church could seat four hundred people, barely one hundred showed up each Sabbath morning for services, and not even all of those on time. But he believed God could work, and so he began spending hours studying the truths of Scripture, seeking for better clarity on how to share the gospel. He spent so much time studying that he had little time left to actually prepare his sermons. So, knowing that only the Holy Spirit could convict hearts and make up for his personal deficiencies, he began to get up early every Sabbath morning to pray earnestly that God's Spirit would be poured out on his congregation. God began to work in answer to his private prayers, and as a result, more and more people began to attend church. By the end of his first year, Sabbath attendance had tripled. But this was only the beginning!

About fifteen months into his time at this new church, he decided to do a series on prayer. He shares how this experience impacted him: "A whole new world opened up for me. Prayer and communion with God became much more real and concrete. My relationship with Jesus grew much closer than ever before. I finally realized how most of us seem to live our lives three inches below the water-line: we know we're drowning but assume this is our lot in life, ignorant of the fact that just above us is a whole new world."[1]

As a result of this prayer series, the Holy Spirit began to move on his church even more powerfully and the members began to really pray. Not only were they praying during the mid-week prayer meeting, but they started praying together every Sabbath afternoon during daylight saving time. During standard time they met Friday evenings to pray. But this wasn't enough. Realizing that some of his church members were under demonic attack, Pastor Clouzet invited his elders to join him at 5:00 A.M. one day for a time of special intercession. Seven of his ten elders came, and the time of prayer was so powerful that they decided to meet and pray together every week. Then they added Fridays, and then Sabbath and Sunday mornings. Then deacons asked if they could join the morning prayer time. Then members asked if they could join and the growing group began praying every morning of the week.

As God's Spirit was poured out, Pastor Clouzet saw more and more spiritual victories among the church members. Church leaders who had never been interested in prayer before now didn't want to be late for their board meetings, since the first thirty minutes were devoted to prayer. As a result of the Holy Spirit's blessing, evangelism took off, and the fellowship hall was transformed into the Better Living Center, where dozens of health, finance, and family seminars were hosted for the community. As a result, more and more people were baptized.

The second year, Pastor Clouzet was convicted to do a series on the Holy Spirit, and more blessings followed. Many small groups were formed, and another church plant was started. Because God's power was dramatically changing the lives of the members, they added a "testimony time" to their regular Sabbath service, so people could share. Pastor Clouzet reports that some members would drive for hours to get to church, just so they could hear what God was doing in the lives of their fellow church members.

As I reflect on this amazing testimony, I am reminded of what Ellen White once wrote: "The descent of the Holy Spirit upon the church is looked forward to as in the future; but it is the privilege of the church to have it now. Seek for it, pray for it, believe for it. We must have it, and Heaven is waiting to bestow it."[2]

It's hard to summarize Pastor Clouzet's testimony as God continued to bless more and more. During the five years he spent with this congregation, tithe quadrupled and evangelism offering rose a whopping 5,000 percent! The church membership tripled and most of the members became active in some type of ministry. Almost two hundred people were baptized. As he states, "This may not be unusual for some places in the world,"[3] but for us here in the comfortable Laodicean communities of the West, this was truly an act of God.

Let us not forget that what God did for this congregation began with one man who was willing to wrestle in his private prayer closet. This is where the true work began, and this is where it also begins for us! Inspiration confirms this: "The greatest victories to the church of Christ or to the individual Christian are not those that are gained by talent or education, by wealth or favor of men. They are those victories that are gained in the audience chamber with God, when earnest, agonizing faith lays hold upon the mighty arm of power."[4]

While things may start small, we need to keep praying. Eventually, others will join us and the work will grow. What God did for Pastor

Clouzet and his congregation, He can do for anyone, or for any church willing to take seriously His promises and the power of prayer.

The blessings of corporate prayer

In the book of Joel, we find a nation in great spiritual distress. As a result of this distress, the spiritual leaders were commanded to call a solemn assembly and gather the people together for fasting and prayer. "Let the priests, the ministers of the LORD, weep between the porch and the altar, and let them say, Spare thy people, O LORD, and give not thine heritage to reproach, that the heathen should rule over them" (Joel 2:17).

What would be the result of this time of corporate fasting, supplication, and intercession? The prophet Joel continues,

> Then will the LORD be jealous for his land, and pity his people. Yea, the LORD will answer and say unto his people, Behold, I will send you corn, and wine, and oil, and ye shall be satisfied therewith: and I will no more make you a reproach among the heathen: . . . And I will restore to you the years that the locust hath eaten, the cankerworm, and the caterpiller, and the palmerworm, my great army which I sent among you. And ye shall eat in plenty, and be satisfied, and praise the name of the LORD your God, that hath dealt wondrously with you: and my people shall never be ashamed (verses 18, 19, 25, 26).

But this wasn't all that would happen. A few verses later, we are told about a great spiritual outpouring that would take place. "And it shall come to pass afterward, that I will pour out my spirit upon all flesh; and your sons and your daughters shall prophesy, your old men shall dream dreams, your young men shall see visions: And also upon the servants and upon the handmaids in those days will I pour out my spirit" (verses 28, 29).

Ellen White comments, "If this prophecy of Joel met a partial fulfillment in the days of the apostles, we are living in a time when it is to be even more evidently manifest to the people of God. He will so bestow

His Spirit upon His people that they will become a light amid the moral darkness; and great light will be reflected in all parts of the world. O that our faith might be increased, that the Lord might work mightily with His people."[5]

Pastor Mark Finley tells how amazed he and his wife were a few years ago when they attended the Shenyang Church in China (located just north of North Korea). This church is one of the largest Seventh-day Adventist churches in the world today, with a membership of over six thousand. The church started with only nine members and now has spawned over three hundred church plants, with as many as fifty to several hundred in each plant.

When Pastor Mark Finley asked the pastor what the secret was to their amazing growth, he was told it was prayer! "We meet each morning from 4:30 a.m. to 6:00 a.m. to pray and 150 or so of our people come every day. These seasons of prayer unleash God's power for growth and revival.

"Then Mark asked why at 4:30—so early! The pastor said it was because the people are busy professionals who need to go to work, mothers with children to take care of, and also busy students who must go to school." So they came to pray before they started the responsibilities of the day.[6]

J. Edwin Orr, historian on worldwide revivals, once wrote, "No great spiritual awakening has begun anywhere in the world apart from united prayer—Christians persistently praying for revival."[7] Let us take advantage of the gift we've been given, the privilege of both private and corporate prayer. We are promised, "When the way is prepared for the Spirit of God, the blessing will come. Satan can no more hinder a shower of blessing from descending upon God's people than he can close the windows of heaven that rain cannot come upon the earth."[8]

Desperate for God to work

Many of us could learn some valuable prayer lessons from our Chinese brothers and sisters. They should inspire us to ask, "Are we desperate to see the Holy Spirit poured out in our lives and ministries? Are we desperate for personal revival today? Are we desperate enough to step out of our comfortable routine to join our brothers and sisters in prayer?"

I once heard of a man who asked his pastor what it would take for a true Holy Spirit revival to come upon his life and ministry. His pastor explained that he'd have to baptize him in order to show him. The man thought this was a bit strange but agreed. In the baptismal tank, the pastor covered the man's nose and gently lowered him under the water. Rather than lifting him back up, the pastor continued to hold him under the water. The man, not sure what was happening, began to struggle a bit, but the pastor's grip was firm. After a few moments, panic seized the man, and thinking that maybe the pastor was trying to drown him, he began to thrash about violently, trying to get free. At this point the pastor brought him to the surface.

Visibly shaken and gasping for breath, the man shouted, "What in the world are you trying to do? Do you want to drown me?"

The pastor calmly replied, "When you are as desperate for revival as you were just now for that next breath of air, then the Lord will send revival."

We have great zeal when it comes to seeking worldly success and honor. Athletes are applauded for their stamina and men of influence are esteemed for their perseverance and dedication. But what about our persistence for the Pearl of great price? What about our zeal for heavenly treasure?

> Desires for goodness and true holiness are right so far as they go; but if you stop here, they will avail nothing. Good purposes are right, but will prove of no avail unless resolutely carried out. . . .
>
> . . . Most professed Christians have no sense of the spiritual strength they might obtain were they as ambitious, zealous, and persevering to gain a knowledge of divine things as they are to obtain the paltry, perishable things of this life. *The masses professing to be Christians have been satisfied to be spiritual dwarfs. . . .*[9]

[Thus] many will be lost while hoping and desiring to be Christians; but they made no earnest effort, therefore they will be weighed in the balances and found wanting.[10]

Let us not be weighed in the balances and found wanting. According to Dwight Nelson, pastor of Pioneer Memorial Church, our prayers should be *desperate, urgent,* and *expectant.*[11] God delights to honor desperate prayers, especially when His people press together in unity, standing with faith upon His Word. Yes, heaven moves when God's people pray!

Chapter 7

God Still Works Miracles Today

The Power of United Prayer

> *Again I say unto you, That if two of you shall agree on earth as touching any thing that they shall ask, it shall be done for them of my Father which is in heaven.*
>
> *—Matthew 18:19*

I will never forget the day my friend Julia called me on the phone. Her father, who had not given his life to Christ, was dying from a sudden illness. "Please pray with me," she pleaded, "that God will work a miracle in his heart before it's too late!"

In times past, I probably would have prayed on the phone with my friend and then gone back to my work. After all, while I cared about Julia, I didn't know her father *personally*. However, that day God challenged me to do more. He challenged me to stand in the gap with Julia as He showed me that *each soul* is of infinite value to Him—whether I knew them or not. So after we prayed on the phone, I felt convicted that God was asking me to continue to fast and pray with Julia until we saw spiritual breakthrough.

I was quite busy, but I put my work aside and began to pray. However, I didn't make it through that first night because a small area of compromise stood in the way. At first I argued with God, "This is ridiculous, it's so small! I can't let this go." But then I felt His Spirit convicting my heart, *"Is it more valuable than a soul for whom I died?"* Ashamed, I surrendered my sin of compromise to God, and as I did, new power flooded my prayers.

For the next night and several days thereafter, I prayed with Julia incessantly—almost without stopping—for this miracle. It was a fierce spiritual battle and at times Julia and I both felt discouraged and wanted to give up. But God heard our prayers of agreement and in the end—praise the Lord—the spiritual victory we prayed and fasted for was accomplished before her father died.

God is calling all of us to deeper, more persistent prayers of agreement. He's calling us not just to pray *for*, but to perseveringly pray *through*. We all know how to pray *for*; we pray for our meals, we pray for safety on the road, we pray for a class or meeting, we pray for our friends and loved ones, and we pray for anything else that randomly crosses our path—and this is as it should be. But praying *through* means, "I'm committing to pray with persevering faith *until* I see victory or until I see an answer come!" Praying *through* is not easy because we must be committed for the long haul—maybe years. And we must be willing to put away any known sin of compromise. But when we are willing to pray *through* with a surrendered heart, God will give us the breakthrough!

Inspiration encourages us, "To every sincere prayer an answer will come. It may not come just as you desire, or at the time you look for it; but it will come in the way and at the time that will best meet your need."[1] Wesley Duewel writes:

> How long were the disciples to tarry in Jerusalem? "Until [they had] been clothed with power from on high" (Luke 24:49). How long did Moses keep his hands raised to God in prayer? Until Amalek was totally defeated (Exod.17:13). How long did Joshua hold out his javelin toward Ai while the army attacked? Until Jericho was

destroyed (Josh. 8:26). How long did Elijah stay on his knees in prevailing prayer after three years' drought? Until rain clouds formed in the sky (1 Kings 18:44). How long did Jesus pray in Gethsemane? Until Satan was defeated. How long did the disciples continue in prayer in the Upper Room? Until the Holy Spirit came upon them. No matter what our prayer request, if God has led us to pray for a need that we believe is the will of God, how long should we pray? Until the answer comes.[2]

Praying *through* can be successful only if we are rooted in God's Word. It's not about our determination to outlast God's. No, it's about our confidence in His faithfulness. "We should not present our petitions to God to prove whether He will fulfill His word, but because He will fulfill it; not to prove that He loves us, but because He loves us."[3]

God still works miracles today!

When we give our lives to Christ, we become part of a large community and family. God never intended for us to be little private independent units working all alone. We are to be a collective body made up of many members, working together in unity to exhort, encourage, and spread the gospel. This unity should also influence the way we pray.

Writing to Brother and Sister Farnsworth on the topic of united prayer, Ellen White stated:

> We are encouraged to pray for success, with the divine assurance that our prayers will be heard and answered. "If two of you shall agree on earth as touching any thing that they shall ask, it shall be done for them of My Father which is in heaven. For where two or three are gathered together in My name, there am I in the midst of them" (Matthew 18:19, 20). . . .
>
> The promise is made on condition that the united prayers of the church are offered, and in answer to these prayers there may be expected *a power greater than that*

which comes in answer to private prayer. The power given
will be proportionate to the unity of the members and
their love for God and for one another.[4]

Referring again to Matthew 18:19, 20, Ellen White exclaims, "Precious promise! Do we believe it? What marvelous results would appear
if the united prayers of this company were to ascend to God in living
faith!"[5]

Let me share an amazing story that happened not too long ago in
Vietnam.

After experiencing the joy of God in their own lives, lay pastor
Hanh[6] and his house-church members were convicted to fast and pray
specifically for the unreached villages in Vietnam. They began by focusing their prayers on a village 150 miles away, a village where not one
Christian lived. They chose this village because it was the hometown of
one of the couples in their group. This couple, the Wins,[7] had unconverted relatives in this village who they longed to win for the Lord. So
pastor Hanh, the Wins, and the house-church members began to pray.

Not long after, the aunt of the Wins—a lady named Yen[8] who
was suffering from terminal stomach cancer—came to their city seeking medical care. Her nephew, Mr. Win, invited Yen to pastor Hanh's
house-church where they attended each Sabbath. She came and there she
heard of Jesus Christ and was given her own Bible. Yen eagerly accepted
Christ as her Savior, and everyone rejoiced—especially Mr. and Mrs.
Win. However, because Yen was in the last stages of cancer, the doctors
offered her no help; her only hope was in the Master Healer. And so the
house-church members began praying fervently for a miracle.

The cancer made it impossible for Yen to keep food down, but her
insatiable appetite for the Word of God sustained her. After two weeks
in the city, she returned home to her family in the village. But her condition worsened. About one month later, Yen's sister-in-law called Pastor
Hanh with the sad news that Yen was about to die.

The Wins, along with their house-church family, had been continuing to pray for Yen, as well as for her village, but when they heard
this news, they immediately gathered to pray earnestly that God would

intervene. They prayed intensely for two hours, claiming Psalm 30 for her life. They reasoned with God, asking Him, "If You let Yen die, who will praise Your name in this village?" At the close of their prayer, they felt peace and assurance that God would heal her.

After another season of united prayer the next day, Pastor Hanh called to see if Yen's health had improved. He discovered she was in an unconscious state and was barely holding on to life. Talking to Yen's sister-in-law, an unbeliever, he pled with her earnestly, "Do you love Yen? If you do, listen to me! We have been praying that God will heal Yen. He is the only One who can help now! Please go get Yen's book called the Bible, open it to Psalm 30, kneel down beside Yen and read the words, putting Yen's name in the verses. God is able to heal and re-store her," he persisted. There was silence on the other end of the phone line. When Pastor Hanh hung up the phone, he was not sure if Yen's sister-in-law would do what he asked, but the group continued to join together in united prayer, trusting in the Lord.

A few days later, Pastor Hanh, along with the Wins, went to visit the village. They were met with shouts of joy from a fully restored Yen, from her sister-in-law, and from a host of former unbelievers, all praising the Lord.

"Not long after Pastor Hanh called, Yen stopped breathing," her sister-in-law reported. "I had already cleaned her up and was preparing to dress her body for burial when I remembered what Pastor Hahn had said to me on the phone." Turning to Pastor Hanh, she continued excit-edly. "I had no hope left other than your plan. After I did what you said, Yen started to move inside the blankets she was wrapped in. I stared in amazement and fear as she started vigorously kicking the blankets off, trying to free herself. She then sat up. I couldn't believe it because she had not sat up in two weeks! She asked for some food, which she kept down. It's a true miracle!"

Yen had not only come back to life, but she had also been completely healed. With this new open door, Pastor Hanh and the Wins, as well as others in the house-church, began reaching out to the village, sharing about the loving Author of life and His powerful words in the Bible. Over fifty people have already accepted Christ, and news of the miracle and of God's love is spreading to other unreached villages in the area.[9]

Would this miracle have happened if the believers in this small house-church in the city hadn't been willing to fast and unite in prayer for this village? What would happen if we would follow the example of our Vietnamese brothers and sisters in praying for the unreached in our communities and in our areas of influence?

Returning to the basics

While I have grown up reading stories about the Adventist pioneers and how they loved to pray and study their Bibles long into the night, it's not been until recent years that I've begun to experience a small taste of what those amazing days must have been like.

In 2009, God brought a group of us together with a passion to help God's people experience genuine biblical revival *personally*. Under the leadership of Pastor Ivor Myers,[10] and with the help of many other pastors and Bible teachers from around the world, our goal was to put on training conferences that would give people practical tools to help them get into the Word of God for *themselves*.

Within six months of starting to brainstorm, we hosted our first event on the Soquel campgrounds in Central California. Since this was our first conference, and most of us on the team were ministry amateurs (with the exception of Pastor Myers and maybe one or two others), we planned for an attendance of only two hundred to three hundred people.

We weren't sure what would happen, but as it turned out, God blessed *exceedingly abundantly above* our expectations. This first event maxed out with over 350 attendees. And although we'd started in the red financially and given discounted attendance to many (as we didn't want to turn away anyone who wanted to learn how to study the Bible), instead of the ten thousand dollars in offering we'd prayed for to make ends meet, God gave us almost thirty-five thousand dollars in donations. We could hardly believe it! We knew without a shadow of a doubt that God was blessing and that He wanted us to press forward as a ministry, daring to ask for greater blessings and for more souls.

With God's blessing, the ministry grew. More people came to each conference and each time the Holy Spirit seemed to be poured out more powerfully than before. As time went on, we received more and more testimonies of what God was doing in the lives of our attendees as they were going home and applying what they'd learned. And as their lives changed, so did ours.

It's been over five years now since we started ARME[11] Bible Camp Ministries, and just recently, we completed our twentieth Bible study training event.

Amazingly, over these last few years, we've been able to watch God touch the lives of thousands of attendees from all over the United States, the United Kingdom, Indonesia, Africa, Europe, Asia, and even Middle Eastern countries and cities like Dubai and beyond. We've not only watched many surrendering their lives to Christ, but we've seen young people who were not interested in spiritual things falling in love with the Word and with the power of prayer. We've seen marriages on the brink of divorce restored. We've seen families reunited. We've seen church leaders revived. We've seen schools being turned upside down as students went back to their studies passionate about Bible study and prayer. We've seen spiritual mountains moved. We've even seen physical healings. But most importantly, we've seen God's remnant church coming to life as we've never seen before. Why has God blessed so abundantly? I'll give you one small hint. *It has to do with united prayer!*

At ARME, we begin every morning of our conference with at least thirty minutes of united prayer—and this isn't just a dozen or so who meet to pray backstage. Often a hundred or more join us in this daily prayer time. We also have a prayer meeting going on *all day long* during the meetings. Here our attendees gather together throughout the day, praying for the speakers, for each other, and for a greater outpouring of the Holy Spirit.

We've also begun holding one all-night prayer meeting during each conference, in which the vast majority of our attendees participate. During this meeting, we intercede for a greater outpouring of the Holy Spirit on our church, and we also spend time lifting up the individual needs of those present. James 5:16 tells us, "Confess your faults one to another, and pray one for another, that ye may be healed. The effectual fervent prayer of a righteous man availeth much."

Many have shared that this time of all-night prayer is one of the most impacting parts of the whole conference because of the spiritual healing they experience there, as well as a love and unity that they've never before witnessed among fellow believers.

We have discovered that God is not hemmed in by a lack of resources, talent, or experienced professionals. The thing that matters most to Him is our *heart*. Are we surrendered? Are we obediently following His will? Are we following His Word?

Pastor Paul Ratsara, president of the Southern Africa-Indian Ocean Division, has been to several of our ARME events already and has spent time personally mentoring our team. He told me recently, "I think we get too busy today creating specialized formulas for success, when our formula is already written in the Bible and through the testimony of God's prophets. We don't need to baptize a new method or new plan. The Holy Spirit has already baptized the method and plan God has given us. We just need to follow it. We need to return to the basics. When we do, we will see Pentecost repeated!"

Inspiration tells us, "God depends upon you, the human agent, to fulfil your duty to the best of your ability, and he himself will give the increase. If human agents would but co-operate with the divine intelligences, thousands of souls would be rescued."[12]

We must remember that it is only the power of the Holy Spirit that can bring real conviction and change to lives. This isn't our work! This is God's work! However, when the Holy Spirit is present, and when we combine Bible study with significant time in prayer, it's like adding fire to dynamite—*Holy Spirit dynamite*! And as a result, there will be massive revival explosions, touching the lives of many.

Of course, what we've experienced personally is just a glimpse of what God is already doing all around the world. *But He longs to do more!* I believe what we see happening currently is just the tip of the iceberg in comparison with what He's waiting to do. He wants to see our whole world turned upside down, just as it was in the days of Pentecost. And the key to this work will be found in returning to the basics—in turning back to deeper Bible study and pressing together in greater unity

through prayer. Are we willing to allow God to redefine our n
vision today, even if it means stepping outside our comfort zones o₁ sim-
plifying our methods? What if how God is blessing our church today is
only the beginning of the opening of the door to much greater blessings?

The miracles we've seen resulting from united prayer represent just
a glimpse of what God has been doing around the world for centuries,
through the Old Testament men and women of God, and then through
the apostles of the early church.

I think of Moses' and Aaron's united prayers for Israel and the work
God did as a result. I think of the revivals that came during the times of
Ezra and Nehemiah as God's people united in prayer and repented of
their sins. I think of the deliverance God gave to the Jews when Esther
called for corporate prayer and fasting. I think of Pentecost and what
happened in the upper room, and later around the world, as God's men
and women united in prayer, humbling themselves before His throne. I
think of how God fueled the Reformation in the 1500s through united
prayer. I think of Count Zinzendorf and the one-hundred-year prayer
meeting that started with the Moravians in the 1700s because of an
outpouring of the Holy Spirit in answer to united prayer. I think of the
Welsh Revival and the many other revivals that have occurred over the
last couple hundred years because of united prayer and people seeking
to make their lives right with God. I think of our early Adventist pioneers who would often meet together with weeping and pray all through
the night, begging for more of God's Spirit.

Time and time again, I have seen what a difference united prayer has
made when families, churches, conferences, unions, and divisions have
made united prayer a priority. Prayer is changing our church from the
inside out. And I know that many leaders in the Seventh-day Adventist world church would agree, as I often hear their testimonies about
what God is doing around the world in answer to united prayer: greater
unity in committee meetings; success to our large evangelism explosion
campaigns; increases in tithes, offerings, and church attendance; revival
in churches and schools worldwide. Prayer, especially *united prayer,* is
behind much of the blessings we've received as a church.

But shall we settle, congratulating ourselves on the successes we've achieved? No! Until the work is finished, we must continue pressing together, and we must continue daring to ask for more! For what we've seen is only the beginning of what God is waiting to do!

Chapter 8

Daring to Ask for More

The Audacity of Humble Faith

> *Now unto him that is able to do exceeding abundantly above all that we ask or think, according to the power that worketh in us.*
> —*Ephesians 3:20*

*O*ne of my favorite modern-day testimonies of audacious, faith-filled prayer comes from my friends Pastor Jerry and Janet Page and their prayer partners from the Central California Conference.

Back in 1995, when Pastor Page was elected as the Central California Conference president, he and his wife Janet arrived to find the conference struggling financially. Monterey Bay Academy was almost two million dollars in debt, and the conference leadership was considering closing the annual Soquel camp meeting, even though many members wanted to see it continue.

As Pastor Page discussed all the problems needing solutions with his wife, Janet, she suggested he ask church members in the conference to become "prayer partners" for the Central California Conference. He did, and over three hundred members responded. He also persuaded the conference committee to conduct one more Soquel camp meeting, so they could see how things were working and seek God's will for the future. Pastor Page then sent out a newsletter to the new prayer partners, asking them to pray earnestly over the next upcoming camp meeting. The prayer partners were asked to pray that attendance would increase and that God would fill the meetings with His presence in such a mighty way that it would be obvious to all that God wanted the camp meeting to continue.

Janet, a true believer in the power of prayer, was strongly led by the Lord to begin recruiting local prayer partners to come pray at the conference office for the burdens and needs of the conference. Before camp meeting that year, she and some prayer partners also began walking the Soquel campgrounds.

Not long after, amazing things began to happen. Drivers, coming to deliver trailer rentals, would share that when they drove through the gates they sensed something special about the place.

When that year's camp meeting began, God's blessing was evident in a new and powerful way. Each person attending was prayed with at the gates as they entered. Many who came said they had never experienced the Lord's presence so strongly before. Young adults shared that they had felt compelled to attend, which is just what the prayer partners had prayed for.

The preaching was with such power that many came forward giving their lives to the Lord. Additionally, the evangelism offering, which had always been coming in short, for the first time reached the one hundred thousand dollar goal mark. People couldn't believe it. But this was just the beginning.

During camp meeting, the Pages put out paper slips on all the chairs with an invitation to join the conference prayer partners. Over three hundred *more people* joined the prayer team.

To keep everyone updated on what to pray for, they began sending out conference prayer requests every quarter. The prayer challenges were many, but at the top of the list were that Monterey Bay Academy could get out of debt and that God's blessings would be felt in a mightier way at the yearly Soquel camp meeting.

God answered both prayers in amazing ways. Within approximately two years, Monterey Bay Academy was completely out of debt, and more and more miracles began happening at Soquel camp meeting.

Janet and her prayer partners continued meeting each week at the conference office to pray. Because of all the answered prayers those first two years, they were convicted that *more people* needed to see the power of prayer. So they began praying that God would give them a "special token"—something to show the conference members that there was truly power in united prayer. Of course, their greatest burden was that God would really turn the lives of the attendees around. They wanted people to see that their struggling marriages did not need to be lost, that backslidden children could be redeemed from darkness, and that God's work could still go forward with power, even when circumstances looked discouraging and times were hard economically.

After praying about this "special token" for many weeks, their small prayer group became convicted to pray that at the next camp meeting the evangelism offering would not reach just $100,000, but $125,000. They knew this would be a powerful testimony that would encourage the conference membership that God can do great things when people unite together in faith and prayer. When camp meeting began, Janet asked the camp meeting prayer team to pray for this, as well.

That next year, God answered their united prayers and the evangelism offering reached a whopping $138,000—well above their prayer goal! They rejoiced for they knew it was only because God was working.

When the conference members found out that the prayer partners had been praying for this very blessing as a sign of God's power, many began to cry. Inspired, more conference members began to pray, and as a result, more lives were revived and changed.

The next year, after listening to God in fervent prayer and much sacrificial giving, over $250,000 came in.

While the evangelism committee was reluctant to set higher financial goals, the prayer partners continued to pray audaciously, some not only asking God to make the offering increase, but also asking God what amount they should pray for. When God impressed them with a specific dollar amount, they began to pray boldly for this amount, knowing many lives were being changed as a result of what was taking place at Soquel camp meeting each year.

By the fourth year, the evangelism offering went up to half a million dollars. Again, this inspired more giving and more praying.

Through united prayer, the Central California Conference began to thrive. The conference hired multiple Bible workers, planted churches, started many youth and young adult ministries, and kept full-time evangelism teams busy. God worked miracles in the personal lives of conference members by restoring marriages, bringing lost children back to the church, and winning spiritual battles.

Many, including Pastor and Mrs. Page, after time in prayer, were impressed by the Lord to pledge by faith beyond their monetary means to support the yearly evangelism offering. However, each year they watched with joyful amazement as God provided. One by one, conference members testified how God had supplied the money they each had sacrificially pledged for His work.

It was as if God was reminding them all of His promise, "Give, and it shall be given unto you; good measure, pressed down, and shaken together, and running over, shall men give into your bosom. For with the same measure that ye mete withal it shall be measured to you again" (Luke 6:38).

After eight years of this exciting prayer journey seeing God bless the conference in unimaginable ways, the evangelism offering reached one million dollars. Everyone was praising God. The next year, this miracle happened again! However, the prayer partners did not grow content, but continued asking God what they should pray for next.

The tenth year, a few of the prayer partners were convicted to pray that God would *double the offering* and bring in two million dollars. Some of the conference leaders felt this was impossible, but the prayer partners prayed anyway.

Saturday night, during the final weekend at camp meeting that next year, as Pastor Page was getting ready to go up to speak, a man came up and asked him how the offering was coming along. Pastor Page

responded that it was coming along very well and that they would probably reach one million dollars again, although a few of the prayer partners, he confided, seeming to be going a little crazy, had felt impressed
to pray for two million dollars. The man's eyes got big. "Really?" he
asked in amazement? "Are you kidding me? The prayer team is praying
for two million dollars?"

"Yes!" Pastor Page responded.

The man then began to share how just that afternoon he and his
brother had decided to ask God what they should do to help with the
evangelism offering that year. At first they were both thinking of giving one hundred thousand dollars to help, but as they talked, God impressed them that they should put one million dollars on top of what
all the others gave. Now it was Pastor Page's eyes that grew wide with
amazement. God had once again heard and answered prayer!

After fifteen years in the Central California Conference, Pastor Jerry
Page and his wife, Janet, were called to work at the Seventh-day Adventist World Church Headquarters in Maryland.[1] But even after they left
the Central California Conference, the evangelism offering has continued to be over one million dollars every year. It's very evident that God
has continued to work in a mighty way in the Central California Conference as the prayer partners have continued to pray bold, audacious,
faith-filled prayers.

While we should never be demanding or presumptuous in our
prayers, I believe that God likes it when we make large, even *audacious*
requests of Him, especially if these prayers will glorify His name. Of
course, it's important that, just as the Central California prayer partners
did, we first go to God and ask *what it is* that we should be praying for.
If we first seek to align ourselves with God's will, then, knowing that the
Holy Spirit has guided our prayers, we can pray boldly and audaciously.
John 15:7 tells us, "If ye abide in me, and my words abide in you, ye
shall ask what ye will, and it shall be done unto you."

Imagine what God would do if, instead of trying to do all the work
in our own strength, we would listen to His voice, learn to abide in
Him, and then spend significant time in prayer!

Inspiration tells us, "The same compassionate Saviour lives today, and He is as willing to listen to the prayer of faith as when He walked visibly among men. The natural co-operates with the supernatural. It is a part of God's plan to grant us, in answer to the prayer of faith, that which He would not bestow did we not thus ask."[2]

Reading the Pages' testimony, some may shake their heads in disbelief thinking, *It's great God did this for their conference! They had hundreds if not thousands of people involved. But what about my little church? We don't have enough members to run any more ministries, and we can barely collect two hundred dollars a month in offerings. How could we ever do anything really great for God? How could we dare to ask God for more? We are only a few!*

Well, let me share just such a story.

The little church that could!

The English branch of the Seattle Central Korean Seventh-day Adventist Church in Washington State witnessed powerfully how God can answer prayer when everyone steps out in faith together, expecting great things.

Martin Kim, a pastor and prayer evangelist, shares their story in his own words:

> In December, our church, being convicted that we all needed to become more actively involved in fulfilling the Great Commission and in helping missions, began designating all loose offerings for foreign missions. Typically, loose offerings amounted to about $200 each month. It wasn't much, but we knew that overseas this money would go a long way to feed the physically and spiritually malnourished.
>
> After our second collection of around $200 in January, I listened to a powerful message by an overseas missionary who shared story after story of how God had provided and moved the work forward. And then I was really challenged when the missionary asked if we would ever have enough money to finish the work. No! Of course not! Not even

$10 million or $100 million would be enough; thus, we should learn to move forward by faith, trusting the God of infinite resources to provide.

Agreeing with this challenge, I knew that if we didn't step forward in faith and trust God to do what only He could do, we would never finish the work. After all, the Jordan River didn't part until the first priest put his feet in the water. God always wants to see His people move in faith.

So I began to pray, "Lord, I want to step forward in faith. I want to see You do the kinds of things that this missionary talks about. Lord, what do You want us to do in our little church?"

I began thinking about our special offering for foreign missions. Initially, I wanted to challenge our church to pray for a $500 offering, but I decided that $500 did not require much faith at all. After much prayer and thought, I finally concluded that it would definitely require *a lot* of faith to ask God for a $1,000 offering.

Since our last offering collected in January had gone to provide rice for the people of Vietnam, our group decided to provide Bibles for the Vietnamese in February. So the following Sabbath, I put this challenge to our members, asking them to pray for an offering of $1,000 so we could provide two hundred Bibles to the people of Vietnam.

Every Sabbath and through the weekly church announcements via e-mail, our members were reminded to pray for this special gift. I reminded them that when we pray, God moves and does that which only He can do. We also encouraged our members with promises from God's Word.

Ellen White writes, "Many whom God has qualified to do excellent work accomplish very little, because they attempt little. Thousands pass through life as if they had no definite object for which to live, no standard to reach.

Such will obtain a reward proportionate to their works."[3]

On the other hand, Christ's disciples "expected much, therefore they attempted much."[4] His disciples give the pattern we are to follow today.

In February, God blessed us, not with $1,000 but with $4,382! Instead of giving the Vietnamese 200 Bibles, we were able to provide 876![5]

What do you do after you witness the power of prayer and see God move in such a mighty way? We decided that praying for the same amount would show no faith. So we decided to take the last amount and round up. We prayed that God would bless us with a $4,500 offering in March. This time we wanted to use the funds to provide bamboo churches for Cambodia. If we raised $4,500, we could provide at least eight churches.

In March, God blessed us with an offering of $6,684! Rather than building eight churches, we were able to build twelve![6] Once again we had witnessed God's power and grace.

To make a long story short, we continued each month to dare to ask for more and more, and over the course of that year, we saw over $120,000 come through our church—just for foreign missions alone. It was almost unbelievable, *except we were all there and saw it happen month by month.* Can you tell me that God doesn't answer audacious prayer? He not only answers, but He's just longing to pour out blessings *exceedingly abundantly above* our greatest expectations!

Prayer is not a part of the work; it is the most important work. "When we work, we work; but when we pray, God works."[7] How true this is!

Interceding for the deliverance of nations

Rees Howells, a twentieth-century missionary to Africa and later to

Europe, dared to ask for more. Not only did he pray for more resources to do the Lord's work and more souls for the kingdom, but he also prayed for the deliverance of nations so that the gospel work could go forward unhindered.

This powerful revivalist and intercessor built a Bible college in Wales just a few years before World War II began. Once the war began, recognizing the threat of Hitler's regime to the spread of the gospel, he immediately rallied his staff and students—about a hundred—to begin interceding that God would counteract the work of Hitler and the enemy of souls.[8]

All during the war, the Wales Bible College staff and students devoted from 7:00 P.M. until midnight every night in prayer. This was in addition to an hour-long prayer meeting in the morning and at noon. During the hardest days of battle, they often fasted and prayed all throughout the day and often all night.

As Hitler's Nazi regime brought tragedy and destruction to the lives of millions, Howells and his students prayed four specific prayers about four specific aspects of the war.

The first prayer was that Hitler would not succeed in invading Great Britain. As history tells us, Great Britain did not fall to the Nazis, but if the Germans had kept up their bombing just *five more minutes* on that last horror-filled day, Great Britain would have fallen into their grasp.[9] The second prayer was that Hitler would not attack Egypt and gain Alexandria. The third prayer was that he would not succeed in overthrowing Moscow. And the fourth was that he would not succeed in his attack against Stalingrad.

Toward the end of the war, military commentator General J. R. C. Fuller published an article titled "Hitler's Four Blunders," listing four reasons for the impending doom of Hitler and the Nazis. First, Hitler failed to invade Britain. Second, he did not attack Egypt and gain Alexandria. Third, he did not capitalize on his advantageous position to invade and overthrow Moscow. And fourth, he was defeated in the great attack on Stalingrad.[10]

Were these "four blunders" merely Hitler's failures, or did they happen because God heard the prayers of this small group in Wales desperate to see deliverance so that the gospel would not be hindered? While many may speculate, I believe that the latter is the answer.

The last great prayer battle for Howells and the praying intercessors at Wales Bible College was for the opening of the Western front. After months of wrestling prayer on behalf of the Allied troops, in May 1944, God assured them that He was going over before the Allied troops and that they would have no setback.

One month later, on June 6, 1944, Allied forces successfully landed unmolested on the beaches of Normandy, France. It was the largest amphibious invasion in world history, with 175,000 soldiers brought over on 5,000 ships and in 11,000 planes in *one night*. Now known as D-Day, this was a great turning point in the war against Hitler. We have since learned that this night was the *only night* of the war that no Nazi U-boats patrolled the English Channel.[11]

What would have happened that day if Rees Howells and his students at Wales Bible College had not been praying? Inspiration tells us, "Success does not depend upon numbers. God can deliver by few as well as by many. He is honored not so much by the great numbers as by the character of those who serve Him."[12]

Just imagine!

Rees Howells's testimony should challenge and convict us today. What if God's church rose up unitedly in persevering prayer for those nations still locked in darkness? What if we fasted and prayed and kept daring to ask for deliverance of our brothers and sisters who don't yet know Christ? These are big prayer requests, but don't we serve a big God?

Just imagine what would happen if we once again took the Word of God seriously, putting away our differences, humbling our hearts, and praying in unity for the work to go forward—until God answered! What would happen if, instead of talking *about* each other, we took the time to pray *for* each other—through the night if needed, to see healing and victory? Just imagine the many *more* miracles we would see in our lives today!

In the book *In Heavenly Places,* Ellen White counsels, "Prayer is a heaven-ordained means of success. Appeals, petitions, entreaties, be-tween man and man, move men and act a part in controlling the affairs of nations. But prayer moves heaven."[13]

God is looking for intercessors. He's looking for men and women who will dare to ask for more, who will dare to intercede on behalf of His land (Ezekiel 22:30). We may be only one or two, but each of us plays a valuable part in this great work of intercession.

E. M. Bounds writes,

> We are constantly on a stretch, if not on a strain, to devise new methods, new plans, new organization to ad-vance the church and secure enlargement and efficiency for the gospel. This trend of the day has a tendency to lose sight of the man or sink the man in the plan or organiza-tion. God's plan is to make much of the man, far more of him than of anything else. Men are God's method. The church is looking for better methods; God is looking for better men. . . .
>
> What the church needs today is not more machinery or better, not new organizations or more and novel meth-ods, but men whom the Holy Spirit can use—men of prayer, men mighty in prayer.[14]

We need a bigger vision in prayer. We need God's vision! Let's keep praying and daring to ask for more—for God's glory, that the gospel may go into all the world, into all nations, that Jesus may come!

Part II

Divine Keys to Answered Prayer

Chapter 9

Overcoming the Distraction Dilemma

Putting Life's Priorities in Proper Order

> *Martha, Martha, thou art careful and troubled about many things: But one thing is needful: and Mary hath chosen that good part, which shall not be taken away from her.*
>
> —Luke 10:41, 42

*M*ost everyone in the world today is searching for a magic key—the key to unlock the door to success, fame, and fortune; the key to finding the right spouse, keys to living happily ever after, keys to raising smart kids, keys to staying young and beautiful, and on and on and on. While some seem to have grasped what appears to be a magic key, without an anchor and purpose in Christ, they will continue to drift aimlessly through life.

Although heaven's definition of success is not the same as the world's, God has given us specific keys for success. Indeed, all the keys that we need to be effective in our relationships, in our families, in our ministries, in our prayers, and even in staying healthy, He has already given us in His Word. We have an anchor!

However, although God has given us all the keys we need to live a successful Christian life, these keys will not bring any benefits unless we use them. Most of heaven's keys sit on our shelf gathering dust because we are too busy to pick them up. To illustrate, let me share an imaginary story.

Have you ever wondered what it might be like to sit in a planning session that Satan and the enemy forces hold to discuss how to disrupt the lives of God's children? Well, one author felt inspired to write the following, and he's probably not too far off the mark. Let's listen in:

> One day Satan called a worldwide meeting to discuss how to keep Christians from having a deep and powerful walk with Christ. The huge crowd hushed as he stepped up to speak.
>
> "We can't keep Christians from going to church," he began. "We can't keep them from reading their Bibles and knowing the truth. We can't keep them from conservative values, but we can do something." He paused. Everyone listened. "We can keep them from forming an intimate, abiding experience in Christ. If they gain that connection with Him, our power over them is broken. So let them go to church, let them have their conservative lifestyles, but steal their time, so they can't gain that deep experience in Jesus. This is what I want you to do. Distract them from gaining hold of their Savior and maintaining a vital connection throughout their day!"
>
> "How shall we do this?" shouted his angels.
>
> "Simple!" he replied. "Keep them busy, busy, busy in the nonessentials of life and invent un-numbered schemes to occupy their time and attention. Tempt them to spend and spend, then borrow and borrow. Keep them from their children. Convince the wives to go to work and the

husbands to work six and seven days a week, ten to twelve hours a day, so they can afford their expensive lifestyles. Tell them they are doing it for their children. Ha! That one works well. As their families disintegrate, soon their homes won't offer an escape from the pressures of work, and they will just work all the harder." Then Satan paused.

"But this is the most important thing. Overstimulate their minds so that they cannot hear the still, small voice of God any longer. Entice them to play the radio or music whenever they drive or relax. Entice them to keep the TV, DVDs, MP3s, iPods, radios, and any other distracting noises going constantly in their homes. This nonstop noise and activity will clutter their minds and break their union with Christ.

"Fill their homes with magazines and newspapers. Pound their minds with the news twenty-four hours a day. Invade their driving moments with billboards. Flood their mailboxes with junk mail, sweepstakes, mail-order catalogues, every kind of newsletter and promotional offering, free products, services, and false hopes. Keep them distracted with constant noises, e-mails, text messages, and phone calls from the time they first wake up until they fall exhausted into their beds at night.

"Even in their recreation, let them be excessive. Don't let them go out to enjoy the simple joys of nature. Instead, send them to amusement parks, sporting events, concerts, and movies.

"When they meet for spiritual fellowship, involve them in gossip and small talk so that they leave with troubled consciences and unsettled emotions. Don't let them encourage or uplift each other. Keep those who are the gifted encouragers especially busy and worn out!

"And above all, when they get together, keep them from praying for one another. If they must, let them be involved in ministry. But crowd their lives with so many good causes that they have no time to seek power from Christ. Soon they will be working in their own strengths, sacrificing their health and family unity for the good of the cause. And we will be victorious!"

It was quite a convention in the end. And the evil angels went eagerly to their assignments trying to cause Christians everywhere to get busy, busy, busy, and to rush here and there.[1]

If Satan truly has an agenda to distract us, it appears that he's been pretty successful at it, hasn't he? When we evaluate the society and life-style of most of us Christians today, especially in the modern world, this is our reality. We are *busy, busy, busy*! Satan doesn't mind if our lives are consumed in ministry or service to God (like Martha), as long as we don't have time to sit still at Jesus' feet. He doesn't mind so much if we are out teaching and preaching and doing the Lord's work, just as long as we do not have personal time to spend with the Lord of the work. After all, if he can keep us from abiding in Christ, the Living Vine, our labors will be fruitless (John 15:5).

Making time with God a priority

The last few years, life and ministry seem to have gotten more and more time consuming for me. There are never enough hours in a day to get everything done that needs to be done. However, I've learned that I must make my quality time with God one of those non-negotiables in my daily schedule, for I need His strength and guidance to move forward safely.

Making time for daily devotions is not something we do so we can check it off our to-do list for the day. It's so we can know our Savior and King. If you love someone, you don't ask, "How much time must I spend with him or her?" but rather, "What can I possibly do to rear-range my life and schedule so we can spend *even more* time together?" While I don't believe God wants us to be "clock watchers," the more we get to know Him, the more time we will want to spend in His presence.

Some may take more time and some may take less, but the most important thing is that we get enough time with Him each day to know that He is with us and is ready to walk with us. Ellen White writes, "Do not leave your closet until you feel strong in God."[2] Until we have this peace, we must not leave our time with Him. This is not about fitting Him around our agenda, but making ourselves available to *His* agenda. She writes further:

> Many, even in their seasons of devotion, fail of receiving the blessing of real communion with God. They are in too great haste. With hurried steps they press through the circle of Christ's loving presence, pausing perhaps a moment within the sacred precincts, but not waiting for counsel. They have no time to remain with the divine Teacher. With their burdens they return to their work.
>
> These workers can never attain the highest success until they learn the secret of strength. They must give themselves *time to think, to pray, to wait upon God* for a renewal of physical, mental, and spiritual power. They need the uplifting influence of His Spirit. Receiving this, they will be quickened by fresh life. The wearied frame and tired brain will be refreshed, the burdened heart will be lightened.[3]

My friend Pavel Goia, whose life story is shared in the book *One Miracle After Another*,[4] shares how when he was first converted and still living in communist Romania, he made the commitment to God that he was never going to leave his place of prayer and worship in the morning for any reason until he knew that God was with him and would accompany him through his day. He stuck fast to that promise, even when he accidently slept in one day, and he knew that if he kept his commitment to God, he would miss an important class at school taught by one of the strictest communist professors he'd ever had. Although fearing what the repercussions would be because of his absence, he took the time with God he needed (about two hours). When he arrived at school, he found that the class he had missed had been canceled because his professor was sick.

Another time, Pavel accidently slept in again. This time, he had an important meeting with the county building commissioner, as he had been denied wages by an unruly supervisor. Realizing he only had fifteen minutes to spare, he grabbed his clothes and prepared to leave when God reminded him that they hadn't had their time together yet. Pavel knew it would be horrible to miss such an important appointment, and that his job could be on the line, but he knew that his appointment with God was more important. So he stopped rushing and sat down to read his Bible and pray.

Two hours later, he headed toward the appointment he had missed, unsure of what he would find, but certain that God was with him. When he arrived, he gladly discovered that the building commissioner had been tied up all morning in meetings and that he hadn't even missed the appointment. However, just then, the man opened his office door and came out to the secretary's desk where Pavel was waiting. Pavel was able to share his problem and the issue was quickly resolved.

Time and time again throughout his life, and even while serving in the Romanian communist military, God worked miracle after miracle as Pavel made his daily time with God his first priority.

Ellen White herself was known for her hours spent in the Word and in prayer. Often rising as early as 2:00 A.M. or 3:00 A.M., she would spend hours pleading with the Lord for wisdom and direction. Staying up all night in prayer was not out of the ordinary. Although weak and frail in health for most of her life, her strength she gained through prayer. And it's obvious that God blessed, as her Holy Spirit–filled life has impacted millions even to this day.

John Wesley once stated, "I have so much to do that I spend several hours in prayer before I am able to do it."[5] Martin Luther agreed: "If I fail to spend two hours in prayer each morning, the devil gets the victory through the day."[6] S. D. Gordon wrote:

> The great people of the earth today are the people who pray! I do not mean those who talk about prayer; nor those who say they believe in prayer; nor those who explain prayer; but I mean those who *actually take the*

time to pray. They have not time. It must be taken from something else. **That something else is important, very important and pressing, but still, less important and pressing than prayer.** There are people who put prayer first, and group the other items in life's schedule around and after prayer. These are the people today who are doing the most for God in winning souls, in solving problems, in awakening churches.[7]

Speaking of mighty men of prayer, I don't think we have a better example than our Lord and Savior Jesus Christ. It wasn't any easier for Jesus to get away and pray than it is for us today.

No other life was ever so crowded with labor and responsibility as was that of Jesus; yet how often He was found in prayer! How constant was His communion with God! Again and again in the history of His earthly life are found records such as these: "Rising up a great while before day, He went out, and departed into a solitary place, and there prayed." "Great multitudes came together to hear, and to be healed by Him of their infirmities. And He withdrew Himself into the wilderness, and prayed." "And it came to pass in those days, that He went out into a mountain to pray, and continued all night in prayer to God." Mark 1:35; Luke 5:15, 16; 6:12.[8]

We may be busy—very busy—but that is no excuse to miss daily quality time with God. We are not busier than Jesus, and we never will be. Jesus was so busy that He often didn't even have time to eat as he dealt with the needs of those pressing around Him. Yet it was often during these busiest times that He spent His nights in prayer. As a result, He came back to His work renewed and invigorated. We have much to learn from His example.

The small belief we have in the true effectiveness and power of prayer is painfully evidenced by the little time we give to it in our daily lives. If we truly understood the gift God has given us in the *divine appointment of prayer,* we would no longer be fitting prayer around our schedules, but we would be seeking to fit our schedules around prayer. We would be praying throughout our days, and every decision that arises, rather than stretching our tired brains, would be an instant call to prayer.

Charles Spurgeon, a famous revivalist known for his success in ministry due to prayer, stated, "Sometimes we think we are too busy to pray. That is a great mistake, for praying is a saving of time."[9]

If God is truly going to be free to work powerfully in our lives, something has to change—and that something is our priorities.

> Heaven with its attractions is before you, an eternal weight of glory, which you may lose or gain. Which shall it be? Your life and your character will testify the choice you have made. I feel the more anxious because I see so many indifferent upon the subjects of infinite importance. They are always busy here and there about matters of minor importance, and the one great subject is put out of their thoughts. They have no time to pray, no time to watch, no time to search the Scriptures. They are altogether too busy to make the necessary preparation for the future life. They cannot devote time to perfect Christian characters and in diligence to secure a title to heaven.[10]

In the next chapter, I will share more practical tips about how we can *intentionally* rearrange our priorities so we can have undistracted time with God each day.

For now, we may be busy, but let us not be too busy to pray and spend time in God's Word. Our lives and eternal destinies depend upon it. God is not asking for much, but if we are going to dare to ask for more, He's asking for more too!

Chapter 10

Safeguarding Our Set-Apart Time

Making First Things First

> *But seek ye first the kingdom of God, and his righteousness; and all these things shall be added unto you.*
>
> —*Matthew 6:33*

A professor pulled out a large glass jar filled with fist-sized rocks. She then asked her class if the jar was full.

"Yes," they all responded. Then she brought out a pail of pea-sized chunks of gravel and shook them into the jar down around the larger rocks. "Is the jar full now?" she asked again.

"Probably not," was the response. Then she brought out a container of sand and poured it into the jar. It filled all the cracks around the small and large rocks. "What about now?" she asked.

"No!" they responded with certainty, "It's still not full." She smiled. "You are right," she said as she brought out a pitcher of water and poured it into the jar. The water soaked down through the sand and around the rocks. She stepped back with a smile. "So what am I trying to teach you through this object lesson?"

One student piped up, "You're telling us that no matter how busy we are, we can always squeeze a bit more into our schedule." Everyone laughed.

But she shook her head. "Learn to put the big rocks in the jar first, and then fit everything else around them! You have to set your priorities in life consciously, otherwise the details of life—the sand and the gravel—will swallow up your time."

And so it is with our lives. Spiritually, physically, financially, and emotionally, we need to learn to prioritize and put the big rocks—the most important things in our lives—in the jar first, before they get crowded out by the mundane daily details of life.

For those of us in ministry, we often fool ourselves into thinking that serving God is the equivalent to knowing God. But it is not! God is calling us to *be with Him* and *know Him* before we go and serve Him (see Mark 3:14). We cannot give to others what we have not received ourselves sitting at His feet. Nothing is so important in our lives that it's worth holding on to at the risk of losing our own souls.

Ellen White warns, "Beware how you neglect secret prayer and a study of God's word. These are your weapons against him who is striving to hinder your progress heavenward. The first neglect of prayer and Bible study makes easier the second neglect."[1]

As we learn to make time with God our daily priority (even if we skip a little sleep or cut out something else), we will discover that everything else in life will begin to flow more smoothly. Instead of taking all day to accomplish a project, it will take just a few hours because we are running on supernatural strength and wisdom. Instead of feeling anxious and stressed, although many things demand our attention, we will have perfect peace because God's in control. While it doesn't always make sense by human standards, whenever we give to God, He always gives back *much more*.

Guarding your set-apart time

Now that we've recommitted to put God first, how do we protect and guard our time with Him each day? The following are some of my personal tips.

Find your own solitary place to meet with God. In Mark 1:35, we are told, "And in the morning, rising up a great while before day, he [Christ] went out, and departed into a *solitary place,* and there prayed."

It's helpful to have your own solitary place where you have your devotions each day. It might be a favorite chair by your fireplace, or it might be in a literal *closet* where prying eyes don't see. My family has some dear friends, the Chapmans, who have eight children still at home. As you can imagine, they stay quite busy keeping up with daily life and homeschooling. To safeguard their personal devotion time each day, they have built a small cabin on their property—more like a small tool shed—that is reserved specifically for the parents and older children to take turns having solitary time with God to read the Bible and pray without distraction. I've never seen anyone do this before. What an inspiring example of priority to guarding that solitary place with the Lord. If there's a will to spend time alone with God, we will find a way!

Of course, there's nothing magic about a *place.* After all, God is not confined within walls or space. He goes with us, via the Holy Spirit, wherever we go. The point is, if you have a designated appointment spot, it's easier to remain undistracted during your time with Him than if you have no plan and are moving randomly about your home in the midst of the clutter of daily life.

Develop the habit of going to bed at a reasonable hour. I won't go into the health benefits of adequate sleep, or the fact that Ellen White once said that the sleep we get before midnight is twice as beneficial as what we get after midnight.[2]

However, unless we plan ahead, even the night before, it will be very difficult to get up and spend time with God the next morning because we are simply too tired from staying up late. There are legitimate reasons that will keep us up late (like taking care of sick children or meeting a ministry deadline), but these should be the exception and not the rule.

When we choose to do our own thing late into the night, we've already made the choice to put God in the backseat the next day. If our prayer lives are going to change, this pattern must change. We have to be intentional about saying No to some things at night so we can say Yes to the Lord in the morning.

Develop the habit of getting up early. E. M. Bounds writes, "The men who have done the most for God in this world have been early on their knees. He who fritters away the early morning, its opportunity and freshness, in [sleep or in] other pursuits than seeking God will make poor headway seeking him the rest of the day. If God is not first in our thoughts and efforts in the morning, he will be the last place the remainder of the day."[3]

Robert M'Cheyne, a minister in Scotland in the early 1800s, struggled with making early prayer a habit, but he felt the difference when it was lacking. Most of us can probably relate with his thoughts:

> I ought to pray before seeing any one. Often when I sleep long, or meet with others early, it is eleven or twelve o'clock before I begin secret prayer. This is a wretched system. It is unscriptural. Christ arose before day and went into a solitary place. David says: "Early will I seek thee"; "Thou shalt early hear my voice." Family prayer loses much of its power and sweetness, and I can do no good to those who come to seek from me. The conscience feels guilty, the soul unfed, the lamp not trimmed. Then when in secret prayer the soul is often out of tune, I feel it is far better to begin with God—to see his face first, to get my soul near him before it is near another.[4]

Of course, some reading this book may work nights or have different sleeping habits. Whenever your day starts, try to make it a priority to get up extra early to have that sacred undistracted time with God before you begin your daily (or nightly) duties. And if you don't think you *can* get up—well, just ask God to wake you up. He'll do it if you give Him permission.

John Bunyan, author of *The Pilgrim's Progress,* once stated, "He who runs from God in the morning will scarcely find Him the rest of the day."[5] May this *not* be our testimony!

When you get up, don't get distracted! Ellen White counsels, "Consecrate yourself to God in the morning; make this your very first work."[6]

When you get up in the morning, it is absolutely vital that you avoid turning on the radio, television news, or any distracting noise that would pull your attention from God. Also, refrain from checking your e-mails, text messages, social media accounts, or any other electronic communication.

Cell phones—especially smartphones—are probably the biggest distracters when we first wake up. Because of this, I have learned to utilize the "airplane mode" in the early morning. Whatever you do, seek to avoid nonemergency phone conversations or replying to text messages until you've had that sacred time with God. This may seem petty, but I've found this to make a huge difference in the quality of my devotional time because God knows that *He comes first* and that He's the most important Person in my life.

If you find your devotional time interrupted by thoughts of your long to-do list or other unrelated thoughts, instead of feeling guilty, just take a second and jot them down on a separate sheet of paper so you can remember them after your devotional time is over.

Admittedly, for those with young children, finding quality time alone is always a struggle. If you can't manage to wake up before your children do, or you don't have help from a spouse in giving you some undistracted quiet time, just do the best you can with what time you have. It may not be ideal, but remember that God always honors our *sincere efforts*. Even if it's just a few minutes here and there, He can multiply the blessing just as He multiplied the loaves and fishes.

On the other hand, if our lack of quality devotional time is due to laziness or mismanaged priorities, we shouldn't expect God to make up the difference. He's asking us to put Him first, not just in theory, but literally. Once we start doing this, everything else in our day will fit together!

Make a plan and be consistent! While we need to always be open to the Holy Spirit's leading, it's important to have a tentative plan each day of how we are going to spend our time with God. That way, we won't get distracted trying to figure out what to study when we wake up.

There's not a right or wrong way to have devotions. The important thing is that *we have them*! However, it's crucial that we make time for both Bible study *and* prayer. We shouldn't neglect one for the other—the two go hand in hand.

I usually start my devotions with my prayer time, as it just seems natural to start my day talking with God. I also want the Holy Spirit's blessing before I start reading His Word.

As there are many things and people I pray for daily, I've written my routine prayer requests down on flash cards, often with a Bible verse on the other side. Then I put the flash cards on a key ring so they all stay together, and I can carry them with me wherever I go. Once a specific request is answered, I take the card off the ring and fold it up, putting it in a jar on my shelf. It has encouraged my faith to watch the prayer jar being filled up as God answers my prayers!

One of my favorite parts of prayer each morning is praise and worship. If I'm not in danger of disturbing someone, I will sing during my prayer time. Inspiration tells us, ". . . Singing is as much an act of worship as is prayer. Indeed, many a song is prayer."[7]

Another favorite part of prayer for me is praying the Word. I can't emphasize this enough! I think many people miss out because they don't see the connection between God's Word and their prayer lives. The Bible isn't meant just to be read through; it's meant to be *prayed through*.

The Word of God contains thousands of promises. Once we start to take hold of the promises of Scripture, we will never lack subjects for our prayer lives.

After taking time for prayer, I will engage in more focused Bible study. I will either study out a specific Bible topic or story, or I will follow a daily Bible reading plan, such as the Revived by His Word initiative.[8]

I like to read cross-references, as well as look up the original words in Hebrew and Greek to gain a better understanding of a Bible passage. This is powerful! However, even if we become the best scholars in the world and don't allow the Bible to change our hearts and lives, what has been gained? Thus, as I study and read God's Word, I'm constantly asking myself, "How can I apply this to my life today? What is God trying to teach me through this passage today? How can I become more like Him today?"

I also like to read any corresponding material found in the Conflict of the Ages series or other resources from the Spirit of Prophecy. Reading these *along with* my Bible study has given me much greater understanding and appreciation for the Word itself. Although I grew up with these resources right under my nose, it's only been in recent years that I've discovered the "gold mine" we Adventists have been given in the inspired writings of Ellen White. [9] It's incredible!

Of course, nothing can replace the power of the Word itself. While there are many popular devotionals out these days, it's very important that we *do not* let contemporary devotionals—or even Spirit of Prophecy compilations and devotionals—powerful as they may be, take away from actual time in God's Word. Nothing can replace God's Word!

> There is nothing more calculated to strengthen the intellect than the study of the Scriptures. No other book is so potent to elevate the thoughts, to give vigor to the faculties, as the broad, ennobling truths of the Bible. If God's Word were studied as it should be, men would have a breadth of mind, a nobility of character, and a stability of purpose rarely seen in these times. [10]

For more Bible study tips, including how to go deeper in study, check out the free online booklet that Armando Miranda, vice president of the General Conference, and I recently put together and titled *Revived by God's Word: A Mini-Handbook for Bible Study*. [11]

Again, the key point is not that you follow a certain plan or method every day, but that you take *time each day consistently*, and that during this time, you give priority to prayer and Bible study, being open to what God is trying to teach you.

Treat God with respect, as the King He really is! Inspiration remind us, ". . . We should come before [God] with holy awe. The angels veil their faces in His presence. The cherubim and the bright and holy seraphim approach His throne with solemn reverence. How much more should we, finite, sinful beings, come in a reverent manner before the Lord, our Maker!"[12]

Many people desire an audience with the powerful and influential Zulu king in South Africa, but few get it. A few years back, God opened up a rare opportunity for one of my friends to spend an entire day with him, and they became good friends. Later, when the king's daughter was married, my friend was invited to the wedding.

You can imagine the respect my friend showed the king when in his presence. He didn't interrupt their conversation to take a phone call or to answer a text message. He wasn't running off to do this task or that. He stayed in the king's presence and just enjoyed the day, talking and getting acquainted.

If this is the kind of respect we give earthly dignitaries, shouldn't we show the same kind of respect to our Lord and King of the universe when we meet with Him?

My friend Leslie Ludy shares a story about the great Reformer John Wesley. He had been invited to spend an evening with Lord Byron, the most powerful man in England. This was a great honor, as people would wait months and months to get an audience with this man. However, before the evening was over, John Wesley got up and excused himself, saying that he needed to leave.

Lord Byron was almost offended. "Why are you leaving when the night is still young?" he asked. "Don't you realize that I am a very important man and many people beg to spend time with me at my table?"

Wesley replied, "I don't mean to offend you, sir, and I feel very honored for this time together. But I have an appointment with the King of the universe now, and I dare not be tired and I dare not be late."

Talk about a real-life example of keeping your priorities straight! You might be thinking, *Yeah, but it seems there could have been a little exception there, don't you think? After all, Wesley was with an important dignitary. He could always spend time with God later. God would surely understand.*

God does understand. He understands that we are weak, frail, and in desperate need of a continual connection with Him—a connection that needs to be stronger than any earthly ties and more important than any earthly honor. He is, after all, the King of kings and the Lord of lords. Prayer is our "divine appointment"—the appointment above all others. When we miss it, we are putting ourselves on enemy ground.

Inspiration tells us, "The darkness of the evil one encloses those who neglect to pray. The whispered temptations of the enemy entice them to sin; and it is all because they do not make use of the privileges that God has given them in the divine appointment of prayer."[13]

Keep God with you as you go throughout your day. Even after our morning devotions are over, God is to go *with* us, to stay *with* us, and to abide *with* us. Like Enoch, we should learn to walk with God each day. When problems arise, and we are in need of wisdom, we are to pray. Indeed, "We may keep so near to God that in every unexpected trial our thoughts will turn to Him as naturally as the flower turns to the sun."[14]

Ellen White, addressing ministers and church leaders, spoke strongly: "None need feel that they are too busy to pray, too full of business cares to spend an occasional fifteen minutes to seek counsel from God. My brethren, make God your entire dependence [as you go through your day]. When you do otherwise, then it is time for a halt to be called. Stop right where you are, and change the order of things."[15]

We may have good intentions (and most of us do), but when those good intentions do not carry over to good discipleship, it is usually due to a lack of intentionality on our part. So let's learn to be *intentional*!

Having a close, deep relationship with God will not develop by accident or by random visits. We must take time for *intentional* cultivation. We must guard our set-apart time with God as sacred, for it belongs to God just as much as our tithe. Remember, Daniel saw his time of worship and prayer as so significant that he was willing to go to the lions' den rather than give it up! Are we this committed today?

As we move forward, let us dare to put God first each and every day! After all, He isn't just anyone. He is our Savior and King!

Chapter 11

Putting Away All Pretense

Heart Reform From the Inside Out

> *For he is not a [Christian], which is one outwardly. . . . But he is a [Christian], which is one inwardly.*
>
> —Romans 2:28, 29

One of the saddest realities of Christianity today is that there are many Christians, but few disciples. There are many intellectually convinced believers, but few converted. Many have knowledge about God, but most do not know Him experientially. Most have the spiritual keys in their possession, but these keys don't impact their day-to-day lives. As a result of this sad reality, God cannot work as He desires. And in actuality, our own spiritual pretense, without true heart conversion, is actually holding back heaven's blessings.

A number of years ago in the Congo, there was a pop star singer who was very popular. The Lord touched his heart and he gave his life to Christ. He thought that when he came into the church he would escape from the world. Instead, he found the world already in the church.

Sadly, this is too often what we find today.

> Many who call themselves Christians are mere human moralists. They have refused the gift which alone could enable them to honor Christ by representing Him to the world. The work of the Holy Spirit is to them a strange work. They are not doers of the word. The heavenly principles that distinguish those who are one with Christ from those who are one with the world have become almost indistinguishable. The professed followers of Christ are no longer a separate and peculiar people. The line of demarcation is indistinct. The people are subordinating themselves to the world, to its practices, its customs, and its selfishness. The church has gone over to the world in transgression of the law, when the world should have come over to the church in obedience to the law. Daily the church is being converted to the world.[1]

Ellen White, addressing the church during the late 1800s, makes the shocking statement that not even *one* in twenty, whose names are registered in church books, are prepared to end their earthly history. She continues that if they did, many would find themselves without hope and without God, just as any other common sinner.[2] If this was the case with many in the church then, what would be our story today?

Sadly, things aren't getting any better. The most popular religion of today is actually the *religion of form*. Far too many Christians have become content with a "form of godliness" without the power of true godliness (2 Timothy 3:5). Their profession has become nothing more than pretension; they are *pretending to be something they are not*.

When I speak, I often ask congregations, "What would happen if a movie screen was played today for the whole church to see your personal activities from this past week? What would we see about the way you lived your life, about the way you talked to your family members, about your conversations with your coworkers, about what you listened to in the car, about what you looked at on the Internet, about your thought life towards those around you? Would you be OK if that movie was shown for all of us to see?"

Of course, it's not what our fellow church members see that is most important. It's what God sees! The Bible tells us, "The LORD seeth not as man seeth; for man looketh on the outward appearance, but the LORD looketh on the heart" (1 Samuel 16:7). God is concerned with our *hearts*. What goes on in our minds? What do we enjoy when no one is watching? What is the motive of our thoughts and actions? Are we really seeking Him, or are we just trying to hold up a respectable reputation?

If there's anything that God does not accept, it's pretenders. *Pretense,* another word for *hypocrisy,* actually holds back His Spirit and His blessing. Inspiration tells us soberly, "The influence most to be feared by the church is not that of open opposers, infidels, and blasphemers, but of *inconsistent professors* of Christ. These are the ones that keep back the blessing of the God of Israel and bring weakness upon His people."[3]

"There must be no pretense in the lives of those who have so sacred and solemn a message as we have been called to bear. The world is watching Seventh-day Adventists, because it knows something of their profession of faith, and of their high standard; and when it sees those who do not live up to their profession, it points at them with scorn."[4]

Has our profession turned into *mere pretense*? While we may be able to fool ourselves some of the time, and we may be able to fool others most of the time, remember that we can't fool God at any time. If we truly want to see our prayers answered and be effective in ministry—not to mention being prepared to meet Jesus—all our pretentious Christianity must stop. Period!

Heart reform from the inside out

In Zambia, there is a unique river named the Luapula. The name *Luapula* means "cutting through." The reason it got this name is because it cuts through one lake, then through mountains and valleys, then through another lake, then through more valleys, and then through a third lake before it finally reaches the ocean. What makes this river unique is that as it cuts through these three lakes, it does not change its speed, nor does it mix with the lakes through which it passes. It keeps its own identity. Fishermen report that fish from the lakes and fish from the river are different. They also report that water from the lakes and water from the river taste different.

We as people of God should be like this river. We are traveling on our way to heaven. On this journey, we travel through many mountains and many valleys. We travel through the world (the three lakes), but we are not to become like the world. We are to be dead to the world—undiluted, separate, and *set-apart*.

While remaining separate and set-apart, we should attract the world to the Christ we serve and the life we live. Just as the Luapula River's strong current will pull people into its flow, so we should be so strong in the Lord that people will be pulled into His flow. But if we allow ourselves to be swallowed by the world, we not only lose our identities as believers, but we have no power to bring people with us to heaven. For this very reason God tells us, "And be not conformed to this world: but be ye transformed by the renewing of your mind, that ye may prove what is that good, and acceptable, and perfect, will of God" (Romans 12:2).

This transformation of heart and mind only God can accomplish as we yield to Him. No matter how much we esteem this fragrant divine nature from Christ, we are not capable of producing it in our own strength. That's why we are admonished, "We need to be converted daily. Our prayers should be more fervent; then they will be more effectual. Stronger and stronger should be our confidence that God's Spirit will be with us, making us pure and holy, as upright and fragrant as the cedar of Lebanon."[5] It's not easy to die to self daily, but if we will surrender our heart and will to Christ, if we will consent for Him to do the work, He will do it.

Ellen White writes:

> Many are inquiring, "*How* am I to make the surrender of myself to God?" You desire to give yourself to Him, but you are weak in moral power, in slavery to doubt, and controlled by the habits of your life of sin. Your promises and resolutions are like ropes of sand. You cannot control your

thoughts, your impulses, your affections. The knowledge of your broken promises and forfeited pledges weakens your confidence in your own sincerity, and causes you to feel that God cannot accept you; but you need not despair. What you need to understand is the true force of the will. This is the governing power in the nature of man, the power of decision, or of choice. Everything depends on the right action of the will. The power of choice God has given to men; it is theirs to exercise. You cannot change your heart, you cannot of yourself give to God its affections; but you can *choose* to serve Him. You can give Him your will; He will then work in you to will and to do according to His good pleasure. Thus your whole nature will be brought under the control of the Spirit of Christ; your affections will be centered upon Him, your thoughts will be in harmony with Him.[6]

That's the amazing wonder of the power of God. When we give Him permission, He changes us from the inside out! This is the key!

We don't have another two thousand years as a church to fool around with the Great Commission that we've been given. We probably don't even have another one hundred years if we look at the signs of the times in which we live. Time is running out. Jesus is coming soon. And the gospel message must go out to the entire world. But before Christ can use us, before He can answer our prayers, we must put away all pretense. We must be consecrated *personally*. When we are, His Holy Spirit can be poured out!

The Lord did not lock the reservoir of heaven after pouring his Spirit upon the early disciples. We, also, may receive of the fullness of his blessing. Heaven is full of the treasures of his grace, and those who come to God in faith may claim all that he has promised. If we do not have his power it is because of our spiritual lethargy, our indifference, our indolence. Let us come out of this formality [religion of form] and deadness.

There is a great work to be done for this time, and we do not half realize what the Lord is willing to do for his people.[7]

The gospel still possesses the same power it had in apostolic times. God's promises have not changed—*His people must change*. He's looking for disciples—consecrated, committed followers. He's given us all we need for life and godliness (2 Peter 1:3), but He is asking us to walk a higher road. This time, He is the One asking *us* for more!

Chapter 12

Dangerous Truth Distortions

God's Word: The True Character Test

> To the law and to the testimony: if they speak not according to this
> word, it is because there is no light in them.
>
> —Isaiah 8:20

*I*n Bible times, the strength of a fortress or city (and sometimes a nation) was determined by the strength of its walls.
Some walls were built anywhere from ten to twenty feet
wide and would stretch on for miles. A classic example is the Great Wall
of China, which was built around 7 B.C. and was almost thirty feet wide
at the base in some parts. This wall stretched on for thousands of miles
and served to provide protection and fortification to China for many
years.[1]

When strong walls obstructed its path, it was virtually impossible for
an opposing army to take control of a city or nation. Because of this,
army commanders realized they needed to use subtle battle tactics if
they were going to be successful in war. One of these tactics was to send

out scouts to find a breach, or weak spot, in the wall. These scouts were also looking for a gate that was not as closely guarded.

The devil works much the same way in his attack against Christians today. He doesn't want to waste time trying to beat down a strong wall when he can sneak in through a small crack. Thus he's constantly looking for a breach. He's constantly testing the bricks around our spiritual fortress to see if he can find a weak spot or *one loose stone* that he can pull out and sneak through. He's constantly checking to see if we've accidently left the back gate unlocked or dropped the key.

The devil doesn't care what the breach in our wall is called or how small it is. It might be called "impatience," "lust," "vanity," or "refusing to forgive." It might even be called "unbelief" or "distortion of truth." As long as he can find a breach, he can squeeze through and do all the damage he wants within the spiritual fortresses of our lives. Sad to say, he's been all too successful in the Christian realm.

> Most Christians today live in a constant state of distress, hounded on all sides by the enemy. There are no protective walls around us, and we are defenseless against Satan's attacks upon our lives. As a result, we go around nursing anger toward God for allowing bad things to happen to us, all the while forgetting that we have an enemy that is hell bent on destroying us, and he will succeed as long as we leave our battle weapons untouched on the ground and the wall around our city in shambles.[2]

While God *does* allow trials and suffering into our lives to purify our characters and grow us (I will talk more about this in a bit), one of the most effective ways Satan tears down our walls of spiritual fortification is by getting us to blame God for the very things that Satan himself has orchestrated. And he has been very successful with this spiritual battle tactic.

The facts of Scripture tell us that God cannot lie, that He is just, that He is merciful, and that He is loving, tenderly looking after His own. Yet, Satan has successfully convinced many in the Christian world that the opposite is true—that God actually comes to steal from, kill, and destroy *His own children,* purely so we will learn a spiritual lesson. This couldn't be further from the truth.

As we evaluate this subtle battle tactic of the enemy, let's review some basic truths of Scripture regarding the character of God and the character of our destroyer. Understanding these truths will affect *how we pray.*

God's Word—*the true character test*

The following outline, compiled by my friend Leslie Ludy,[3] contrasts the character of our Savior and the character of our destroyer, Satan. Understanding these differences will help us more quickly and accurately recognize the weak spots or breaches in our spiritual walls—breaches which all too often are only lies distorting God's true character.

Light versus darkness. First Peter 2:9 says that God has called us out of darkness into His marvelous light. Think about the qualities of light: clear, not confused, not blurry, bright, cheerful, and hopeful. The opposite of light is darkness. Satan is the prince of darkness, meaning he is the prince of all things fearful, confused, indistinct, dim, and forbidding. *Anything of confusion, fear, or darkness is not from God.*

Life versus death. John 10:10 says: "The thief cometh not, but for to steal, and to kill, and to destroy: I am come that they might have life, and that they might have it more abundantly." Here we see that Christ came to give abundant life, not death. The qualities of abundant life are joy, health, wholeness, strength, purity, spiritual success, and multiplication of blessings. The characteristics of death are disease, sickness, blindness, deafness, muteness, lameness, disorder, feebleness, erosion of spiritual and physical strength, erosion of blessings, and erosion of resources. *Anything that breeds these qualities of death in our daily experience is not from God.*

Inspiration informs us, "Sickness, suffering, and death are work of an antagonistic power. Satan is the destroyer; God is the restorer."[4] With this in mind, rather than accepting *every* vitality-robbing physical or spiritual ailment as *always* being God's will, we should claim the promise of Luke 10:19, where God tells us, "Behold, I give unto you power to tread on serpents and scorpions, and over all the power of the enemy:

and nothing shall by any means hurt you."

Claiming promises like this may seem a bit radical, and we tend to shy away from anything that might sound too bold and daring. After all, we know that the "name it and claim it" gospel is a faulty one. But if we as Christians are sincerely seeking to put away all wrong and to follow the Lord with radical abandonment—as the seventy elders Christ sent out—we can ask God to fulfill this promise in our lives today, as well.

Of course, we must keep in mind that God does not usually interfere with the law of cause and effect. When we make destructive choices, He often allows the resulting destructive consequences. If we live unhealthily, we shouldn't be surprised if we get sick. If we live immorally, we shouldn't be surprised when we reap the sad results. However, God is a God of mercy, and He can still restore.

Additionally, not all suffering and sickness is because of the bad choices we've made. Some of it is simply the work of our enemy—the destroyer—trying to stop God's work from being accomplished in our lives.

Over and over again, the Bible tells us that it is the Lord who heals us—both physically and spiritually.[5] Obviously, we do not know *when* He will choose to heal us physically. It could be instantly, slowly over time, or not until the resurrection. Therefore, we must trust His sovereign will. However, we do know without a doubt that it is His will to heal us *spiritually* today, here and now. And it is His will that we have life—and life more abundant!

Father of lights versus father of lies. James 1:17 says that God is the Father of lights in whom is no shadow of turning. In Scripture, the Father of lights is defined as the Giver of good and perfect gifts, merciful, long-suffering, gentle, quick to forgive, strong to protect, able and eager to rescue us, and a tender Deliverer from all that would ensnare us. The enemy, on the other hand, is the father of lies: a snuffer-out of life and hope, a condemner, a whisperer of fault, a noisome critic of the soul, a doubter of God's ability, a persecutor of the spirit, an advocate for the flesh, and one constantly seeking to diminish God's fatherly nature. *Anything that causes us to lose hope or degrades our confidence in God is not from our Lord.*

Have you ever thought, *Look at all the mistakes I keep making! How could God ever save me? I should just give up and stop trying!* If you've ever had these thoughts, know that they are not from God. These thoughts are from the enemy, and he's a deceiver!

Inspiration encourages us: "Do not listen to the enemy's suggestions to stay away from Christ until you have made yourself better; until you are good enough to come to God. If you wait until then, you will never come. When Satan points to your filthy garments, repeat the promise of Jesus, 'Him that cometh to Me I will in no wise cast out.' John 6:37. Tell the enemy that the blood of Jesus Christ cleanses from all sin."[6]

Romans 5:8 tells us, "But God commendeth his love toward us, in that, while we were yet sinners, Christ died for us." Yes, even while we were yet sinning, Christ had already paid the price for our ransom.

However, the good news is that He doesn't leave us where He finds us. As the author Paul Washer writes, "It is a long-standing gospel truth that the greatest evidence of having been justified is that we presently are being sanctified. We have assurance that God has saved us from the condemnation of sin because He is currently saving us from its power."[7] One of my favorite promises comes from 2 Corinthians 5:17: "Therefore if any man be in Christ, he is a new creature: old things are passed away; behold, all things are become new."

In the future, when you hear that voice whispering doubt or despair, remember that it's not God speaking but your destroyer. God always speaks hope, not hopelessness. We are told: "Jesus loves to have us come to Him just as we are, sinful, helpless, dependent. We may come with all our weakness, our folly, our sinfulness, and fall at His feet in penitence. It is His glory to encircle us in the arms of His love and to bind up our wounds, to cleanse us from all impurity."[8]

Discipline versus abuse. Hebrews 12:5–7 compares godly discipline to the discipline of a loving, devoted Father. This kind of discipline is expressed tenderly, in love. It is minimized to the level of need, brings about greater strength and health, and is always presented with the hope of reconciliation and the fostering of even deeper intimacy with Him. The enemy works only in the arena of abuse. He is cruel, angry, harsh, extreme, and breathes threats of abandonment and forsaking. Satan's abuse injures, makes sick, breaks the spirit, and disrupts intimacy. *Anything of an abusive nature that comes against us is not from God.*

Often in life, I have experienced very *real* pain as God cut something of "self" out of my life. Whether it was an inordinate affection I had toward something or someone, a selfish habit, or something of pleasure that I had put in the place of God, it wasn't fun to let it go. *It hurt!* But this is different from the pain the enemy brings. The enemy cuts to kill, but God—as a surgeon—cuts to restore!

When God disciplines us by asking us to surrender something to Him, it's always so that we can grow closer to Him. The Bible tells us that God's discipline is like that of a vinedresser pruning vines so that they will bear *more fruit* (see John 15:1, 2). In the book *The Ministry of Healing,* Ellen White expands our knowledge of God's discipline:

> Many who sincerely consecrate their lives to God's service are surprised and disappointed to find themselves, as never before, confronted by obstacles and beset by trials and perplexities. They pray for Christlikeness of character, for a fitness for the Lord's work, and they are placed in circumstances that seem to call forth all the evil of their nature. Faults are revealed of which they did not even suspect the existence. Like Israel of old they question, "If God is leading us, why do all these things come upon us?"
>
> It is because God is leading them that these things come upon them. Trials and obstacles are the Lord's chosen methods of discipline and His appointed conditions of success. He who reads the hearts of men knows their characters better than they themselves know them. He sees that some have powers and susceptibilities which, rightly directed, might be used in the advancement of His work. In His providence He brings these persons into different positions and varied circumstances that they may discover in their character the defects which have been concealed from their own knowledge. He gives them opportunity to correct these defects and fit themselves for His service.

Often He permits the fires of affliction to assail them that they may be purified.

The fact that we are called upon to endure trial shows that the Lord Jesus sees in us something precious which He desires to develop. If He saw in us nothing whereby He might glorify His name, He would not spend time in refining us. He does not cast worthless stones into His furnace. It is valuable ore that He refines.[9]

In Malachi 3:3, we see the Lord depicted as a Refiner purifying His silver—that's us!—for His soon coming. Of course, this refining process is not easy, but if we allow ourselves to be transformed in His hands, He will make us beautiful specimens for His glory! And like Job, we can say, "When he hath tried me, I shall come forth as gold" (Job 23:10).

So if you are being pruned by afflictions, take heart, because it shows that God still sees possibilities in your life, and this is good news!

Bridegroom versus harsh husband. Christ is called our loving Bridegroom all throughout Scripture. A loving bridegroom is a patient listener, affectionate, an advocate and rescuer, willing to give up his life to save, quick to respond to the needs of his bride, constantly speaking words of love and kindness, and continually praying for the benefit of his beloved. The enemy is like a harsh husband: impatient, cold and haughty, never pleased, distant, demanding, controlling, trying to catch us doing wrong, verbally and physically abusive, selfish, and feigning tenderness only to get what he wants. *Anything of the nature of a harsh husband that comes against us is not from God.*

Shepherd versus roaring lion. John 10:11–15 defines Christ as the Good Shepherd who lays down His life for His sheep. As our Shepherd, He is deeply interested in even the smallest matter, watchful, constantly alert to the needs of His own, never tiring or sleeping. He is always looking upon His lambs with an affectionate gaze, ready to fight and defeat any fiend that would dare attack those under His care. Satan is defined as a roaring lion in 1 Peter 5:8. A roaring lion is the opposite of a good shepherd. He looks to control through fear instead of love. He rules through intimidation, not respect. He makes demands and threatens severe punishments if not obeyed. He makes the soul anxious and tense, compared with the absolute peace that is promised by the Shepherd in Psalm 23. The enemy roars loudly about his power and constantly yells, "Beware! The enemy is more powerful than you!" *Anything of the roaring lion nature that comes against us is not from God.*

Those coming out of witchcraft and the occult world share that the characteristics of a "harsh husband" and "roaring lion" are often seen through manipulation and control. If they do not perform certain rituals correctly or give enough reverence to the spirits, destruction, curses, and sometimes even death might follow. I remember facing this head-on when I was a student missionary in the jungles of South America. The natives, some of them even Adventist Christians, still lived in constant fear of offending the spirits.

In contrast to a roaring lion out to destroy us, we serve a Shepherd of love. The beautiful theme throughout Scripture is redemption. Rather than an angry taskmaster trying to catch His people doing wrong, we find a God of love, leading His people to righteousness. However, when His people steadfastly choose to continue in sin, God has no choice but to allow them to receive the wages of sin—death (Romans 6:23). But He finds no pleasure in bringing judgment upon the wicked. He's always quick to restore when His people return to Him (Ezekiel 33:11).

It's important to remember that because we live in a battle zone— our planet—we will continue to suffer the casualties of war—many times without understanding why—until Jesus comes to take us home. But let's not be confused any longer about the character of our God. Rather than being a destroyer, He has come to save us, the lost sheep. He is our Good Shepherd, who has come to rescue us from the roaring lion. When we understand this, we will be significantly closer to sealing up the spiritual breaches of our soul and being fortified to stand strong and victorious against the attacks of our archenemy.

Remember, the true character test of our God is revealed in His Word. If we don't know the Word, we won't know Him. Therefore, let us acquaint ourselves with His Word today!

Chapter 13

Looking for Spiritual Breaches

Discovering the Enemy's Battle Tactic

> *And he shall set engines of war against thy walls, and with his axes*
> *he shall break down thy towers. By reason of the abundance of his horses*
> *their dust shall cover thee: thy walls shall shake at the noise of the horsemen,*
> *and of the wheels, and of the chariots, when he shall enter into thy gates, as*
> *men enter into a city wherein is made a breach.*
>
> —*Ezekiel 26:9, 10*

*N*ow that we've made a clear distinction between God's character of love and hope in contrast to the deceiver's character of lies and hopelessness, let's take some time to evaluate the different avenues in which Satan often attacks and seeks to overcome us spiritually.

The following areas are broad in scope (like a disease) but are often a symptom of smaller breaches (poor lifestyle habits) in our spiritual wall of fortification: spiritual defeat and discouragement; spiritual doubt and mental confusion; spiritual fogginess and lethargy; spiritual restlessness and discontentment; spiritual burnout; feeling overwhelmed with life or ministry; depression and despair; living in a state of frustration or anger; true or false guilt; worry; anxiety; and constantly feeling stressed or anxious.

In addition to the above, Satan also attacks us through relationship struggles, health struggles, financial struggles, ministry struggles, and the list goes on and on.

The fact that we feel the attack in these areas doesn't always mean we have a breach—it may just mean we are on the right path and he's doing everything he can to counter our effectiveness for the Lord. We must remember that we wrestle not against flesh and blood, "but against principalities, against powers, against the rulers of the darkness of this world, against spiritual wickedness in high places" (Ephesians 6:12).

However, if despair, doubt, or other unhealthy mind-sets (as mentioned here and in the previous chapter) are part of the equation, or if we are growing resentful toward God rather than growing closer to Him through the trials, we are most likely suffering from some type of spiritual breach in our lives.

Most Christians don't recognize that there is a deeper cause of many of their struggles. They don't recognize that Satan has snuck in through a back door and is binding them with his chains of deception. Thankfully, Christ came to set the captives free, to make our crooked ways straight, and to break apart the chains that bind us (see Isaiah 58:6 and Isaiah 45:2)!

As we recognize that the enemy is trying to weaken our spiritual fortresses so he can overcome us, we should prayerfully ask the Lord to search our hearts (Psalm 139:23, 24). Before we can move forward effectively by repairing the breaches in our spiritual walls, we have to know exactly *where* the holes are and what access points he has into our lives.

Although not exhaustive, the following is a list of common spiritual breaches[1] to get you started as you pray. It would be good to create your own personal "breach list" as God brings things to mind. We'll talk about what to do with this list in the next couple of chapters.

Unconfessed sins. This includes anything we've done wrong toward God, His law, or others and not made right. (See the following categories.)

Idols. In this case, I am not talking about "graven images." I am referring to anything that comes between God and us, or anything that is more important in our lives than God. If we have an idol, it will often consume our attention, focus, and thought life to the exclusion of other healthy activities, family needs, or ministry tasks. Idols can be inappropriate relationships; activities; lifestyles; hobbies; expensive clothes, toys, or gadgets; food; misused talents; material wealth or status—and they can even be *ourselves*! Self-idolatry is the worst sin, because we place "self" on the throne above God. That's what Satan tried to do in the beginning and is why we are all living in a world of sin today.

Addictions. These breaches could be the same as our idols, or they might be different. An addiction might be a physical substance or food, video gaming, novel reading, pornography, uncontrolled thoughts and fantasies, and so on. Or it might be a seemingly innocent activity such as surfing the Internet, spending hours on social media sites, or having to read *every* news story that comes across our computer screens. It could be how we spend our downtime, such as watching movies, sports, or other favorite television programs. Addictions can even be cravings to be "liked" so that we do things simply from the motive of gaining the applause of others rather than seeking the esteem of God. Addictions could be something good that has taken over the focus of our lives, such as becoming the top man or woman at work, making lots of money, or being so consumed with staying physically fit that we spend every spare moment at the gym.

We often justify addictions because they appear to fill perceived needs in our lives. Thus, we allow them to crowd out our time with God and with those we love. Addictions are always something that we can't imagine giving up, but if God is to remain the King of our lives, He must be the Lord of our lives! *He* must be our addiction. Nothing else should come between us and Him!

Ungodly mind-sets. Ungodly mind-sets are the most prevalent sins in Christianity today simply because of their apparent respectability. While we look upon immorality and vile behavior with abhorrence, sins of the mind often go unrebuked. Why? Because everyone, it seems, struggles with them! How can anyone preach against them when we are all guilty?

Yet, these areas, when unaddressed, can become major breaches in our spiritual lives.

The most popular ungodly mind-sets include, but are not limited to, pride—in our achievements, spiritual accomplishments, talents, leadership, and status; a feeling of superiority over others; arrogance; self-righteousness; selfishness; self-seeking; self-promotion; greed; lust; jealousy; envy; vanity; gluttony; anxiety; irritability; impatience; anger; bitterness; resentment; refusing to forgive; discontent; a lack of thankfulness; fear; self-pity; pessimism; doubt toward God; spiritual apathy; unbelief; hate; victimization; unteachable in spirit; disrespect for those in authority; unholy thoughts and desires; and seeking our own interests more than that of others.

Not only do we need to attack the breach (ungodly mind-set, addiction, etc.), but we also need to make sure we hack out its roots. For example, if we read magazines or surf Internet sites that feed the worldly, greedy cravings of our selfish nature, we are opening the door for materialism and worldliness to take root within our hearts. Likewise, if we read magazines or watch movies, online videos, or television shows that promote sensuality, we shouldn't be surprised when lust and sexual compromise become struggles in our lives. That's why it's so important that the branch, root, and whole tree all get pulled out together when we go to battle. Then the enemy will have fewer weapons to use against us in future conflicts.

Ungodly conversations. These breaches are also seldom addressed, yet they are quite prevalent, even in the lives of sincere Christians. They include, but are not limited to, gossip—even spiritual gossip justified by the motive of edifying others; hurtful sarcasm; criticism; backbiting; insensitive judgment; complaining; murmuring; exaggeration; lying; inappropriate flirting; vulgar language; vocalized disrespect; cynicism; and expressing doubt toward God, the church, or the success of ministry. God tells us, "He that *hath* no rule over his own spirit *is like* a city that is broken down, *and* without walls" (Proverbs 25:28; emphasis added).

Ungodly behaviors. Some of these breaches may be quite normal in the society in which we live, but they are not acceptable to God. These behaviors include, but are not limited to, self-promotion;

self-aggrandizement; manipulation; taking advantage of others' weaknesses; practicing fraud; cheating; abusing others' trust; failing to honor our word; being lazy on the job; being greedy; being gluttonous; stealing; backstabbing; disrespect of those in authority; tearing down another's character; wasting time, money, or resources; dressing immodestly or flaunting our bodies to draw attention to ourselves rather than God; using people to get what we want; expecting to be waited on hand and foot; the constant attempt to prove we are right; and being defiant when we are corrected. Of course, we cannot forget the sin of breaking God's Ten Commandments! Any time we break any of His commandments, even in small, seemingly insignificant ways, we are creating another breach and foothold for the enemy. (Just look at Exodus 20 and Deuteronomy 8 for a deeper understanding of the significance of this!)

Ungodly relationships. Ungodly relationships can be as innocent looking as a "codependent friendship," where our happiness is based on the love and attention of another instead of on God, to the many other inappropriate unbiblical relationships we may be tempted to form. The most common relationship breaches come from inappropriate relationships with the opposite sex (both inside and outside of marriage), unbiblical sexual relationships between those of the same sex, and romantic relationships between a believer and an unbeliever. God tells us, "Be ye not unequally yoked together with unbelievers: for what fellowship hath righteousness with unrighteousness? and what communion hath light with darkness?" (2 Corinthians 6:14). Emotional adultery could also fit in this category. Of course, if you've already fallen in one of these areas, or in any of the other breaches we've mentioned already, do not lose heart! There is always hope in Christ!

Worldly preoccupations. Satan's goal is to get us to love the world rather than God. And to a great extent, he has achieved this. Many of God's people have become so consumed with worldly things that they are not even aware when a spiritual breach is created by a *preoccupation* with status; love of money; shopping; expensive name-brand labels; buying of material possessions, such as luxuriously large homes, big toys, and electronic gadgets; technology; worldly music or movies; television soap operas, talent shows, and other programs; honor of celebrities or sports figures, and so on. God tells us, "For where your treasure is, there will your heart be also" (Matthew 6:21).

Ellen White laments:

> Why is it that men, standing on the very threshold of the eternal world, are so blinded? . . . Many Seventh-day Adventists fail to realize the responsibility which rests upon them to cooperate with God and Christ for the saving of souls. They do not show forth to the world the great interest God has in sinners. They do not make the most of the opportunities granted them. *The leprosy of selfishness has taken hold of the church.* The Lord Jesus Christ will heal the church of this terrible disease if she will be healed. The remedy is found in the fifty-eighth chapter of Isaiah.[2]

Satanic strongholds. As Bible-believing Christians, there are certain things with which we should never be involved! Mind-altering drugs, tobacco, alcohol, and any other addictive substance; consultation with fortune-tellers; tarot cards; horoscopes; hypnosis; séances; Ouija boards; skull-and-crossbones emblems on our clothes; and any activities of the occult world are completely off-limits for professing followers of Christ. It's alarming that even in Adventist circles, Satan has been bringing in his innocent-looking amusements of darkness by the trainload. Whether it's enjoying movies or books featuring magic, spiritualism, mysticism, science fiction, witches, vampires, murder mysteries, and more, or participating in Halloween (the high day of worship for the entire occult world), Satan does not care, just as long as he has us.

We must remember that anything that glorifies sin or plays with spiritual power aside from God (no matter how attractive or innocent Hollywood has made it appear) is to be avoided at all cost. This means that books, movies, or television shows such as the Harry Potter series, *Star Wars, Charmed, Buffy the Vampire Slayer, Angel,* and many others like these shouldn't even be in our homes, let alone playing on our television screens. Neither should rock and roll, heavy metal, or any of their satanically inspired cousins be playing from our radios and CD players, for these styles are the trademarked music of darkness. The Bible tells us that there is to be *no* fellowship between light and darkness. If any of this darkness is part of our lives, not only do we have a serious breach, but our walls are crumbling, and we must go running to Christ and plead for Him to change us if we hope to be saved.

A few years back, a friend of mine was traveling as a missionary in South America. To pass the time as he bounced over the mountain roads on a public bus, he asked the stranger sitting next to him what he did for a living.

The man replied, "I'm a witch doctor. I cast spells on people. I make people sick, and I also make people well. I make people get rich, and I can also send them a curse where they will lose all their riches." He continued boastfully, "If you want, I could cast a spell and make your wife leave you, and I could bring you the woman of your dreams."

"Oh no! You couldn't cast a spell on my household!" David responded firmly.

"Yes, I could!" the witch doctor countered.

"No, you couldn't!" David stood his ground.

"Let me ask you some questions!" the witch doctor insisted.

"OK, fine. Go ahead."

"Do you ever view pornography?"

"No."

"Do you ever watch magic or movies having to do with the occult?"

"No."

"Do you ever watch soap operas?"

"Never."

"Do you read worldly magazines like . . . [and he named a few common to the region]?"

"Not a chance."

"Do you ever listen to rock and roll [and he named some other worldly music styles common to the region]?"

"Nope!" David began to grin, as he could tell where this conversation was leading.

After the witch doctor had exhausted his list, he looked at David with new respect. "You are right! I can't touch you or your family! But the moment you take part in any of those activities, I can exercise all the power in the world over you!"

Whether we live in a South American jungle, in a village in Africa, or in a bustling city of Europe or North America, the devil's power and the devil's presence is very real. And all he needs is a little foothold of sin to sneak into our domains and work havoc in our lives. While his tools and methods of operation may vary slightly from place to place, his tactics are always the same: he's looking for a breach in our walls. He's looking for a way to get in and tear our walls down. And it doesn't take much for him to be successful!

Inspiration cautions us, "Satan will so shape circumstances that unless we are kept by divine power, [these circumstances] will almost imperceptibly weaken the fortifications of the soul."[3] That's why we must cling to God's power to fortify our walls and make them strong. We cannot stand against the attacks of the enemy alone!

Before we move on, there's one more category of breaches that is very easy to overlook!

Sins of omission. We often congratulate ourselves on what we aren't doing wrong and fail to recognize what we aren't doing right. Sins of omission in the attitudes and lifestyles to which God has called us are so numerous that we could hardly list them all here. However, a few of the most glaring omission breaches include a lack of truly seeking after God with our whole hearts; a lack of complete heart surrender; a lack of abhorrence for our sins and those things that wound Christ afresh; a lack of earnestness to receive more of the Holy Spirit—the only thing that will give us victory over sin; a lack of spiritual zeal and life; a lack of the fruit of the Spirit in our lives (see Galatians 5:22, 23); a lack of faith, humility, and trust in God's Word; a lack of sincere interest in deep Bible study and prayer; a lack of spiritual fortitude and backbone when the battle around us increases; a lack of self-control; a lack of warmth and love towards our brethren; a lack of friendliness towards strangers and those different from us; a lack of kindness and willingness to sacrifice for the poor and for the "least of these"; a lack of willingness to be inconvenienced to help others in need; a lack of taking up our crosses daily and denying ourselves for the sake of the gospel; a lack of willingness to wrestle and agonize in prayer for others; a lack of desire and effort to stand in the gap as intercessors for a perishing land; and the list goes on and on.

As we can see, being fortified spiritually is not just important, *it is vitally important*! And Satan knows this. That's why he's doing everything he can to gain a foothold in our lives so that he can break down our walls of spiritual protection. If he can do this, he knows our prayers will be ineffective.

In the next chapter, I will discuss how we can fill in the breaches in our walls and overcome the enemy's strongholds in our lives. But let us end this chapter on a note of encouragement.

When you evaluate your life and all the breaches in your wall, it might be very disheartening. You might hear the voice of the enemy whispering in your ear, "You have so many holes in your wall, it's pointless to even begin! You will never be able to build your walls strong!" But don't listen to this voice. God always speaks hope and courage. Just the fact that you recognize your weaknesses and many sins gives evidence of the fact that God is already at work in your life.

Self-evaluation is indeed painful at times, and because of this, we shy away from it. But self-evaluation is needful so that we can see ourselves *as we truly are* and recognize our desperate need of Christ. Take to heart the following:

> But we must have a knowledge of ourselves, a knowledge that will result in contrition, before we can find pardon and peace. The Pharisee [speaking of the story found in Luke 18] felt no conviction of sin. The Holy Spirit could not work with him. His soul was encased in a self-righteous armor which the arrows of God, barbed and true-aimed by angel hands, failed to penetrate. It is only he who knows himself to be a sinner that Christ can save. . . . We must know our real condition, or we shall not feel our need of Christ's help. We must understand our danger, or we shall not flee to the refuge. We must feel the pain of our wounds, or we should not desire healing.[4]

So let us take heart! Christ is asking for more, but the work of restoration and transformation is a work that only He can do. He simply asks us to surrender to Him and let Him do it. It may not look easy right now, but we have made a very important first step—acknowledging our great need. When we call upon God, all His strength will be ours and we will be *more* than conquerors (Romans 8:37). He promised, and He cannot lie! So let us press forward in building our spiritual walls strong! And let us continue *daring to ask for more*!

Chapter 14

Building Up the Walls

Practical Steps to Spiritual Fortification: Part 1

> *And they that shall be of thee shall build the old waste places: thou shalt raise up the foundations of many generations; and thou shalt be called, The repairer of the breach, The restorer of paths to dwell in.*
>
> *—Isaiah 58:12*

As I've traveled in Third World countries, I've witnessed the devastating effects of malnutrition. Those who are malnourished succumb to any sickness that comes along. It doesn't matter what it is. Their bodies simply can't handle any type of physical onslaught, because they don't have proper food and have become weak. As a result, those in malnourished regions are dying from all types of diseases.

This is exactly what the devil is trying to do in our lives today. He is trying to starve our relationship with God. He is trying to keep us from eating God's Word and drinking from the fountain of Living Water in prayer. If he can keep us spiritually malnourished, he knows that any sickness (sin) that he brings our way will cause our spiritual downfall. His main goal, which he's been pretty effective at accomplishing, is to keep us from our daily food, feed us with junk food in place of good nutritious stuff, or just simply starve us until we have no strength to stand and our walls crumble. When hungry and harassed and attacked by the enemy, our focus often turns inward. We don't pray or reach out to others because we have too many of our own problems. And that's exactly what Satan wants.

Thankfully, if we cast ourselves upon God, stand upon the power of His Word, and by faith claim His promises, *we can obtain deliverance and victory.* God is greater than all the powers of darkness (see 1 John 4:4; John 12:31). As Romans 8:31 says, "If God be for us, who can be against us?"

Inspiration adds, "They are to contend with supernatural forces, but they are assured of supernatural help. All the intelligences of heaven are in this army. And more than angels are in the ranks. The Holy Spirit, the representative of the Captain of the Lord's host, comes down to direct the battle. Our infirmities may be many, our sins and mistakes grievous; but the grace of God is for all who seek it with contrition. The power of Omnipotence is enlisted in behalf of those who trust in God."[1]

The key to victory is learning to strengthen ourselves in the Lord, for He's promised that He will fight for us.

Forming a battle plan. In recent chapters, I've talked about the need for strong walls, about the importance of spiritual fortification, and about the many breaches that give the enemy an inroad into our lives. Now it's time for business. Now it's time to take up our spiritual weapons and start filling in those cracks and making our walls strong once again.

This process of rebuilding our spiritual walls won't happen overnight. It's going to be a battle, and it's going to take persistence. And again, it's not something that we should attempt to do on our own. But with God's strength, and with the tools He's given us, we can succeed at rebuilding our spiritual walls of fortification and making them strong!

So let's begin!

Choose your target. Before you start praying, you need to know what your target is—that is, you need to know exactly what you are trying to overcome! This is why 2 Corinthians 13:5 tells us to "examine ourselves." Taking time for a thorough heart evaluation is not only important but *crucial* to achieving spiritual victory.

As you think about your battle target, write down whatever God brings to your mind. It may be a breach I mentioned in the previous chapter, or you may need to pray and ask God to show you your specific weak spots. Remember that sometimes even good things can become a breach if we allow them to stand between us and God, so what may look innocent to others may be an actual breach in your life.

This list is just for you and God. You may share it with your spouse or prayer partner if you wish, but the main purpose is for you to know where to begin in Bible study and prayer.

Pick up your sword. Standing on the promises of God's Word by faith through prayer will be your most effective approach in achieving spiritual fortification. Once you know where the breaches are in your spiritual wall, it's time to pick up your sword! "The soul must be barricaded by prayer and study of the Scriptures. Armed with these weapons, Jesus encountered our wily foe on the field of battle, and overcame him."[2] You will be able to pray with increased confidence and faith when you can take the Bible in your hands and hold it up to God, saying, "Here's Your promise. I claim it for this specific breach in my life! You do not lie, and I will not let go until You fulfill Your Word."

Martyn Lloyd-Jones, a Welsh Protestant minister from the early 1940s, when speaking on how important it is to claim God's Word in prayer, wrote, " 'Pester Him, as it were, with His own promises. Tell Him what He said He is going to do. Quote the Scripture to Him. . . . It pleases Him. . . . God is our Father, and He loves us, and He likes to hear us pleading His own promises, quoting His own words to Him, and saying, "In light of this, can You refrain?" It delights the heart of God.' "[3]

Yes! God loves to have us pray like this! He wants us to ask big things of Him. And we are told that when we come to Him confessing our sinfulness and unworthiness, He will answer. The honor of His throne is at stake for the fulfillment of His Word because He cannot lie.[4]

Here are a few powerful promises to get you started. But remember, we don't just pray and claim Bible promises; we must also act on our prayers. These prayers God will answer, and deliverance will come.

Victory for those who confess their sins—1 John 1:9; Hebrews 7:25. No sin is too great for God to handle. He sent His Son that we might find deliverance and victory. No matter what we've done, if we desire to be forgiven and set free, the gift is ours. We just have to claim it! When we confess our sins, it's also important that we actively turn away from those sins and seek to walk a new way. We cannot do this in our own strength, but God will help us when we lean on Him.

Victory over idols—Ezekiel 36:25–27; Jeremiah 24:7. It's important to remember that if we want victory over "idols" in our lives, we don't wean ourselves away from them gradually. We have to destroy them— *remove them completely* from our lives so they have no more access to our hearts—just like the young King Josiah did when he came to power in the days of ancient Israel (see 2 Chronicles 34).

Victory over addictions—Luke 18:27; Psalm 55:16–18. Addictions are difficult to break, but it's best if we just go cold turkey and walk 180 degrees in the opposite direction!

If you are addicted to worldly music, movies, magazines, sports icons, something in the occult world, or even some type of unhealthy food or substance, it might be time to clean house and have a bonfire party with just you and God. You'll be amazed at the peace and strength you will feel afterwards as you *decidedly* walk a new way.

In Acts 19, when the gospel of Christ was preached, the people came and openly confessed their evil deeds. A number who had practiced sorcery brought their scrolls together and burned them. Because of this, the Word of God grew and prevailed. And more and more people came to accept the gospel because they saw the gospel changing people's lives.

There are many things, while not inherently evil, that can become idols and detract from our quality time with God. In these cases, it might be good for us to go on a complete or lengthy fast until these things no longer have a controlling hold on our hearts. By this, I'm not meaning fasting from a specific food (unless that is your addiction), but rather fasting from *the specific thing* that is causing our spiritual compromise.

In the past, I have found it extremely beneficial in restoring my spiritual perspective and priorities to "fast" from different forms of media and entertainment that were distracting me. This includes the extremely popular social media Web sites. While I have always been careful about what I read or watch, I've realized that these sites often tend to blur my spiritual boundaries. I think these (and other online media sources) have become some of the *greatest obstacles* to maintaining our spiritual focus and consecration if not kept in control. Why? It is simply because they numb our spiritual sensitivities with a barrage of meaningless and frivolous thoughts, and they also rob us of valuable time that could be devoted to more effective study or service to God.

The biggest key in overcoming addictions (or any sin) is to give God our entire heart and turn our focus completely upon Him. If we become consumed with Him, knowing Him, studying His Word, sharing Him with others, we won't be so tempted to waste time or look at the things of the world.

Victory over ungodly mind-sets—Isaiah 26:3; Psalm 119:165; Philippians 4:8. Besides prayer and time in the Word, one of the best ways to obtain victory over ungodly mind-sets is to learn to replace the ungodly thoughts with positive, godly thoughts. If you are jealous toward someone, start praying for him and speaking words of kindness to him, and your thoughts will change with God's help. When tempted to think evil, start repeating a Bible promise or sing a praise song and the bad thoughts will leave. (Some may think I'm joking, but this *really works!*)

Ellen White advises, "When the enemy comes with his darkness, sing faith and talk faith, and you will find that you have sung and talked yourself into the light."[5]

Victory over ungodly conversations—Isaiah 6:5–7; Ephesians 4:22, 23, 29. If you are always griping about something, make yourself speak words of thankfulness every time you are tempted to complain. Challenge yourself to go two weeks replacing every negative, ungodly word that you are tempted to speak with words of thankfulness or praise to God. Before you know it, you will develop a new habit of biting your tongue rather than complaining, gossiping, or tearing others down, and you will see more clearly all your reasons to praise God. Remember, when we speak negatively about life or others, we influence others negatively, and God holds us responsible for the ripple effects our words make.

Victory over ungodly behaviors—Romans 12:18–21; 1 Corinthians 10:31. Again, replace ungodly behaviors with godly habits. Heap coals of fire upon the head of those who offend you. Above all, ask God to give you purity of motive and action, and purity of heart, even if no one is watching. *After all, God is watching!* If we can't learn to live by godly principle and walk with integrity now for God's glory, we won't do it when the hard times and real tests come.

This is why Inspiration tells us, "Repentance includes sorrow for sin and a turning away from it. We shall not renounce sin unless we see its sinfulness; until we turn away from it in heart, there will be no real change in the life."[6]

Victory over ungodly relationships—2 Corinthians 6:4; 1 Samuel 16:7. If you are in an ungodly relationship, it's often best to cut ties and walk away, hard as this may seem. If you continue to compromise, you're asking for spiritual disaster. When I speak of ungodly relationships, I speak of those outside of marriage. If you are already married and unequally yoked, then your task is to do the best where you are within that marriage and hope and pray that your influence will win your unbelieving spouse to the truth. (First Corinthians 7 deals with this topic more deeply.)

Whatever you do, don't play with fire! Seek godly counsel if needed. Ask God to change your heart and give you a new love for Him and find friends who will encourage you in your spiritual walk. The flesh may be weak, but God promises strength. And as we draw closer to Him, we will find that He provides more fulfillment than any human relationship ever could.

Victory over worldly preoccupations—Colossians 3:1–3; Romans 12:1, 2. I'm reminded of the old song written by Helen H. Lemmel: "Turn your eyes upon Jesus. Look full in His wonderful face, and the things of earth will grow strangely dim, in the light of His glory and grace."

This is the best way to overcome worldly preoccupations: look at Jesus and give Him all the keys of your heart. And as you do, take an extended spiritual fast from the things of the world. Turn off the television and stay away from online social networks, shopping malls, or anything else that pulls you toward the world until the ties that bind you are broken. I recommend you take your Bible and journal and go for a day out alone with God in nature. It's wonderful for helping you refocus on your heavenly priorities.

Victory over satanic strongholds—2 Corinthians 10:3, 4; Psalm 40:2, 3. Again, the best way for deliverance from darkness is turning to the Light. Choose Christ and give Him your will! We can't play with darkness and be on the winning team. Destroy anything that is of darkness in your life or anything that compromises your relationship with God. The devil won't be happy and he will put up a big fight, but God will help you! Remember, "In the whole Satanic force there is not power to overcome one soul who in simple trust casts himself on Christ. 'He giveth power to the faint; and to them that have no might He increaseth strength.' Isa. 40:29."[7]

Forgiveness for the sins of omission—Ephesians 2:8, 9. It's important to remember that just as God forgives our sins and then gives us strength to walk a new way, no matter how many good works we do, these works don't save us and never will. Only Christ can save us, and only He can give us power to live up to our full potential. Of ourselves, we could never possibly succeed in avoiding all the "sins of omission," for we are told, "God's ideal for His children is higher than the highest human thought can reach."[8]

This is why I think the most important thing we should ask and pray for is more of the Holy Spirit, for this is what gives power to our testimony and effectiveness to our labors. Our greatest "sin of omission" is in rushing ahead in service before we receive this gift.

> Christ declared that the divine influence of the Spirit was to be with His followers unto the end. *But the promise is not appreciated as it should be; and therefore its fulfillment is not seen as it might be.* The promise of the Spirit is a matter little thought of; and the result is only what might be expected—spiritual drought, spiritual darkness,

spiritual declension and death. Minor matters occupy the attention, and the divine power which is necessary for the growth and prosperity of the church, and which would bring all other blessings in its train, is lacking, though offered in its infinite plenitude.[9]

We've talked about picking up our sword—the promises from God's Word—and in the next chapter I'll address moving forward and claiming these promises in prayer. This battle may seem daunting, but don't despair. We serve a great God, and nothing is impossible with Him! *Keep daring to ask for more!*

Chapter 15

Putting on God's Whole Armor

Practical Steps to Spiritual Fortification: Part 2

> *Wherefore take unto you the whole armour of God, that ye may be able to withstand in the evil day, and having done all, to stand.*
> —*Ephesians 6:13*

*T*here are many important parts to the armor of God: the belt of truth, the breastplate of righteousness, the shoes of the gospel of peace, the shield of faith, the helmet of salvation, and, last but not least, the sword of the Spirit. While each one is deeply significant, they are so simple that most of our children could place them correctly with a Sabbath School felt set. But in the heat of the desperate spiritual battles for our very souls, we adults all too often leave God's armor behind! Then we wonder why we are constantly being overcome by the enemy.

"Temptations often appear irresistible because, through neglect of prayer and the study of the Bible, the tempted one cannot readily remember God's promises and meet Satan with the Scripture weapons."[1]

Wearing God's *whole armor* is crucial to our being spiritually fortified as Christians.

There is one significant part of God's armor that we didn't mention. It is one of the most overlooked keys in our spiritual fortification. It's not something we put on or hold in our hand—at least symbolically speaking. Rather, it's something we do. It's a mind-set. I call it *watchful prayer.*

Ephesians 6:18 states simply, "Praying always with all prayer and supplication in the Spirit, and watching thereunto with all perseverance and supplication for all saints."

Praying always means to pray without ceasing (see 1 Thessalonians 5:17). Luke 18:1 states it this way, "Men ought always to pray, and not to faint." Matthew 26:41 gives yet another view of why this piece of armor is so significant. "Watch and pray, that ye enter not into temptation: *the spirit indeed is willing, but the flesh is weak*" (emphasis added).

This is our problem. Our spirits are indeed willing, but our flesh is dreadfully weak. This is why, as we go forward seeking to stand strong against the attacks of the enemy, we must constantly be in a state of watchful prayer. We must be alert, on our guard, ever in tune with the Holy Spirit's promptings, anticipating danger or compromise *before it occurs* so the enemy cannot sneak up and catch us unawares. Inspiration tells us, "*No man* is safe for a day or an hour without prayer."[2]

Christ Himself, when facing the biggest trial of His life in Gethsemane, asked His disciples to "watch and pray" (Matthew 26:41). They failed to do this, being too sleepy. Inspiration tells us, "It was in sleeping when Jesus bade him watch and pray that Peter had prepared the way for his great sin [denying Christ three times]. All the disciples, by sleeping in that critical hour, sustained great loss."[3] What loss might we personally—and corporately—be sustaining today because we are too busy, or too sleepy, or too lazy, to take time to *watch and pray?*

Moving forward on our knees. Now that we have put on our spiritual armor, chosen our weapons (specific promises from the Word of God), and have determined to make drastic changes in our lifestyle and focus, it's time to pray. This is not a half-hearted, lazy kind of praying. It is not the type of praying we do when rushing out the door for an appointment or when in direct line of fire from the enemy—although we should be praying during these times too! This is a time we set apart for specific and wrestling prayer. We are fighting a very real enemy who has attacked us in very real and specific ways. So we must fight back in a very real and specific manner!

As Jacob wrestled through the night, we, too, must wrestle until the breaking of the day. We must hold on to God, saying, "I will not let You go until You bless me! I will not let go until You give me deliverance in this area of my life!" This is not a presumptuous prayer. We aren't praying for our own selfish, fleshly desires. We are praying for victory over the spiritual breaches in our lives. We are praying for spiritual fortification. We are praying to have a new heart and a new spirit. These are things that God has promised to give us.

If we haven't received victory yet, it is most likely because we haven't *really* been asking for it, or we haven't been willing to hold on in wrestling prayer until victory comes. Remember, the prophet Daniel prayed and fasted for twenty-one days before God's deliverance came (Daniel 10:12, 13). While God began to work the *very moment* Daniel first prayed, there were powers of darkness that held up the angel of deliverance. But as Daniel persevered in prayer, Satan was overcome.

Inspiration promises us that "the earnest prayer of faith will baffle [Satan's] strongest efforts."[4]

It's important that we are earnest and persevering in prayer. Though weak and faulty, if we hold on with faith, we can be assured that God will give us the victory we seek. It might not come immediately. But it will come.

> Jacob prevailed because he was persevering and determined. His victory is an evidence of the power of importunate prayer. All who will lay hold of God's promises, as he did, and be as earnest and persevering as he was, will succeed as he succeeded. Those who are unwilling to deny self, to agonize before God, to pray long and earnestly for His blessing, will not obtain it. Wrestling with God—how few know what it is! How few have ever had their souls

drawn out after God with intensity of desire until every power is on the stretch. When waves of despair which no language can express sweep over the suppliant, how few cling with unyielding faith to the promises of God.[5]

Let us cling with unyielding faith to the promises of God. Let us hold on and not let go until every brick is back in its rightful place in our wall, and until all strongholds of the enemy are broken down. If we don't *feel* like praying, *this is the time we especially need to pray*. As we keep pressing forward in faith, the feelings will come, and soon victory will, as well.

Seek to live in obedience. Now we must follow the promptings of the Holy Spirit. We must continue to turn from our habits of sinful thinking and behavior and learn to live in obedience to God's Word. As we follow the Holy Spirit's promptings, He will lead us to take action in specific ways. For each of us, the work may look different and the battle may be different, for He alone knows our areas of weakness and need. Yet the result will be the same—a closer and closer walk with Him. "If the heart has been renewed by the Spirit of God, the life will bear witness to the fact. While we cannot do anything to change our hearts or to bring ourselves into harmony with God; while we must not trust at all to ourselves or our good works, our lives will reveal whether the grace of God is dwelling within us. A change will be seen in the character, the habits, the pursuits. The contrast will be clear and decided between what they have been and what they are."[6]

For each of us, obedience may look different. For me, living in obedience has meant choosing to live without a television and putting boundaries around my Internet and social media activities. Rather than they controlling me and eating up so much of my time and attention, I allow God to control them. This may seem rather extreme to some, but if you think about it, how much of what we find on the big screen and flashing on the Internet headlines these days draws us closer to God? Very little! Most of it directly violates the principles of Scripture (see Philippians 4:8 if you have any questions). It's all about superficial pleasures, worldliness, gossip, crime, lust, adultery, and taking God's name in vain. We may not agree with these behaviors personally, but we actually condone them by allowing them into our homes via the television, Internet, and many movies we watch. The Bible tells us not to put any wicked thing before our eyes for a reason (Psalm 101:3). When we constantly watch these types of things, we are weakening our spiritual walls of fortification, and before long, we may even begin to take part in the activities.

Obedience might seem difficult at first, even extreme. However, when we surrender daily to God and partake of the abundant goodness He's waiting to pour upon us, we won't even miss the superficial amusements, activities, and sins that we once enjoyed. His gifts are *much* better! I can attest to this a thousand times over!

It's important that we stay on guard and not let Satan use our obedience against us. Often, when certain reforms begin to take place in our lives, pride soon follows. We must remember that we are saved "not by works of righteousness which we have done, but according to his mercy" (Titus 3:5). Because of this, we should routinely ask God to search our hearts (Jeremiah 17:10) and make sure that no self-righteousness or other spiritual compromises sneak in.

Ellen White writes, "When all known wrongs are righted, we may believe that God will answer our petitions. Our own merit will never commend us to the favor of God; it is the worthiness of Jesus that will save us, His blood that will cleanse us; yet we have a work to do in complying with the conditions of acceptance."[7]

So whatever God asks you to do, whether it's throwing away books, magazines, music, DVDs, or something else that does not honor Him, or whether it is cleaning out your personal e-mail files, computer hard drive, or pantry, or whether it is making something right with a ministry colleague whom you've wounded—whatever He asks, do it today and don't delay! And don't just throw out the bad. Actively and persistently learn to replace the bad with the good.

Fight against any enemy intrusion. As you begin walking through the steps to spiritual fortification that I've shared, don't expect the enemy to lie by quietly while you take back his territory. You have declared war, and he will not back down without a fight. You must continue to watch and pray, asking God to strengthen you so that you can boldly attack any compromise that sneaks back into your life, "hating even the garment spotted by the flesh" (Jude 23).

I hate wasps and bees and anything with stingers in them, so much so that if one comes into my house, I cannot rest until it is killed. One time, a wasp snuck into my bedroom in the middle of the night, and in my attempts to end its life, I accidently swatted it into some crevice. (I discovered later that it was the air conditioner.) However, I didn't know where it had gone, and I was awake for two hours in the middle of the night ransacking my room trying to find it. I should have just given up the search and gone back to bed, but I couldn't sleep knowing that it was *somewhere* in my room.

Later, my family laughed as I told them the story of the midnight wasp-hunting escapade, and I laugh now too. But I think there is a profound spiritual illustration here. What if we attacked every hint of sin or compromise that attempted entrance into our lives as I went after that tiny wasp? What if, when the enemy finds a hole in our spiritual fortification, we do not rest but go after that specific breach with a vengeance in prayer until the intruder can no longer claim that foothold in our life? What would our lives look like today if this were the attitude we had toward preserving the integrity of our spiritual walls and fortification?

The problem is that we have grown complacent to these little breaches. They don't seem like such a big deal. "After all," we reason, looking around at our companions, "their breaches are much bigger than mine. So I don't have to be so hard on myself." But nothing is small in the sight of God. And to Satan, he doesn't care how he gets a foothold, as long as he has one.

A few weeks ago, I was flying back home from a speaking engagement in Canada. Since crossing the border between Canada and the United States is not a big deal, I didn't even think as I packed my lunch for the plane ride home. And so, along with nuts and crackers also came a couple of oranges and a couple of apples.

Expecting to breeze right through border patrol and customs, I was filling out the entry slip for the United States when the question suddenly popped up on the computer screen, "Are you carrying any kind of fruit or vegetables?" I could have lied, but my conscience knew better, so I checked "Yes," hoping it wouldn't delay my getting to my plane. When I got to the officer's desk at the checkpoint, he frowned, "Oh no! We can't let you bring this fruit into the United States. You will have to go meet with our officers in this side room."

As it ended up, I spent forty-five minutes waiting for the officers in the side room to meet with me and I nearly missed my plane home—and all because of those four harmless pieces of fruit!

As I was thinking about it afterward, the spiritual implications were deafening. It all seemed so small, so minor, just like certain sins I'm prone to cherish. But these sins, if not surrendered, may very well keep us out of heaven! No sin is considered small in the sight of God. Inspiration states, "Even one wrong trait of character, one sinful desire, persistently cherished, will eventually neutralize all the power of the gospel."[8]

It may be an impatient remark, a rolling of the eyes, a slip of the tongue, going against our conscience in even the smallest way, or something else rather small and insignificant. But if we let one "character breach" in, more are sure to follow, and each one Satan holds up against Christ. "Every sinful desire we cherish affords [the enemy] a foothold. Every point in which we fail of meeting the divine standard is an open door by which he can enter to tempt and destroy us. And every failure or defeat on our part gives occasion for him to reproach Christ."[9]

The enemy will keep testing our wall, looking for loose bricks, trying to gain a foothold. We can expect this as long as we live in the domain he claims as his. But we are promised, "With watchfulness and prayer [our] weakest points can be so guarded as to become [our] strongest points, and [we] can encounter temptation without being overcome."[10]

There is nothing as satisfying as knowing you have been in direct conflict with the enemy of darkness and you have prevailed. Victory is possible in Christ! Just keep holding on to Him until the victory is accomplished. If we stand upon the Word of God, we cannot fail. No matter the obstacles before us, no matter the enormity of the mountains nor the seeming insignificance of the details, let us follow God's call to rebuild our spiritual walls and fortify ourselves in Him. For in Philippians 1:6, He has promised that the work which He began in us, He will carry forth to completion, for His glory and His honor.

Let us cling to Him, daring to stand in a generation where many are falling. Let us dare to stand fully clothed in God's armor, and as we stand, let us dare to ask for *more*!

Chapter 16

Fact Versus Feeling

The Battle Over True Faith

> *Now faith is the substance of things hoped for,*
> *the evidence of things not seen.*
>
> *—Hebrews 11:1*

For many years, and down through multiple generations, the children of Israel looked forward to God's promise of deliverance from slavery and a return to their Canaan home. Finally, after being miraculously set free from their Egyptian taskmasters, and after traveling through the hot, dusty desert, they found themselves camped at the very border of Canaan. One can only imagine the eager expectancy that filled their hearts as they joyfully realized, "We are almost home!" But first, God had one more test of faith for His people.

In preparation to take the land of Canaan, God told Moses to send twelve spies (one from each tribe) to see what kind of people and what kind of land Canaan held. These twelve set out and after forty long days returned, bearing amazing tales and magnificent fruit.

However, ten of the spies also brought magnificently bad news. "The people are strong, the cities are walled, and giants live in the land. We are not able to go up against the people, for they are stronger than us. We are like grasshoppers compared to them. They will overcome us!"[1]

As the congregation began to cry in despair, Caleb and Joshua, two of the twelve spies, stood up in protest. "It's true that the people are great, but the land is a good land that flows with milk and honey, and if the Lord delights in us, He will give it to us. Let us go up at once to possess the land, for we are well able to overcome them! Hasn't God promised to give it to us?"[2]

But having been discouraged by the bad report of the ten spies, the hearts of the people were already resigned to the impossibilities of the conquest. And the ten spies bearing the evil report would not be moved. Forgetting that God had delivered them from slavery, brought them through the Red Sea, and given them victory over the Amalekites, they persisted in discouraging Israel from moving forward.

The Bible reports, "And all the children of Israel murmured against Moses and against Aaron: and the whole congregation said unto them, Would God that we had died in the land of Egypt! or would God we had died in this wilderness!" (Numbers 14:2.) "In their unbelief [Israel] limited the power of God and distrusted the hand that had hitherto safely guided them."[3] And what could God do now? Reward their lack of faith? Hardly!

We can only imagine the wonder and anger that must have filled God's heart as He looked down upon His unbelieving children who were so close, and yet so far, from reaching their promised home. "How long will this people provoke Me?" He asked Moses. "How long will it be before they trust My word? How many signs and wonders do I have to show them to prove that I can take care of them and give them victory over their enemies?"[4]

Right then and there, after being tempted ten times (see Numbers 14:22) by Israel's unbelief, we are told that God was ready to disinherit Israel, and He would have destroyed them and started over had Moses not *interceded earnestly* on their behalf. But because Moses stood in the gap, pleading on their behalf, God did not destroy them instantly. However, because of their lack of faith, He had no choice but to punish them. How would He do this? By fulfilling *the very words* they had spoken.

"Tell them," He told Moses, "that as you have spoken in My ears, so will I do to you. You don't want to go to Canaan! That's fine. You will not go in. Your carcasses shall fall in the wilderness. You shall not see the land that I promised to your fathers. Only your children shall enter in. Forty years you will wander in the wilderness, one year for every day that you searched out the land in unbelief. Only My faithful servants, Caleb and Joshua, shall enter the land. For they spoke faith, and as a result, I will honor their words."[5]

It's enlightening that after God told the children of Israel, "OK, you don't think you can conquer this land? Well then, you won't!" that it was *then* they decided they *could* conquer the land. And against the command of the Lord, they actually attempted to go to battle to take Canaan. But here they acted foolishly again. Moses was not with them, Caleb and Joshua were not with them, the ark was not with them, the Lord was not with them, and they suffered a great loss. And this will always be the case when God's people speak disbelief and then move forward presumptuously in their own strength, for God cannot bless.

Seeing the record of God's dealings with His people, we might wonder in amazement how the children of Israel could have ever doubted God along their long journey to the Promised Land. But are we any different today?

> Many look back to the Israelites, and marvel at their unbelief and murmuring, feeling that they themselves would not have been so ungrateful; but when their faith is tested, even by little trials, they manifest no more faith or patience than did ancient Israel. When brought into straight places, they murmur at the process by which God has chosen to purify them. Though their present needs are supplied, many are unwilling to trust God for the future, and they are in constant anxiety lest poverty should come upon them, and their children be left to suffer.[6]

Even today, we are nearing our Canaan home, but do we have any more faith than Israel did? God is giving us one last test. He wants to know if we will trust Him even when our senses and everything around us tell us that victory is impossible. He wants to know if we will believe His Word, even when we have not yet received the promises, and even when the whole world mocks our stand. He's ready to take us home, but He's wondering, "When I come to deliver My people, will I find faith on the earth?"

Learning to live by faith

George Müller, an evangelist preacher and missionary in England during the early 1800s, is best known for his *rare faith* and implicit trust in God to provide for his daily needs as he worked taking care of thousands of orphans.

His famous journey of faith began when, as a preacher, he would travel around the countryside visiting his parishioners and asking how their time with God was. He was disheartened because more times than not, they would reply sarcastically, "What time with God? Don't you know we have to work fourteen hours a day to keep food on our tables so our families don't starve?"

Convinced that God is the One who supplies all our needs, Müller quit his paid ministry as a pastor and asked God to use him as a testimony to show the world that if we put God first, He will supply. As he stepped out in faith, he made a compact with God that while he worked for God, he would share his needs with no one except for God. As a result, God began to answer his prayers of faith and provide. By faith, Müller started one orphanage and then another. Eventually, he was caring for thousands of orphans, all the while without the security of a monthly paycheck.

Sometimes he didn't know where that day's food would come from until the children had sat down at the table and there would be an unexpected knock on the door with someone bringing food. But God always provided. Müller's life was a powerful testimony to the power of prayer, and in later years he testified knowing of at least fifty thousand specific answers to prayer that he had received.

During his lifetime, over seven million dollars (about seventy-two million dollars in today's U.S. currency) passed through his hands to help the orphans and those in need, and not one dollar of it was ever solicited. It all came in answer to prayer.

When asked about his secret to power in prayer, Müller responded: "There was a day when I utterly died." And as he spoke, he bent lower until he almost touched the floor. "I died to George Müller, his opinions, preferences, tastes, and will—died to the world, its approval or censure—died to the approval or blame even of my brethren and friends—and since then I have studied only to show myself approved unto God." When George Müller physically died in 1898, his earthly possessions were valued at around eight hundred dollars. He had truly given all to the cause of Christ!

Like George Müller, we need to test and prove God for ourselves. We need greater faith in daily living. Rather than looking at our limited resources, we need to begin looking at God's unlimited power. Of course, that doesn't mean that we act presumptuously, practice poor stewardship, spend beyond our means, or accumulate huge debt. Rather, it means we learn to move forward in faith when God gives us a vision, knowing that if He's giving the vision, He will also make provision for its accomplishment.

Rather than moving forward by faith, too often, like Israel of old, we lament our lack of resources. But the Bible already has one book of Lamentations. Let's not write another. Instead, let's continue the book of Acts—God's acts!

Ellen White writes, "Let none waste time in deploring the scantiness of their visible resources. The outward appearance may be unpromising, but energy and trust in God will develop resources."[7]

The necessity of faith

Often, when we don't have success in our personal lives or ministry, rather than dealing with the root of the problem, we focus on method improvement. While our methods can always be improved upon, in God's kingdom, methods are usually not the problem—nor are the lack of resources or lack of talent. *The problem is a lack of faith.* Inspiration boldly tells us, "Every failure on the part of the children of God is due to their lack of faith"![8]

As we quickly find when we study the Bible, having faith is not optional in the Christian walk—not if we plan to go to heaven! (See Hebrews 11:6; Revelation 21:8.) So if we are people prone to doubt, how do we develop faith?

The most powerful way to build faith is through the Word, for we are told, "So then faith cometh by hearing, and hearing by the word of God" (Romans 10:17). Ellen White strongly supports this: "Faith that enables us to receive God's gifts is itself a gift, of which some measure is imparted to every human being. It grows as exercised in appropriating the word of God. In order to strengthen faith, *we must often bring it in contact with the word.*"[9]

In early days, Adventists were known as "people of the Book." They carried their Bibles with them everywhere they went, and they were always ready to answer for their faith. When they read the Bible, they didn't rationalize or try to explain certain parts away. They didn't take what God said and try to wiggle it around to fit their own ideas or desires. No, they took it as it was—the divinely inspired Word of God (2 Timothy 3:16). And they held its every thought as sacred. We need this same attitude toward God's Word today. "The Bible is God's voice speaking to us, just as surely as though we could hear it with our ears. If we realized this, with what awe would we open God's word, and with what earnestness would we search its precepts! The reading and contemplation of the Scriptures would be regarded as an audience with the Infinite One."[10]

In Matthew 8:5–13, we read about the centurion who came to Christ pleading for healing for his servant. Jesus responded, "I will come to your home and heal him." Most would have been delighted at this offer, but the centurion responded, "Oh Lord, I'm not worthy for You to come under my roof. Just *speak the word only* and my servant will be healed."

This Gentile had faith in *Christ's word alone*! It was a faith even Israel had not shown. That's why Christ marveled. Israel had the Old Testament Scripture, they knew it by heart, they boasted of being "people of the Book," the people of God. They read the Word of God, they preached it and taught it, but they didn't believe it. However, this centurion believed that there was power in the spoken word *alone,* and as a result, Christ healed his servant that very hour.

This is the kind of faith we need today—faith that stands on God's Word alone! This is why we need to spend much time in the Word and why we need to cultivate the habit of talking faith. If we give more expression to our faith, we will actually develop more faith. Ellen White emphasizes this concept time and time again: "Talk and act as if your faith was invincible. The Lord is rich in resources; He owns the world. Look heavenward in faith."[11] In another place, she adds, "Never give place to a thought of discouragement in the work of God. Never utter a word of doubt."[12]

Imagine how different our life would be if we put a guard over our mouth and made "talking faith" the habit of our daily lives!

Fact versus feeling

If we study our Bibles, we find that faith is one of the most emphasized gifts in all of Scripture. This is because it is the *gateway* to our receiving all other gifts.

The sick are healed by faith (Matthew 9:22); by grace we are saved through faith (Ephesians 2:8); we are justified by faith (Romans 3:28); the disciples worked by faith (Acts 6:8); we carry a shield of faith (Ephesians 6:16); the just live by faith (Romans 1:17); the righteous walk by faith (2 Corinthians 5:7); we are children of God by faith (Galatians 3:26); and in the end, the thing that counts the most is the faith that works by love (Galatians 5:6). The very foundation of Christianity is faith and the gospel is rendered powerless in our lives without it. This is why the devil is so intent on bringing doubt and unbelief into our lives today! Not only will our ministries fail to thrive if we don't live by faith, but we *ourselves* will spiritually wither.

As Christians, we fight a daily battle, a battle between *fact versus feeling.* The outcome of this very significant battle will determine what type of faith we hold. Let me explain.

Fact is what we find in God's Word. Although built upon unseen realities and invisible promises, fact does not waver, as it reflects the unchanging nature of God: He cannot lie (Titus 1:2); He will not change (James 1:17); He is the same yesterday, today, and forever (Hebrews 13:8); and He is more eager to give us good gifts than we are to give good gifts to our children (Luke 11:13). When we base faith on fact, we have a firm foundation to weather any storms.

Feeling, on the other hand, is constantly wavering, as it is based on our personal experiences, changing emotions, anxieties, spiritual lethargy, and unanswered prayers. Rather than consulting the Word of God for its decisions, feeling takes counsel from self, from worldly wisdom, from skeptical friends, and from the past unproductive Christian experience. When we base *faith on feelings,* which come and go, it's as if we are building our house upon the sand. And any storms that come along may knock it over.

When feelings lead the way—whether into ecstasy or apathy—faith always lags behind. Some view warm emotions as being evidences of faith. But faith is not just a sensation you get when you think of something you hope for, or of something God might like to do. Faith must be rooted in the unchanging *facts* of God's Word—not in our changing emotions.

Faith takes God at His word, with or without feeling. It "is the substance of things hoped for, the evidence of things not seen." We can believe our fellowmen, and can we not trust the word of God? When we go to Him for wisdom or grace, we are not to look to ourselves to see if He has given us a special feeling as an assurance that He has fulfilled His word. Feeling is no criterion. Great evils have resulted when Christians have followed feeling. How do I know that Jesus hears my prayers?—I know it by His promise. He says He will hear the needy when they cry unto Him, and I believe His word. He has never said to the "seed of Jacob, seek ye Me in vain."

If we walk in the light, we may come to the throne of grace with holy boldness. We may present the promises of

God in living faith, and urge our petitions. Although we are weak, and erring, and unworthy, "the Spirit helpeth our infirmities." But too often our prayers are moulded by coldness and backsliding. Those who do not deny self and lift the cross of Christ, will have no courage to approach a heart-searching God. We must learn to watch unto prayer, and to be importunate. We must accustom ourselves to seek divine guidance through prayer; we must learn to trust in Him from whom our help cometh. Our desires should be unto God; our souls should go out after Him, and their attitude should always be that of supplication.

When we have offered our petition once, we must not then abandon it, but say, as did Jacob when he wrestled all night with the angel, "I will not let Thee go, except Thou bless me," and like him we shall prevail.[13]

LeRoy Froom, in his book *The Coming of the Comforter,* writes, "Many are looking for physical feelings—joyous thrills and marvelous spiritual shocks—which, if they do not have, they disheartened."[14] In other words, people base their beliefs, the evidence for their closeness with God, and their faith on their feelings, *rather than on the facts of biblical truth.* And that's precisely why Satan is so successful in much of Christendom today. He is breeding a generation of Christians who have come to rely solely on their *feelings and sensations* as faith over the plain evidences in the Word of God. However, Inspiration tells us, "A good emotion is no evidence that you are a child of God, neither are disturbed, troubled, perplexing feelings an evidence that you are not a child of God."[15]

Froom goes on, "Fact, faith, feeling, is God's order." Fact comes first, we choose to believe, and then faith develops based on God's Word, and then finally comes the feelings. "It comes as the result of quiet faith!"[16]

If you are waiting to *feel* like you can trust God completely before you trust God completely, you will probably never trust Him. If you are waiting to *feel* like praying before you pray, you may never pray. God gave us a mind, and He's given us His Word. We need to use them together!

Just imagine how Abraham's *feelings* must have contradicted his faith as he and his son climbed the mountain to the place where God had asked him to offer Isaac as a sacrifice. Yet, he was in the center of God's will. Just imagine how John the Baptist must have *felt* locked up in prison while Jesus was out working miracles. And yet, Jesus said that no greater prophet had been born among women! Just imagine how the Israelites must have been *feeling* when they were trapped against the Red Sea, knowing the mightiest army on earth was coming against them at full speed! And yet God was preparing for one of the greatest miracles of all time.

Inspiration speaks about feeling, "The enemy holds many of you from prayer, by telling you that you do not *feel* your prayers, and that you would better wait until you realize more of the spirit of intercession, lest your prayers should be a mockery. But you must say to Satan, 'It is written' that 'men ought always to pray, and not to faint.' We should pray until we do have the burden of our wants upon our souls; and if we persevere, we shall have it. The Lord will imbue us with His Holy Spirit."[17] Further, when we feel least like praying, this is the time we need to pray the most. "By so doing we shall break Satan's snare, the clouds of darkness will disappear, and we shall realize the sweet presence of Jesus."[18]

One of my favorite quotes on prayer comes from the little book *Steps to Christ*. Here Ellen White writes, "Why should the sons and daughters of God be reluctant to pray, when prayer is the key in the hand of faith to unlock heaven's storehouse, where are treasured the boundless resources of Omnipotence?"[19] The Bible tells us, "According to your faith be it unto you" (Matthew 9:29). It says, "Believe . . . and ye shall have" (Mark 11:24).

You see, prayer is the key, but faith must make the move. Faith is the force that turns the key in the lock and opens the door. And it does so because it trusts God, it trusts that there are amazing blessings behind that closed door. Are we willing to trust God today, regardless of how we feel, and turn the key in the door to heaven's storehouse?

How long will we keep living as though God cannot be

trusted? How long will we keep looking to our feelings to tell us whether or not a path is correct? In these last days God is longing to pour out His Holy Spirit upon His people, but to do it, He needs to know that we can be trusted with Him. He needs to know that we will follow Him, *whether we feel like it or not.* Because when the devil looks and he sees those that will follow Jesus Christ *whether they feel like it or not,* he knows that his days are numbered.[20]

Faith can be described in many ways, but to sum it up best, it is simply this: bold, daring, unflinching, unwavering, un-retreating confidence in God, in His Word, and in His ability to perform that which He has promised—even when we haven't yet seen it.

The Bible encourages, "Blessed are they that have not seen, and yet have believed" (John 20:29). As we dare to ask for more, may we be among this group who can believe before seeing!

Chapter 17

The Power of Prayer and Fasting

Growing Mustard Seed Faith

> *Howbeit this kind goeth not out but by prayer and fasting.*
> —*Matthew 17:21*

*V*ietnam is a communist-dominated country with persecution and harassment often given to those who try to share the gospel. However, the Adventist believers there are learning that what man cannot do, God is able to do—especially when His people unite in fasting and prayer. My friend Julia O'Carey, director of ASAP Ministries, recently shared the following amazing testimony with me.

In one Vietnam city of almost four million, a pastor of a house-church and some of his fellow believers were eager to reach the people of their city for God. Because of this burden, they began handing out gospel DVDs and other materials. But they had little results and often suffered harassment and hours of grueling interrogation from the police because of their efforts.

Not sure what to do next, and desperate to see God work, the pastor asked the believers in his house-church to commit to thirty days of united prayer and fasting. They agreed. And so, fasting three out of seven days a week, they began their thirty-day prayer challenge. They prayed every day for hours, sometimes alone and often together. They spent time putting away wrongs and confessing their sins as they prayed that God would bring breakthrough.

Not long after the thirty days ended, there was a knock on the pastor's door. Opening the door, he instantly recognized the face of a notorious former Viet Cong commander turned mafia gang leader in the city. This man was well known for his illegal activities, drug dealing, and gambling halls and brothels, and the pastor wasn't sure what to expect when the man held up one of the gospel DVDs. With some fear, but overpowered by his love for God, the pastor invited the man into his home. They began to study the Bible together one day at a time for weeks until the man accepted Christ as His personal Savior.

The transformation in the man's life was amazing. He immediately went to work to dissolve his mafia organization and started closing down all his businesses that did not honor God. Everyone noticed the dramatic change, and his men began asking questions. As a result of his witness, forty of his men (along with their families) soon followed his example and accepted Jesus. He was happy, but he didn't stop spreading the message with just his men. He had big goals and wanted to reach the whole city for God.

One day, after much prayer, God gave this former mafia gang leader the idea to hold a "celebration of Christianity." It was a wild idea, but amazingly, God blessed in a remarkable way. This was probably the first time in the history of communist Vietnam that such a large public event was successfully pulled off. Masses of people poured into a rented hall. The pastor who had won the mafia gang leader to Christ was asked to be the guest speaker. The ex-mafia leader also shared his powerful testimony about how God had changed his life. As a result, more came to Christ.

Now more house-churches have been established in the city. The group of ex-gangsters now has over two hundred members and is growing. People are on fire for the Lord and His Word. Over ninety thousand copies of gospel DVDs have been shared with people throughout the city. Many are hearing the everlasting gospel message for the first time and preparing for Jesus Christ's soon coming.[1]

But would this miracle have happened if this pastor and his group had not been willing to fast and unite in prayer, putting away their differences as they pled for God to intervene in their city? Just imagine what might happen in our own lives and ministries if we followed this example and made fervent united prayer and fasting a prerequisite to our mission campaigns and ministry endeavors. Hudson Taylor once stated, "Perhaps the greatest hindrance to our work is our own imagined strength; and in fasting we learn what poor, weak creatures we are—dependent on a meal of meat for the little strength which we are so apt to lean upon."[2]

Growing mustard seed faith

In Matthew 17, we find the disciples in a great dilemma. While they had performed many miracles successfully, when it came to setting free a young boy who was demon possessed, they had no power. Jesus, on the other hand, simply rebuked the demon, he was gone, and the boy was healed.

Later the disciples came to Jesus privately. "Why couldn't we cast out the demon?" they asked. Jesus told them, "Because of your unbelief: for verily I say unto you, If ye have faith as a grain of mustard seed, ye shall say unto this mountain, Remove hence to yonder place; and it shall remove; and nothing shall be impossible unto you" (Matthew 17:20).

> Though the grain of mustard seed is so small, it contains that same mysterious life principle which produces growth in the loftiest tree. When the mustard seed is cast into the ground, the tiny germ lays hold of every element that God has provided for its nutriment, and it speedily develops a sturdy growth. If you have faith like this, you will lay hold upon God's word, and upon all the helpful agencies He has appointed. Thus your faith will strengthen, and will bring to your aid the *power of heaven*. The obstacles that

are piled by Satan across your path, though apparently as insurmountable as the eternal hills, *shall disappear before the demand of faith*. "Nothing shall be impossible unto you."[3]

Picking up with verse 21 of Matthew 17, Jesus wasn't finished with His rebuke to the disciples. "You need this kind of faith!" He told them. "However, this faith that will cast out demons (the most difficult problems) does not come except by prayer and fasting. Obviously, you have *not* been praying and fasting!"[4]

The call to biblical fasting

Fasting isn't a popular topic to preach about these days, and it's often overlooked in the spiritual disciplines we seek to develop. But fasting is a very important part of *effective praying*.

In Matthew 6:16, Jesus made the statement to the disciples, "Moreover when ye fast, be not, as the hypocrites." The hypocrites were noted for their long, rigorous fasting. But rather than a change of heart and lifestyle to see the gospel promoted (see Isaiah 58), their fasting was simply an outward act to show off their "piety."

To counteract the hypocrisy of such fasting, Jesus instructed His disciples, "When you fast, anoint your head and wash your face so that you don't appear unto men as though you are fasting."[5]

It's important to note that when Jesus talked about fasting with His disciples, the implication was not *if* they would fast, but *when* they would fast. In Scripture, fasting is a given. Every major biblical character fasted. And even now Jesus is fasting, as He promised He would not eat again from the fruit of the vine until we are all together in heaven (Matthew 26:29).

There are many misconceptions about fasting. Fasting is not just about making yourself abstain from food for a period of time. That would be called dieting! Neither is fasting something only for religious fanatics trying to earn their way into God's good graces. It's not just for the minister behind the pulpit or for the monk alone in some monastery. It's a spiritual discipline that normal, everyday Christians should practice as they seek to grow their walk with God and achieve greater personal victory in their lives.

Typically, fasting can mean anything from abstaining from specific foods for a time, to a juice fast, to a complete water fast (not recommended for long periods), to fasting on a simple, non-stimulating diet of fruits and vegetables—as Daniel did (this is the kind of fast Ellen White often recommended[6]), to fasting from specific activities such as entertainment or television or anything else that might give you more time to devote to your walk with God. Any such fast should *always* be accompanied with deep heart searching and prayer!

In Bible times, fasting wasn't merely just a denial of food. It was most importantly a time of heart evaluation as the petitioner sought God's blessing or deliverance. We must remember that there is no merit in the fast itself; the purpose of fasting is to change our hearts and bring us into deeper consecration to God. Too often, like the Pharisees of old, we feel that the pain we suffer in fasting is what brings God's blessings. How wrong this is!

Referring to the outward type of fasting that the hypocrites practiced, Bible commentator Albert Barnes writes,

> Do we not often [even today] feel that there is something meritorious in the very inconveniences which we suffer in our acts of self-denial? [However] . . . the pain and inconvenience which we may endure by the most rigid fasting are not meritorious in the sight of God. They are not that at which he aims by the appointment of fasting. He aims at justice, truth, benevolence, holiness [see Isaiah 58:6, 7]; and he esteems the act of fasting to be of value only as it will be the means of leading us to reflect on our faults, and to amend our lives.[7]

We must remember that fasting is not a magic bullet—nor is any other spiritual discipline we undertake. We can't earn God's blessings or answers in prayer any more than we can earn our own salvation. Fasting doesn't substitute for obedience or personal surrender. However, it is a means of cleansing the heart of distractions and helping us have a more receptive frame of mind to what God wants to do in our lives and through our prayers. And when in humility of heart we seek for divine guidance, we are told the angels of God will draw near.[8]

If you study out all the fasts throughout the Bible, you will find that every time God's people prayed *and fasted,* God worked mightily on their behalf. From deliverance from their enemies in battle, to supernatural deliverance from prison, to the outpouring of the Holy Spirit at Pentecost, and on and on, we see a pattern. And this pattern repeats itself throughout Christian history.

"John Calvin was called an inveterate [habitual] faster—and lived to see God's power sweep Geneva. The Moravians fasted, as did the Hussites, Waldensians, Huguenots, and Scottish Covenanters. Except for prevailing prayer that included fasting, we would have had no Reformation and no great awakenings over the centuries."[9]

Adventist history also gives record of the supernatural blessing received from fasting.

In the spring of 1865, the General Conference Committee set aside specific days for fasting and prayer. During this time, there was much searching of heart by church members. Some ate simply, and others abstained from food altogether as their health permitted. As a result, James White, *The Review and Herald* editor, wrote that many prayers were answered, and he had never seen such intensity and feeling, nor better times in Battle Creek or the whole world field. The Adventists also dedicated specific days in 1865 to fasting and prayer that the Civil War would end. Not long after this time of corporate fasting and prayer, *the Civil War ended*![10]

Ellen White has written a number of reasons why and when we should consider fasting. Consider the following:

- We should fast when searching out essential truths so our understanding is clear![11]
- We should fast when seeking the heavenly wisdom that God has promised![12]
- We should fast when seeking God's direction in making important plans.[13]

- We should fast when dedicating our talents to God's service.[14]
- We should fast when requesting God's help in a crisis.[15]
- We should fast when contending with demonic oppression.[16]
- We should fast when seeking God for more laborers for the harvest.[17]
- We should fast for unity among church members.[18]
- We should fast when seeking heart cleansing and spiritual renewal.[19]
- We should fast when seeking to overcome spiritual temptation.[20]
- We should fast when seeking to develop an appetite for plain food.[21]
- We should fast when seeking to conquer disease (for a meal or two).[22]

In addition to fasting when specific problems or issues arise, I think there is also an *advance fasting* we should consider. This is what Christ did in the wilderness for forty days *before* He started His ministry. This is what we should do *before* we make big decisions or *before* we go forward in our work!

The disciples couldn't cast out the demon in Matthew 17 because they weren't prepared spiritually. Sometimes, when emergencies arise, it's too late to start fasting. There's no time! Help is needed, and immediately! If we haven't already taken time to fast for God's blessing and strength, we'll likely not be equipped to fight when God needs us most on the battlefield.

Prayer and fasting should go hand and hand! Prayer is the means by which we grasp the invisible things of God while fasting is the means by which we let loose and cast away the visible things upon which we are prone to depend. Ultimately, the goal of true fasting should be the fulfillment of Isaiah 58. This is the kind of fast to which God is calling us.

> The true fast is no mere formal service. The Scripture describes the fast that God has chosen,—"to loose the bands of wickedness, to undo the heavy burdens, and to let the oppressed go free, and that ye break every yoke;" to "draw out thy soul to the hungry, and satisfy the afflicted soul." Isa. 58:6, 10. Here is set forth the very spirit and character of the work of Christ. His whole life was a sacrifice of Himself for the saving of the world. Whether

fasting in the wilderness of temptation or eating with the publicans at Matthew's feast, He was giving His life for the redemption of the lost. Not in idle mourning, in mere bodily humiliation and multitudinous sacrifices, is the true spirit of devotion manifested, but it is shown in the surrender of self in willing service to God and man.[23]

For more inspiration on fasting, I recommend the book *The Daniel Fast for Spiritual Breakthrough* by Elmer L. Towns.[24] Again though, remember that fasting for more effective prayer and spiritual breakthrough is not about *mastering a method* but about having a change of heart. Only as we listen to the Holy Spirit's promptings and allow Him to lead us into deeper surrender will our fasting be truly effective.

Praising God before the blessings come!

A couple of summers ago, we had a severe drought here in the Ozark Mountains where I live—one of the worst in the region's history. For weeks and months, it seemed, we kept praying for rain, but to no avail. It seemed that all the trees were going die and blow away. It was a very difficult time, especially for my mother and others who love to garden.

One day, during our time of united family prayer, my eight-year-old adopted nephew Daniel prayed, "Thank You, God, for all that rain You are storing up in heaven to pour down upon us!" We all chuckled at his prayer, but we agreed and began to praise God for the miracle we had not yet seen.

Two days later, not only did a huge storm come up out of nowhere, dropping over six inches of rain, but it also turned around and came back over our farm a second time. It actually *changed direction,* something I've never seen a storm do in my entire life. Our neighbors joined in our amazement as we watched this miracle happen. Skeptics may disagree, but I think God worked in such a dramatic way that day because of our little Daniel's prayer of praise. I can just imagine Him smiling, "Now that's the kind of faith I'm looking for! And that prayer I simply cannot resist."

Let's beat on the windows of heaven with a holy audacity that will not let go! Let's humble our hearts before God in fasting and prayer, and wrestle until the breaking of day as we dare to ask Him for more. And finally, let's praise God even before we see the blessing we desire! If we hold on, we will receive *more* . . . above and beyond our requests! We will receive a shower of blessings!

Chapter 18

A Rare Commodity

The Test of Persevering Faith

> *When the Son of man cometh, shall he find faith on the earth?*
> *—Luke 18:8*

*M*any have heard of the famous John Knox, who pleaded, "Give me Scotland, Lord, or I die." Knox, like other Reformers, had been convicted of the errors in the Church of Rome and was determined to see Scotland set free from its control. His friends, seeing his passion for God's Word, urged him to preach and teach, but initially he, feeling feeble and incapable for the daunting task, resisted. Finally, he was convicted and took up the work with a passion that would not be swayed. God heard his prayers and at last Scotland was freed from popery.[1]

Inspiration tells us, "If we have the interest that John Knox had when he pleaded before God for Scotland, we shall have success. . . . And when we take hold of the work and wrestle with God, saying, 'I must have souls; I will never give up the struggle,' we shall find that God will look upon our efforts with favor."[2]

I have a Romanian friend who is passionate about serving God and about seeing others fall in love with Christ through prayer, and as a result, she has a powerful prayer ministry affecting young people all over Europe. However, it wasn't always this way.

Raluca, while a Christian from childhood—who dedicated significant time to working in the mission field—will attest that for many years of her early ministry she was better at working than at praying. After ten days of intense prayer with a friend, however, her priorities were completely changed and she recognized where the true power was—kneeling at Jesus' feet!

Not long after, doors began opening for her to reach her fellow Europeans through prayer ministry. She was scared and didn't feel capable, but she moved forward by faith. Eventually, she was accepting prayer ministry and speaking invitations all over Europe.

After a year or so, she was called to lead united prayer at a youth conference in Germany. At the time, few of the German young people seemed to be taking any interest in united prayer. Feeling discouraged and yet desperate to see God work, she stayed up late one night praying for the people of Germany. Surprising herself, she began to pray earnestly, "Give me Germany, Lord, or I die."

The very next day, after spending much of the night in prayer, God began to open doors and melt the hearts of the young people in attendance at the meetings, and many came to pray.[3]

Returning to Germany almost a year later for the same conference, she was amazed to see how God had been working over that past year. Hundreds of young people, both from Germany and from other countries all across Europe, flocked together to prayer each morning and throughout the day. Many shared how they were starting prayer groups in their own churches and youth groups, and others shared the miracles that God had been working in their lives in answer to prayer. Amazingly, the revival fire Raluca had prayed for was beginning to spread, and *is still spreading today*!

God doesn't always work in such dramatic ways. Sometimes there are prolonged waiting periods before we see the answer to our prayers. And sometimes He wants to test us to know if our prayers are truly sincere.

Ellen White writes:

> Many do not have the virtue of a living faith. They think they have faith, but it is only the thought or action of a moment. They do not persevere in knocking at the door and keeping their request before the Lord. . . . Our prayers are to be fervent and earnest as were the petitions of the needy friend who asked for the loaves at midnight. The more you ask, the firmer will be your spiritual union. You may come into that place where you will have increased blessings because you have increased faith. . . .
>
> . . . God has a heaven full of blessings that He wants to bestow on those who are earnestly seeking for that help that the Lord alone can give.[4]

The question we need to ask ourselves is, "Will my faith persevere even when the answers don't come as soon as I hope?"

The test of persevering faith and prayer

Author and speaker Eric Ludy talks about a few basic types of *faith tests*[5] through which God often allows us to walk. I will expound upon these here, as it's so important we learn to hold on in faith and trust God, even when He doesn't work as quickly as we expect.

Test 1—When God appears silent. In Matthew 15:22–28, we find the story of a Canaanite woman who came to Jesus begging Him to heal her daughter. Jesus didn't respond to her initial cries for help. We are told, "he answered her not a word." We immediately think, *If He had just said* something—*anything to soothe her pain and show He cared—it would have helped, but He said nothing.*

As if Jesus' silence weren't painful enough, the disciples urged Jesus, in front of this woman, "Send her away. She's becoming a nuisance as she cries after us."

Finally, Jesus spoke. But rather than words of comfort, He said simply, "I'm sent to help Israel." The implication was that He was *not* sent to help her. In response, she fell at His feet in humble worship, "Lord, help me!"

Again, Jesus spoke. "It's not good to give the children's bread to dogs." Ouch! Not only had Jesus ignored her cries, but now He'd compared her to a dog! If any were looking on, they were probably thinking, *What's wrong with this woman? Doesn't she get it? Jesus isn't going to help her. She's not even a Jew. Who does she think she is, begging Him to heal her daughter?*

But this woman wasn't concerned with who *she* was or with her lack of qualifications for a miracle. She wasn't even concerned if He called her a dog. All she knew was who *He* was! He was the Savior, and she knew He was the *only One* who could help her, and her faith would not let go. And so she responded through tear-stained eyes and quivering lips, "Lord, it's true I may be a dog, but even dogs eat crumbs from the master's table. All I need is a crumb, Lord, just a crumb!"

Then Jesus turned to her with tenderness in His eyes. It wasn't that He didn't care from the beginning; it wasn't that He didn't love her; it wasn't that He didn't want to heal, but He wanted to prove her faith and use her enduring *persevering faith* as a testimony for the thousands who would need to follow her example down through the ages. At last He spoke what she was longing to hear. "O woman, great is thy faith: be it unto thee even as thou wilt" (verse 28). And at that same hour, her daughter was healed.

Would we have endured this faith test? Do we endure today, when it seems God ignores our cries, when it seems He is answering others' needs—while *we are the outcast* He can't possibly help? Do we hold on and worship Him still, and not let go until He fulfills our great need?

The Bible tells us, "And shall not God avenge his own elect, which cry day and night unto him, though he bear long with them? I tell you that he will avenge them speedily. Nevertheless when the Son of man cometh, *shall he find faith on the earth*?" (Luke 18:7, 8; emphasis added).

Test 2—When God appears to have forgotten. In John 11:1–44, we find one of the greatest miracle stories of Jesus' ministry: the resurrection of His beloved friend, Lazarus.

As the story goes, Lazarus became very sick, and Mary and Martha, his sisters, sent word to Jesus saying, "Lord, behold, he whom thou lovest is sick" (verse 3). Knowing how much Jesus loved Lazarus, they expected Him to hurry to their aid. But instead of coming immediately to their side, Jesus sent a simple message: "Don't worry. This sickness is not unto death, but it's for the glory of God." Then He continued to go about His work for another few days. While He lingered, Lazarus *died.* You can just imagine the grief in the hearts of Mary and Martha. "Did Jesus forget His promise? Why didn't He come when we called?"

By the time Jesus finally arrived, Lazarus had already been dead for four excruciatingly long days. Meeting Christ with weeping, Martha cried, "Jesus, if only You had been here *four days ago,* our brother wouldn't have died!"

In assurance, Jesus responded that her brother would rise. But although seeking to believe that God could *even now* do whatever Christ asked, again her response expressed doubt: "Yes, I know he will rise again in the resurrection at the last day," she replied.

But Jesus wasn't talking about the resurrection day; He was talking about today—that day! But her faith couldn't grasp the possibility. Even when Christ asked for the stone to be rolled away from the tomb, Martha still protested. "Lord, You don't want to do that. He's been dead four days! He will stink!"

How often we are just like Martha. We have no problem believing in the God of *yesterday.* We've read the Bible and we've heard the amazing stories. We have no problem believing in the God of *tomorrow,* either. But *today?* "God couldn't possibly perform the same miracles today . . . could He?" we ask in doubt.

Speaking of the written record of miracles in Scripture, we are told, "These things were not written merely that we might read and wonder, but that the same faith which wrought in God's servants of old might work in us. In no less marked a manner than He wrought then will He work now wherever there are hearts of faith to be channels of His power."[6]

As we see in the story of Lazarus, sometimes God delays purposefully, and the delay is just as much an answer to prayer as is the fulfillment when it comes. Although it may have looked like Jesus forgot His promise initially in this story, He hadn't forgotten. He simply needed to prove their faith, and so He also proves ours today, as well. Sometimes He allows our plans, our dreams, and our hopes to die, so that He may prove us and build us and also so that He can give us something better. Will we still trust Him? Ellen White writes, "There is no danger that the Lord will neglect the prayers of His people. The danger is that in temptation and trial they will become discouraged, and fail to persevere in prayer."[7]

Test 3—When the powers of the natural realm seem too powerful. In Matthew 14:28–30, we find the famous story of Peter walking on water. Initially, as Jesus called him out of the boat, he moved forward in faith, and his faith in Christ held him. But then he took his eyes off the Savior and looked at the storms around him, and as he did, he began to sink. "Oh no! What am I doing? I shouldn't have gotten out of the boat!"

How often have we done the same? Jesus has taken us down a road of faith. We've seen Him work in the past; we see Him working even now. But then our eyes get distracted by the storms around us. The natural realm seems too powerful to be overcome. Will we trust Him even then? Or will we sink into despair, thinking, *It's too difficult—impossible! I've gone too far out on a limb. God can't possibly work now!*

Are you tempted to give way to feelings of anxious foreboding or utter despondency? Inspiration encourages us: "In the darkest days, when appearances seem most forbidding, fear not. Have faith in God. . . .

". . . When in faith we take hold of His strength, He will change, wonderfully change, the most hopeless discouraging outlook. He will do this for the glory of His name."[8]

L. B. Cowman, author of *Streams in the Desert,* writes:

> In the lives of all the great Bible characters, God worked thus. Abraham, Moses, and Elijah were not great in the beginning, but were made great through the discipline of their faith, and only thus were they fitted for the positions to which God had called them. For example, in the case of Joseph whom the Lord was training for the throne in Egypt, we read in Psalms, "The Word of the Lord tried him." It was not the prison life with its hard beds or poor

food that tried him, but it was the word God had spoken into his heart in the early years concerning elevation and honor which were greater than his brethren were to receive; it was this which was ever before him, when every step in his career made it seem more and more impossible of fulfillment, until he was there imprisoned, and all in innocency, while others who were perhaps justly incarcerated, were released, and he was left to languish alone. These were the hours that tried his soul, but hours of spiritual growth and development, that, "when his word came" (the word of release), found him fitted for the delicate task of dealing with his wayward brethren, with a love and patience only surpassed by God himself.[9]

Cowman continues, "No amount of persecution tries like such experiences as these. When God has spoken of His purpose to do, and yet the days go on and He does not do it, that is truly hard; but it is a discipline of faith that will bring us into a knowledge of God which would otherwise be impossible."[10]

Oh, that we would keep our eyes on Jesus, the only One with the power to enable us to walk above the waves and the sea. Oh, that we would trust Him, even in the midst of the storms, even when the fulfillment of God's promises seem impossible. He's more powerful—*far more powerful*—than any storm we will ever encounter in this life.

Test 4—The final test, when God seems to have failed. Matthew 27 gives us the painful story of Christ's crucifixion and death. This is probably the hardest faith test we will ever endure as Christians. How do we explain to the world around us our faith in a Savior who *seems to have failed*?

Imagine the grief of the disciples at the cross when Jesus allowed Himself to be tortured, condemned, and finally crucified. "You are the Messiah, aren't You . . . aren't You?" I can almost hear them asking with questioning tears. "If You are who You say You are, how could You let them do this to You?" The Pharisees and Sadducees mocked Christ's followers: "Some savior you followed! He can't even save himself. How could he save you?"

Defeated and with broken hearts, the disciples watched as Satan appeared to have achieved the victory. Yet through what the disciples thought was defeat, God had won a greater victory and a greater glory. The Bible tells us in 1 John 5:4, "This is the victory that overcometh the world, *even our faith*" (emphasis added).

Will we hold on by faith and pray until we see victory? When God appears silent, will we pray through? When He appears to have forgotten, will we pray through? When it seems impossible in the natural realm or when it appears that He has failed, will we still trust Him and pray through?

We are somberly warned, "The season of distress and anguish before us will require a faith that can endure weariness, delay, and hunger—a faith that will not faint though severely tried."[11] At that time, no mere profession of faith will save us. No, "we must have real faith in Christ."[12] This will be our last great test, and only he whose faith endures to the end will be saved (Matthew 10:22).

As we close this chapter, let us remember that if we want to have the rare commodity of *persevering faith* that can stand even when we don't see the immediate answer to our prayers, we must feed our faith with the Word. We must reflect upon the promises. And when trials come, we must cling to the Lord with a faith that will not let go.

In addition, we should fill our minds with the true-life testimonies of those who have walked this path before. There are many such testimonies, even from modern day, and these faith-building stories will encourage our own.[13] Of course, one of the best faith-building stories is told in the book *The Great Controversy*. What a powerful testimony the apostles and Christian Reformers throughout history have left for us. This is the kind of testimony we need today!

Let us walk by faith, talk faith, feed faith, live faith, and persevere in faith! God wants to do more for us, and He's daring us to keep asking Him for more—*in faith*! Remember, regardless of what lies ahead, *our God does not and will not fail*! We can trust Him. We can trust His Word—even when He's silent!

Chapter 19

Holding On When God Says No

God Doesn't Waste Our Pain

> *For I reckon that the sufferings of this present time are not worthy to be compared with the glory which shall be revealed in us.*
>
> —*Romans 8:18*

This may seem like a rather odd chapter title, considering it's in the section "Divine Keys to Answered Prayer." However, I believe God is looking for those who will hold on and trust Him, not just when He answers their prayers the way they hope, but when He also says No! *We must remember that No is an answer too!*

It's inspiring to read stories of faith and how God has answered prayers in miraculous ways in the lives of others. But if you aren't seeing those same kinds of answers in your own life, if you are dealing with some deep sorrow or crushing blow, or if you just feel that God is ignoring your cries, you may be tempted to despair. "What about me, God? I've cried and prayed. Have You forgotten about me?" you may ask.

At times, we've probably all asked these types of questions, and so have countless other Christians throughout history. After all, while God delivered Daniel from the lions' den, there are other "Daniels" whom He's allowed to die. Just read *Foxe's Book of Martyrs* and you will learn of many sincere believers who died for their faith over the centuries. Many are still dying today.

Larry and Mindy,[1] two of my friends from college, know what it's like to suffer loss and wonder about unanswered prayer. As missionaries, they have dedicated their lives to service. But life overseas hasn't been easy. Several years ago, their four-year-old son died of malaria. They prayed, they cried, but still there was nothing they could do. If that wasn't hard enough, just recently, Larry's father Michael,[2] a mission pilot who has served the church for years, was killed in a tragic plane crash. I'm sure Larry's father prayed for protection that morning just as he has every other day. Yet, for some reason, God allowed him to die, along with three of his passengers. Thankfully, despite these unexplained losses, this young couple continues to press on.

We can't really make sense of these types of tragedies outside of heaven; we just have to trust God and hold on to His Word, knowing that we are just experiencing a small part of the suffering that Christ already experienced on Calvary.

The Bible tells us, "Beloved, think it not strange concerning the fiery trial which is to try you, as though some strange thing happened unto you: But rejoice, inasmuch as ye are partakers of Christ's sufferings; that, when his glory shall be revealed, ye may be glad also with exceeding joy" (1 Peter 4:12, 13).

While I've lost loved ones, I haven't dealt with personal tragedy as deeply as many I know. However, there are prayers I've prayed for over twenty years now that I still haven't seen God answer. But that doesn't mean I've stopped praying! There are also people for whom I've prayed for healing—and sadly watched die.

Honestly, I don't think that this side of eternity we will ever be able to understand why God answers some prayers and others He seems to pass by, why He allows some to be healed and others to die, why He works marvelously for some, and others He allows to walk through the valley of suffering and shame. But one thing I know—He doesn't waste our pain!

As my friend Janet Page, who has dealt with personal tragedy, often says, "If we surrender our suffering to God, He will use it for His glory. Nothing is wasted in God's kingdom." The Bible tells us God stores all our tears in a bottle (Psalm 56:8). And even through times of confusion, silence, and loss, He is still at work in our lives.

The story is told of a woman who struggled with unanswered prayer. One night she had a dream in which she saw three other women kneeling in prayer. As they knelt, Christ drew near them. As He came near the first of the three, He put His arms around her as He bent over her with love and tenderness and spoke encouraging words in her ears. She smiled in response. Then He moved on. When He came to the second woman, He stopped and gently put His hand upon her bowed head, giving her a look of encouragement and approval. But no words of love were spoken. The third woman who was bowed in prayer He seemed to pass by without so much as a word or a glance.

The dreaming woman thought to herself, *How much He must love the first woman. To the second one He gave approval, but not the same love, and the third woman must have disappointed Him or hurt Him deeply, for He did not even stop to speak to her or give her even a glance or a touch. I wonder why He has so much displeasure in the third?*

While she was yet in her dream, the Lord came and stood before her, speaking tenderly to her. "Oh woman, how wrongly you have interpreted My actions! Let Me tell you why I acted as I did. The first kneeling woman needs all the evidence of My love and tenderness to keep her feet in the narrow way. Without it, she would fall! The second woman has a stronger faith and love, and I can trust her to trust Me however things go and whatever people do. The third, whom I seemed not to notice and even to neglect, has faith and love of the finest quality, and her I am training by quick and drastic processes for the highest and holiest service.

"You see," He continued, "she knows Me so intimately, and trusts Me so utterly, that she is independent of words or looks or outward intimation of My approval. She is not dismayed nor discouraged by any circumstances through which I arrange that she shall pass through or by the yet unanswered prayers that mark her way; she trusts Me when sense and reason and every finer instinct of the natural heart would rebel, because she knows that I am working in her for eternity, and that what I do, though she knows not the explanation now, she will understand in the future."

The Lord continued, "I am silent in My love because I love beyond the power of words to express, or of human hearts to understand. Trust Me, My child, I have not forsaken, nor forgotten, but I am preparing this woman and you for even greater blessings."[3]

Do you feel forsaken or forgotten by the Lord today? Know that you are not. Even if you don't feel His presence, rest in the assurance that He is near, for the Bible tells us that He will never leave us nor forsake us (Hebrews 13:5). "Through sincere prayer we are brought into connection with the mind of the Infinite. We may have no remarkable evidence at the time that the face of our Redeemer is bending over us in compassion and love, but this is even so. We may not feel His visible touch, but His hand is upon us in love and pitying tenderness."[4]

It may be hard to imagine right now, but we are told, "In the future life the mysteries that here have annoyed and disappointed us will be made plain. We shall see that our seemingly unanswered prayers and disappointed hopes have been among our greatest blessings."[5]

Ellen White writes the following profound statement in regard to unanswered prayer:

> When we do not receive the very things we asked for, at the time we ask, we are still to believe that the Lord hears and that He will answer our prayers. We are so erring and shortsighted that we sometimes ask for things that would not be a blessing to us, and our heavenly Father in love answers our prayers by giving us that which will be for our highest good—that which we ourselves would desire if with vision divinely enlightened we could see all things as they really are. When our prayers seem not to be answered, we are to cling to the promise; for the time of answering will surely come, and we shall receive the blessing we need most. But to claim that prayer will always be answered in the very way

and for the particular thing that we desire, is presumption.
God is too wise to err, and too good to withhold any good
thing from them that walk uprightly. Then do not fear to
trust Him, even though you do not see the immediate answer to your prayers.[6]

Trusting God even when we don't see what He's doing is kind of
like riding in an airplane. I've flown a lot internationally, and I love
the little screen on the back of the seat that tells me where we are as we
fly. Somehow, for some strange reason, watching this screen brings me
comfort. However, not all airplanes are equipped with this beautiful
feature. So even when I can't see where we are, I have to trust that the
plane is still taking me to the right destination, and I choose to stay in
the plane. That's what learning to trust God is all about. Although He
doesn't always show us where we are or where He's taking us, we have to
trust Him, and above all, we have to stay in the plane with Him. If we
don't, we are asking for disaster!

Hold fast to your faith

In closing this section on prayer, I'd like to share the final blog entry
of the late David Wilkerson. Author of the famous book from the 1980s
The Cross and the Switchblade, he spent most of his life on the streets
of New York City ministering to gangs and drug addicts. As a result
of his ministry and passion for Christ, he saw thousands set free from
darkness.

On April 27, 2011, he wrote a simple blog entry as he did most
days. But this day was different, for not long after writing this entry,
he headed to town for a simple errand and was killed in a tragic car accident. As a result of this devastating loss, thousands came to pay their
respects at his memorial.

Considering the life he lived and the way he died so unexpectedly
and unexplainably, his final blog entry is deeply profound, and I believe
it has a message for all of us today. He wrote:

To believe when all means fail is exceedingly pleasing to

God and is most acceptable. Jesus said to Thomas, "You have believed because you have seen, but blessed are those that do believe and have not seen" (John 20:29).

Blessed are those who believe when there is no evidence of an answer to prayer—who trust beyond hope when all means have failed.

Someone has come to the place of hopelessness—the end of hope—the end of all means. A loved one is facing death and doctors give no hope. Death seems inevitable. Hope is gone. The miracle prayed for is not happening.

That is when Satan's hordes come to attack your mind with fear, anger, overwhelming questions: "Where is your God now? You prayed until you had no tears left. You fasted. You stood on promises. You trusted."

Blasphemous thoughts will be injected into your mind: "Prayer failed. Faith failed. Don't quit on God—just do not trust him anymore. It doesn't pay!"

Even questioning God's existence will be injected into your mind. These have been the devices of Satan for centuries. Some of the godliest men and women who ever lived were under such demonic attacks.

To those going through the valley and shadow of death, hear this word: Weeping will last through some dark, awful nights—and in that darkness you will soon hear the Father whisper, "I am with you. I cannot tell you why right now, but one day it will all make sense. You will see it was all part of my plan. It was no accident. It was no failure on your part. Hold fast. Let me embrace you in your hour of pain."

Beloved, God has never failed to act but in goodness and love. When all means fail—his love prevails. Hold fast to your faith. Stand fast in his Word. There is no other hope in this world.[7]

How profoundly spoken! Ellen White writes: "Despondency may shake the most heroic faith and weaken the most steadfast will. But God understands, and He still pities and loves. He reads the motives and the purposes of the heart. To wait patiently, to trust when everything looks dark, is the lesson that the leaders in God's work need to learn. Heaven will not fail them in their day of adversity.

"Nothing is apparently more helpless, yet really more invincible, than the soul that feels its nothingness and relies wholly on God."[8]

My brothers and sisters in the Lord, let us keep running with our eyes on the goal. As the apostle Paul wrote, "Wherefore seeing we also are compassed about with so great a cloud of witnesses, let us lay aside every weight, and the sin which doth so easily beset us, and let us run with patience the race that is set before us, looking unto Jesus the author and finisher of our faith; who for the joy that was set before him endured the cross, despising the shame, and is set down at the right hand of the throne of God" (Hebrews 12:1, 2).

Christ is the Author and Finisher of our faith, and *He's coming back soon*! May we be ready to meet Him! Until then, may we never stop running as we continue daring to ask for more!

Part III

Understanding the Battle Over Prayer

Chapter 20

Controversy in the Sanctuary

The Sanctuary Blueprint

> *Thy way, O God, is in the sanctuary.*
>
> —*Psalm 77:13*

*W*hile the majority of this book has focused on the power of prayer and the divine keys to answered prayer, I am now going to take a little time to focus on the *battle over prayer,* and how we can avoid the counterfeit revival fires sweeping across the modern-day church. However, before we do this, we need to *briefly* review what we can learn of Christ and the path of salvation through the different articles of furniture in the Old Testament sanctuary.

Let me stress that the following is just a *quick nutshell overview* of lessons we can learn from the sanctuary. I encourage you to do further study on your own, as there are so many rich spiritual insights that can be gained. Also, understanding these truths will help us meet the many subtle deceptions that we are sure to face as we get closer to Christ's second coming.

Let's begin!

And God said, "Let them make me a sanctuary; that I may dwell among them" (Exodus 25:8). Not only did God want the children of Israel to have a symbol of *His very real presence* with them as they journeyed toward the Promised Land, but He also wanted them to understand the pathway that would ultimately bring them to reconciliation with Him—a pathway that would remind them of the seriousness of sin while giving them hope of a coming Messiah who would take away all their sins.

Altar of sacrifice—confession and justification by faith. At the door of the courtyard was the altar of sacrifice where the sinner brought a spotless lamb (symbolizing Christ) and confessed his sins upon the head of the lamb before killing it with his own hands. Here we learn the significance of what our sins cost Christ on the cross. Here we are justified. (See Hebrews 9:22; Leviticus 4:22–26; Romans 10:9–13; 1 Corinthians 15:22.)

Just as we must ask God for forgiveness, we also need to forgive others if we hope to be forgiven by God (Matthew 6:14, 15). Ellen White writes, "If we expect our own prayers to be heard, we must forgive others in the same manner, and to the same extent, as we hope to be forgiven."[1]

Laver—baptism and sanctification. The next piece of furniture in the courtyard of the sanctuary was the *laver.* This laver was a brass basin filled with water, which the priests used to wash themselves before they went into the tabernacle. If they didn't wash themselves thoroughly, they would die when they entered the Holy Place, for no uncleanness was permitted in God's presence (Exodus 30:17–21).

Here we see a beautiful symbol of Christ, the Living Water, who cleanses us (baptizes us) from all sin, and who also sanctifies us day by day to prepare us for heaven. (See 1 John 1:9; Ephesians 5:26; John 1:12.)

Table of shewbread—the Living Word of life. Upon entering the Holy Place of the tabernacle, there were three articles of furniture. The first was the *table of shewbread,* which represents Christ as the Living Word. While the priest ate the bread physically in Old Testament times, symbolically, we are to eat this Word daily today. It is what helps us grow to maturity as Christians. (See John 6:51; Matthew 4:4; Jeremiah 15:16; Hebrews 5:12–14.)

Altar of incense—our Intercessor in prayer. The central piece of furniture in the Holy Place was the *altar of incense*. Here, the priest, symbolizing Christ, would stand before the curtain of the Most Holy Place, and intercede on behalf of the people.

While we have direct access to God's throne now (because Jesus completely satisfied the demands of justice at Calvary, there is no more veil of separation—see Matthew 27:51), it's important to recognize that Christ' righteous prayers *still cover our own,* making them acceptable to the Father. Without His intercession, our prayers today would be in vain.

> The religious services, the prayers, the praise, the penitent confession of sin ascend from true believers as incense to the heavenly sanctuary, but passing through the corrupt channels of humanity, they are so defiled that unless purified by blood, they can never be of value with God. They ascend not in spotless purity, and unless the Intercessor, who is at God's right hand, presents and purifies all by His righteousness, it is not acceptable to God. All incense from earthly tabernacles must be moist with the cleansing drops of the blood of Christ. . . . [However] perfumed with the merits of Christ's propitiation, the incense comes up before God wholly and entirely acceptable. Then gracious answers are returned.[2]

The Bible tells us, "he [Christ] ever liveth to make intercession" for us (Hebrews 7:25; see also Hebrews 4:14–16). Praise God for our heavenly Intercessor!

Golden candlestick—Holy Spirit–filled life and witness. The last piece of furniture in the Holy Place was the *golden candlestick* (or seven-branch candlestick), which gave light to the Holy Place and was always burning. This light represents the Holy Spirit, which, day by day as it continues to burn, draws us closer to Christ, convicting us of sin and empowering our lives and witness. (See Exodus 25:31–40; 30:7, 8; John 8:12; 16:13; Psalm 119:105.)

Ark of the covenant—God's dwelling place. The final piece of sanctuary furniture, the *ark of the covenant,* was located beyond the veil (as already mentioned), within the *Most Holy Place.* Here atop the ark of the covenant was the mercy seat, a type of throne, guarded by two golden cherubim, where God Himself came down to dwell with Israel (Exodus 25:22). Only the high priest was allowed to enter the Most Holy Place, and then only once a year on the Day of Atonement.

It's significant to note that the ark of the covenant contained three items: a pot of *manna* (symbolizing the significance of God's daily provision—see Exodus 16), *Aaron's rod*—which had budded and produced almonds (symbolizing the significance of God's appointed leadership—see Numbers 16), and the *Ten Commandments,* written on tables of stone by God's own hand (symbolizing the significance of God's unchanging law—see Exodus 20; 31:18; Malachi 3:6).

Controversy in the sanctuary

Satan succeeded in cutting humankind off from God when he led Adam and Eve to sin in the Garden of Eden. Next, he tried to keep Christ from conquering when He came to earth to die for the sins of fallen humankind. Thankfully, he failed miserably, and the pathway (through Christ) was provided for our return. Now, Satan's chief aim and focus is to keep us from following *this pathway* home. Inspiration tells us, "The adversary seeks continually to obstruct the way to [God's throne] the mercy seat, that we may not by earnest supplication of faith obtain grace and power to resist temptation."[3]

Satan knows what will happen if we truly grasp the biblical truths found in the sanctuary. He knows what will happen if we find our way back to the mercy seat in the Most Holy Place. Because of this, he's been working overtime for centuries not only to nullify these beautiful truths, but also to provide many effective spiritual counterfeits. And sadly, he's been quite successful.

The following outline, compiled by my friend Pastor Ivor Myers in his best-selling book *Operation Blueprint: Earth's Final Movie,*[4] shows how Satan has sought to destroy the truths symbolized in the sanctuary. As we review the following ways God's blueprint has been tampered with, let us re-evaluate where we stand spiritually and "study to shew [ourselves] approved [not to man but] unto God" (2 Timothy 2:15).

The gateway to the sanctuary: In John 14:6, Christ tells us, "I am the way, the truth, and the life: no man cometh unto the Father, but by me." However, for almost six thousand years now, Satan has been attempting to blind the eyes of men, trying to convince them that there are *other ways* they can come to God without going through His Son. We can see how effective he has been as we consider the following.

The altar of sacrifice: While the sacrificial rituals practiced by the Jewish leaders before Christ's coming often became merely a form, so after Christ's coming, due to the secular influences of pagan Rome upon the church in the early centuries A.D., the forgiveness of sins by *faith alone* in Christ's blood was replaced by man-made counterfeits and traditions. Whether through the practice of penance and indulgences, or by the merit of good deeds, or by the observance of rigorous rituals, it was taught that salvation was obtained by human effort and works. While forms have changed over the years, this faulty *doctrine of self-works* is still embraced by many professing Christians today. (This is in direct opposition to the biblical truth of salvation by faith alone: see Ephesians 2:8, 9; Titus 3:5, 6.)

The laver: Baptism by choice and immersion was replaced by infant baptism and sprinkling. Christians no longer had to make a personal choice to be saved. If they'd been baptized as a baby, they were considered saved! This "once saved, always saved" philosophy negates not only free choice, but the whole ongoing process of biblical sanctification, which is accomplished only as we yield to the Holy Spirit's power day by day. Unfortunately, it is still embraced by many Christians today. (This is in direct opposition to the biblical truth of baptism, sanctification, and daily surrender: see Ephesians 4:5; Proverbs 4:18; 1 Thessalonians 4:3–8; Ezekiel 3:20.)

The table of shewbread: As time went on, the truths of God's Word were replaced and superseded by the traditions and practices of the church. The leaven of man-made ordinances began to take predominance over the purity of biblical truth. In fact, for many centuries, the common men were forbidden to read or interpret the Bible for themselves. This was deemed acceptable only to the clergy. Those who tried to live by or preach the true Word, apart from church traditions, were considered apostates and heretics. Unfortunately, today, many throughout Christianity still follow church traditions over that of biblical truth. (This is in direct opposition to the foundation of unchanging biblical truth and doctrine: see 2 Timothy 3:16; Isaiah 8:20; Proverbs 30:5, 6; Revelation 22:18.)

The altar of incense: Instead of going through Christ our Intercessor to communicate directly with our Father in heaven with our confessions and prayers, man orchestrated a confessional booth, where a human priest was to sit in the place of God, hearing the confessions of the people. Thus the gift of forgiveness and mercy was taken from God and placed in the hands of mortal men. This practice is still followed by many Christians today. (As we can see, the removal of the sanctuary doctrine of Christ as our Intercessor is in direct opposition to biblical truth: see 1 Timothy 2:5; Hebrews 10:19.)

The golden candlestick: Unfortunately, in the years following the Pentecostal outpourings (after Christ's ascension), secular entities began to introduce more and more worldliness and compromise into the church. As a result, true Holy Spirit living was replaced by a form of *spiritual pretense* by many in religious leadership. Not only was it "OK" to be in the church and live as one pleased (as long as proper confessions were made and penance was paid), but thousands who exhibited a Holy Spirit–filled life and testimony were burned at the stake, fed to lions, or left alone to rot in cold dark dungeons because of their stand for biblical truth and their Holy Spirit–filled life and witness. This period of great spiritual persecution is what we know today as the Dark Ages. It literally lasted 1,260 years, which matches the biblical prophecy from Daniel 7:25, which predicted this difficult experience for God's people. (This squelching of the genuine Holy Spirit power is in direct opposition to Scripture: see Acts 1:8; 5:32; Isaiah 43:10.

The ark of the covenant: And last, the religious powers, under a guise of religious pretense, not only attacked those who kept God's laws through the Dark Ages, but they literally changed God's law, the very law He wrote in stone with His own finger. They brought images and idols into the worship service, and, most significantly, they changed the fourth commandment from Sabbath to Sunday.[5] (Once again, changing God's law and superseding the Bible with man-made church traditions goes in direct violation to the Holy Scriptures: see Matthew 5:18, 19.)

Ellen White warns, "Satan is constantly endeavoring to attract attention to man in the place of God. He leads the people to look to bishops, to pastors, to professors of theology, as their guides, instead of searching the Scriptures to learn their duty for themselves. Then, by controlling the minds of these leaders, he can influence the multitudes according to his will."[6]

Many in religious leadership are now pushing to bring all religious bodies and denominations back together in unity. They quote Jesus' prayer request "that they all may be one; as thou, Father, art in me, and I in thee" (John 17:21). It is true that as believers in Christ *we are to be one*! However, far too many Christians overlook John 17:19, in which Jesus expresses His wish "that they also might be sanctified through the *truth*" (emphasis added). The Bible doesn't tell us that we are sanctified by unity or by being united with other religious entities. It says that we are sanctified and made one *through the truth*—the truth being found in the Word of God (John 17:17).

With this in mind, how can Bible believing Protestant Christians become reconciled and *one in the truth* with those that for centuries have sought to alter God's truth? God is calling all of us out of spiritual Babylon, out of spiritual confusion and compromise—not back into it (Revelation 14:6–12). It's clear that the prophecy of Revelation 13:3 is being fulfilled before our very eyes today. Let us not sleep as others do. Let us watch and be sober; let us pray!

It is obvious by what is happening in the world around us that we are living in significant times! However, while things may seem confusing and different winds of doctrine will blow and then subside (2 Timothy 4:3), let us keep our focus on Christ, for with His Word before us, we have no reason to be swept away (Ephesians 4:14; 2 Timothy 3:16). We can stand strong in the truth no matter the storms! As the late Hollis Scarbrough said, "In every age, God has ALWAYS had a people—faithful and loyal, the called and chosen—and He still has a special people today."[7]

The question is, Will we be part of this people? Will we be part of His *final remnant* as depicted in Revelation 12:17? To find out where you fit in this sanctuary controversy, as well as to gain an eye-opening overview of Christian history from the beginning war in heaven until present times, I encourage you again to read *The Great Controversy*. This book has inspired me as no other, as it shows where we stand in earth's final battle between truth and error. The question we each need to ask ourselves is, Am I on the right side of this great controversy battle?

God is calling each of us to a deeper study of His Word. He is calling us to a deeper experience with Him. Above all, He is calling us to follow the sanctuary pathway back to His throne. But He doesn't force anyone! The choice to follow is up to us!

Chapter 21

How to Avoid Playing With Strange Fire

Recognizing Counterfeit Revival: Part 1

> *And Nadab and Abihu died, when they offered
> strange fire before the Lord.*
>
> —*Numbers 26:61*

While driving through a little country town in the Ozark Mountains, I saw a sign with big, bold letters: "Revival—Happening Now!" Feeling impressed to check it out, I turned off the road into a church parking lot and joined a group heading into the church.

Now, I should have known from the moment I walked through the door that this was not going to be any ordinary revival service—if revival services can ever be ordinary. The music was very, very loud, and I almost needed to cover my ears as the praise leader egged the crowd on, singing—rather screaming—into the microphone.

Apparently not satisfied with the praise session, the pastor entered the pulpit and yelled at the people that if they truly believed in a great God, they needed to act like it and go crazy for Him. As a result, everyone started waving their arms and dancing while they sang, and some were even jumping up and down and off the stage.

The uproar in the room increased until it was difficult to even understand the words of the songs they were singing. However, I did catch one very telling line of lyrics: "Heaven is real, death is a lie, heaven is real, death is a lie." To me, that sounded very familiar—like something a serpent told Eve about six thousand years ago (Genesis 3:4). It was all I could do to resist getting up and leaving, but I determined to stay a bit longer to see what would happen next.

Soon the preacher, a traveling revivalist, began a very compelling, lengthy appeal for offerings to support his traveling ministry. Concluding this, he proceeded to preach—or rather yell—about our need for a deeper walk with God. This walk, he explained, would be evidenced by a *new supernatural experience.* I began taking notes as fast as I could.

"Now the world frowns at us because of our focus on *the experience,*" he confided. "But that's where God meets us!" I didn't recall a Bible verse supporting that, but I continued to listen intently. He elaborated on that and then transitioned to *the altar.*

"Whoever controls the altar controls the outcome!" he shouted. *How true!* I thought. *But there is more than one altar. The devil has an altar too! To which altar are we referring?*

The preacher continued. "Do you know why it's so important that we control the altar? It's because if we do, this whole state of Arkansas will be shaken! That's what happens when the altar gets hot! Folks, it's time we come forward and take control of the altar!" He was speaking at a higher and higher pitch and began to sweat. People raised their hands in agreement, and behind me I heard someone speaking in tongues. "People, are you hungry for Jesus or aren't you? We've got to stop talking about the fire and *experience the fire.* Forget about those you are sitting beside. Forget about protocol. If you want a *supernatural experience,* if you want to see miracles, *you've got to get up and take control of the altar!*"

I guess this was his way of making an altar call because people began jumping out of their seats and running to the front with their arms in the air. Soon it was difficult to hear the preacher with all the babbling in tongues, weeping, and yelling in the room.

Despite the preacher's earnest appeal, there were still some of us in the congregation who were unmoved. At this, he began to sweat even more as his voice took on a greater intensity and volume. "I don't know what more to say!" he cried in great consternation, seeming to look right at me. *"Do you want the fire or don't you?"* At this point, afraid he might come down, lay hands on me, and try to force me to experience "the fire," I decided it was time to leave.

Driving home, my mind kept replaying the events of the revival service. On one hand, I wish I were a mouse in the corner to see how it all ended. On the other hand, it's probably best I didn't. It was getting a bit crazy. There was a fire going on in that church all right, but it was a *strange fire.*

What is the significance of "strange fire"?

The Bible tells us, "Nadab and Abihu *died,* when they offered strange fire before the LORD" (Numbers 26:61; emphasis added). This may seem quite harsh if we don't understand the story.

Nadab and Abihu were Aaron's sons and had stood highest in Israel, next to Moses and Aaron. They were in the Lord's service, in the Lord's temple, bowing before the Lord's altar. Further, they had been especially honored of the Lord, as they were allowed, along with the seventy elders, to behold the glory of the Lord on the mount.

So why was their sin so grievous? You see, God desired to teach His people that they must approach His throne with holy reverence and awe. When it came to the worship of God in the ceremonial services of the tabernacle, there was a distinct difference made between the common and the sacred. Nadab and Abihu were careless of that difference, and in a state of partial intoxication, they decided to do as they pleased. Instead of burning incense with "sacred fire" that God Himself had kindled, they transgressed His commandments by using "common fire" that they themselves had started. God had pronounced a curse upon those who saw no difference between the common and the holy. He requires exact obedience. And this small yet significant sin could not be ignored, otherwise all Israel would grow careless and lose sight of the holiness of God and the sacredness of His laws.[1]

This testimony is a somber warning to us today! The Bible tells us, "But ye are a chosen generation, a royal priesthood, an holy nation, a peculiar people" (1 Peter 2:9). As such, a greater responsibility rests on Christians than on the average unbeliever. The sin of playing with common, man-made fire is just as deadly as bowing before the wrong altar. We cannot do this and expect God's blessing. However, because God doesn't instantly strike down the disobedient today as He did in Israel's day, many have grown careless and have lost sight of the danger of mingling the common with the sacred. And many in the Christian world have grown content with building their own *man-made fires*.

Let's talk about some of the strange fires being built and taken into God's church today.

When postmodernism goes to church

A subtle and deadly philosophy is taking over the world today. Claiming to promote a new, enlightened way of thinking, it is instead leading men and women into deeper spiritual deception and error. Most of the Western world calls this philosophy—or strange fire—*postmodernism*.

Postmodernism fosters a general suspicion of reason and holds hands with skepticism and relativism. Truth is relative to the observer. You have your truth and I have my truth, and even if they are 180 degrees opposite, that is OK because *truth is relative*. There's no such thing as absolute truth—something that's true under all circumstances, times, and places. According to postmodern philosophy, truth is also migratory. It changes with time and place. What's true in Africa is not necessarily true in America or Europe, and vice versa. In essence, truth is culturally conditioned.

Postmodernism now dominates most of Hollywood, most of higher education in the United States, and most of Western society. It has even crept into the church.

After explaining to a young man the biblical reasons why Adventists keep Saturday as the Sabbath as opposed to Sunday, I was startled by his response: "I think the day we worship is all relative—it just depends on what's best for the person. After all, God knows our hearts." In stating that reality came from *what he felt* rather than from solid answers in the Bible, my young friend articulated how postmodernism has affected our modern church and Christian culture. *Truth has become relative!*

However, for believers, it all comes back to this question: "Do we take the Bible as absolute truth and wholly inspired by God as it claims to be (see 2 Timothy 3:16), or do we define truth based on our life, culture, or spiritual preference?"

Some treat the Bible as just another inspiring piece of literature, but we can't take it as this. It's either a huge hoax (for it makes some outrageous claims about itself and about God, as well as giving very specific unpopular instructions on a variety of topics), or it is indeed divinely inspired and should be treated as such—even today.

Postmodernism wipes out absolute truth, and thus leaves no solid foundation on which to stand. Truth is left to be defined by the whims of a changing culture, and each person can define his or her truth differently. This creates a dilemma for Christians because true Christianity is built upon a foundation of *absolute biblical truth*. It's a truth—or fire— that God has built, not man. As Seventh-day Adventists, this foundation is especially key; we believe truth to be non-negotiable. We base our beliefs on the unchanging and authoritative Word of God—*"Sola Scriptura,"* as the Protestant Reformers used to say.

> But God will have a people upon the earth to maintain the Bible, and the Bible only, as the standard of all doctrines and the basis of all reforms. The opinions of learned men, the deductions of science, the creeds or decisions of ecclesiastical councils, as numerous and discordant as are the churches which they represent, the voice of the majority—not one nor all of these should be regarded as evidence for or against any point of religious faith. Before accepting any doctrine or precept, we should demand a plain "Thus saith the Lord" in its support.[2]

The Bible tells us, "Enter ye in at the strait gate: for wide is the gate, and broad is the way, that leadeth to destruction, and many there be which go in thereat: Because strait is the gate, and narrow is the way, which leadeth unto life, and few there be that find it" (Matthew 7:13, 14).

Finding and staying on the narrow way is not easy in today's culture. If we are not students of the Word, we will likely miss this narrow path that leads to heaven. On the other hand, the broad way is not difficult to find. That's why, if we read the Bible correctly, it should cause us concern if we find ourselves on a path that the whole world is following. If everyone is headed one direction, it might be wise to consider if this is truly the way God has indicated we as Christians should go.

The broad way can take in everyone, no matter what they do or don't believe. Satan's most subtle tactics are directed at the Christian world. He is especially talented at meeting the *felt needs* of his Christian subjects, whatever they may be. If ever there was a "seeker friendly" evangelist, it is he. If people are looking for excitement in religion, he has it. If people are looking for renewal through contemplative, self-focused spirituality, he has it. If people want to bring all their possessions with them on their spiritual journey, they can.

The enemy is famous for telling his "Christian" followers, "You don't have to do anything different. You don't have to give up anything or adhere to any specific truth or doctrines. You don't have to change. You're OK just the way you are!" It's all about meeting *their needs and desires.* And boy has he been successful!

For the next couple of chapters, I am going to talk briefly about what counterfeit revival fire might look like—especially as it relates to prayer—and how we can distinguish it from the true. If we are going to stay on the straight and narrow and have success in ministry, understanding these concepts is vital! However, before we move forward and talk about specifics, let us consider a significant vision Ellen White had.

The danger of bowing before the wrong throne

In the book *Early Writings,* we find the record of a disturbing vision.[3] It portrayed God on His throne in heaven and Christ beside Him in the

Holy Place, interceding for the people. Before the throne were believers from around the world. Some were sincerely seeking a deeper walk with Christ, begging for the Holy Spirit. As a result, Jesus shed a great light upon them. Others had become spiritually complacent. They were content with their spiritual condition and, rather than continuing to grow, resisted the light. The light they'd received from God's throne slowly began to fade away, and sadly, they did not even realize that they were walking in darkness.

What is most disturbing about this vision is what happened next. When God and His Son, Jesus, left the Holy Place and moved into the Most Holy Place, only the true believers who were afflicting their souls and seeking a deeper walk with God saw Them move and followed Them. Satan came undetected to stand beside the first throne and, hiding his true identity, acted like he was carrying on God's work. But it was a *counterfeit work*!

Ellen White writes, "I saw them [the deceived believers] look up to the throne, and pray, 'Father, give us Thy Spirit.' Satan would then breathe upon them an unholy influence; in it there was light and much power, but no sweet love, joy, and peace. Satan's object was to keep them deceived and to draw back and deceive God's children."[4]

For many generations, Christians have been living a "Holy Place" experience: reading the Word, praying, and being witnesses for the faith. That was adequate. But now, at the end of time, God is asking us for *more*! He's asking us to move into a "*Most* Holy Place" experience—a "Day of Atonement" experience.

In Leviticus, we catch a glimpse of what a "Day of Atonement" experience was all about.

> And the LORD spake unto Moses, saying, Also on the tenth day of this seventh month there shall be a day of atonement: it shall be an holy convocation unto you; and ye shall afflict your souls, and offer an offering made by fire unto the LORD. And ye shall do no work in that same day: for it is a day of atonement, to make an atonement for you before the LORD your God. For whatsoever soul it

be that shall not be afflicted in that same day, he shall be
cut off from among his people (Leviticus 23:26–29).

The Day of Atonement was when the sanctuary was cleansed. This
happened once a year in Old Testament times. As Adventists, we believe from the Bible that we are living in the actual heavenly Day of
Atonement, before the final cleansing of the earth—our world. This
means that we need to be afflicting our souls, which means searching
our hearts as never before and making sure every sin has been confessed.
It also means that we need to be living up to the light God has given us
in His Word (John 14:15; 1 John 5:2, 3)—not in order to be saved, for
we can never be saved by righteous living—but to prepare us for living
in heaven. It is this experience that prepares us to receive the latter rain.

This is why we should be so alarmed about the *counterfeit revival
movement* sweeping throughout Christianity today! Not only does the
"anything goes" philosophy of postmodernism lull Christians to sleep
with a false security of salvation, but it leads believers to be content with
a *superficial work*! This in turn leads to worship at the wrong throne, Satan's throne, where believers think they are worshiping God. As a result,
when Christ comes back to take His children home, many will be found
unprepared to receive Him, just like the foolish virgins. *I pray that none
of us will be in this group!*

A revival of primitive godliness

At the end of time, we are told that there will be a revival of primitive
godliness. I believe we are even now beginning to see this revival occur
as young and old alike, around the world, are being spiritually revived
through the power of God's Word and through the power of prayer.
Filled with the Holy Spirit and great joy, and compelled to seek after a
primitive godliness rare for these times, they stand, just like Daniel and
his three friends in the courts of Babylon, saying, "We will not defile
ourselves with a portion of the king's meat or with the wine which he
drinks. We will turn away from the allurements of the world and we will
serve God."[5] As a result of this deepening commitment to God, many
are laying down their lives in sacrificial service to see the Lord's work go

forward. And the work *is* going forward!

Inspiration tells us:

> Before the final visitation of God's judgments upon the earth there will be among the people of the Lord such a *revival of primitive godliness* as has not been witnessed since apostolic times. The Spirit and power of God will be poured out upon His children. At that time many will separate themselves from those churches in which the love of this world has supplanted love for God and His word. Many, both of ministers and people, will gladly accept those great truths which God has caused to be proclaimed at this time to prepare a people for the Lord's second coming. *The enemy of souls desires to hinder this work; and before the time for such a movement shall come, he will endeavor to prevent it by introducing a counterfeit.*[6]

Did you catch that? *Satan is working on a counterfeit!* Can you imagine, given he's had around six thousand years to plan, how good his counterfeit might be? This is a scary thought!

How can we experience that revival of primitive godliness and avoid Satan's counterfeit? I will address the latter in more depth in the following chapters. For now, Inspiration tells us, "It is only as the law of God is restored to its rightful position that there can be a revival of primitive faith and godliness among His professed people."[7]

This is about restoration of truth—not your truth or my truth, but God's truth! This is significant because Adventism was founded on the premise that God is calling us to move forward to a "Most Holy Place" experience as we prepare for Christ's soon coming. Thus, rather than minimizing the truths of His Word and trying to fit in with the Christianity of postmodernism, let us boldly proclaim the truths of the Bible. Especially, let us share the three angels' messages of Revelation 14 that God has given for these last days.

As our understanding of biblical key truths grows, we may feel overwhelmed by what the Lord asks us to do. Because of this, we may be tempted to put off complete obedience and surrender, but this is dangerous. Speaking to ministers specifically, Ellen White writes that "many are in the greatest danger of failing to perfect holiness in the fear of the Lord."[8] They are in danger because, though they may preach the truth of God's Word, if they have not allowed this truth to cut their own hearts, in the end they themselves will be castaways. Eternal life will pass them by. Of course, this is not just a problem for ministers. This is a problem among all of God's children.

> Today a large part of those who compose our congregations are dead in trespasses and sins. They come and go like the door upon its hinges. For years they have complacently listened to the most solemn, soul-stirring truths, but they have not put them in practice. Therefore they are less and less sensible of the preciousness of truth. . . . While making a profession, they deny the power of godliness. If they continue in this state, God will reject them. They are unfitting themselves to be members of His family.[9]

My dear friend, *biblical truth is not relative*! It's not about what we think or feel is right. It's about what God says is right! Whether as a minister of the gospel, or as a stay-at-home mother (or anyone in between), let us not minimize what God has given us in His Word. Let us not play with strange fire or be careless with what God has given us. Rather, let us remember that we are in the final Day of Atonement, and let us be preparing to meet our Lord. As we continue seeking after Him with a heart of surrender, willing to follow Him all the way, He will continue to reveal Himself to us through His Word and take us deeper and deeper in our relationship with Him. And in the end, it will be said of us, "Here is the patience of the saints: here are they that keep the commandments of God, and the faith of Jesus" (Revelation 14:12).

So let us move forward with our hand in His as we plead for His holy fire. This is the fire we desperately need today, and He wants us to ask for it! He wants us to dare to ask for more!

Chapter 22

Reinventing the Way We Do Church

Recognizing Counterfeit Revival: Part 2

> *Beware of false prophets, which come to you in sheep's clothing,
> but inwardly they are ravening wolves.*
>
> *—Matthew 7:15*

*I*n the ancient Aesop fables, we find the story of a hungry wolf looking for a lamb chop dinner. Time and time again, this wolf approached a flock of sheep only to be recognized and driven away. Discouraged and distraught (and feeling even more hungry), he finally thought of a brilliant plan. Taking Auntie Wolf's sheepskin rug from off her floor, he wrapped it about himself and started off. This time he approached the flock slowly and began by eating grass along with the sheep. *Yuck!* he thought. *Eating grass is disgusting!* But he knew eating grass would be worth it once he'd captured a tasty lamb.

As the wolf was now cleverly disguised, the sheep did not recognize the newest member of their flock. And when nighttime came, he was herded into the fold along with the sheep—just what he had hoped for. One of the baby lambs complained to his mother, "That sheep doesn't smell right. I think something is wrong." But the little lamb was only hushed. "Don't be rude," his mother scolded. "Mind your own business." The wolf just smiled to himself. Soon, very soon, when the shepherd went home, the wolf would be having scrumptious lamb for dinner.

However, Mr. Wolf was in for a big surprise, for that night the shepherd decided he wanted lamb for dinner too. And spying what appeared to be the biggest sheep in the flock, the shepherd plucked the wolf right out of the fold.

We can chuckle at the ironic twist to the ending of this story, but in reality, this fable is no laughing matter. The apostle Paul writes to the church elders of Ephesus, "Take heed therefore unto yourselves, and to all the flock, over the which the Holy Ghost hath made you overseers, to feed the church of God, which he hath purchased with his own blood. For I know this, that after my departing shall grievous wolves enter in among you, not sparing the flock" (Acts 20:28, 29).

Christ warned, "Beware of false prophets, which come to you in sheep's clothing, but inwardly they are ravening wolves" (Matthew 7:15). The class of prophets here described profess to be Christians. It is obvious that they have the form of godliness and appear to be laboring for the good of souls.[1] But their doctrines lead people not only to complacency and spiritual compromise, but they also lead the flock away from truth.

Speaking of these false prophets in "sheep's clothing," Paul continued to warn the believers, "For if he that cometh preacheth another Jesus, whom we have not preached, or if ye receive another spirit, which ye have not received, or another gospel, which ye have not accepted . . . such are false apostles, deceitful workers, transforming themselves into the apostles of Christ. And no marvel; for Satan himself is transformed into an angel of light. Therefore it is no great thing if his ministers also be transformed as the ministers of righteousness; whose end shall be according to their works" (2 Corinthians 11:4, 13–15).

It's important to know how to recognize false teachers—teachers who give us a new kind of fire and a new kind of gospel. The above

Bible passage tells us how! Now let's consider more of what is happening in Christianity today.

The new and sensational: Should we join the movement?

Of course, everything *new* is not bad. Pastor Dwight Nelson recently preached a sermon at 3ABN camp meeting on Isaiah 43:19, which states, "Behold, I will do a new thing."[2] We *need* a new thing. We *need* to be awakened from our spiritual slumber. We *need* to be renewed with power from on high. However, there is a *dangerous new* that is misleading thousands, maybe even millions, in many churches of the modern day.

Satan sees the genuine revival coming, and to hinder God's work, he has created a new, exciting counterfeit. Inspiration tells us, "In those churches which he [Satan] can bring under his deceptive power he will make it *appear* that God's special blessing is poured out; there will be manifest what is thought to be *great religious interest*. Multitudes will exult that *God is working marvelously* for them, when the work is that of another spirit. Under a religious guise, Satan will seek to extend his influence over the Christian world."[3]

So far, this doesn't really sound that bad, but let's read on.

> There is an emotional excitement, a mingling of the true with the false, that is well adapted to mislead. Yet none need to be deceived. In the light of God's word it is not difficult to determine the nature of these movements. *Wherever men neglect the testimony of the Bible, turning away from those plain, soul-testing truths which require self-denial and renunciation of the world, there we may be sure that God's blessing is not bestowed.* And by the rule which Christ Himself has given, "Ye shall know them by their fruits" (Matthew 7:16), it is evident that these movements are not the work of the Spirit of God.[4]

During the revival service I attended (mentioned in the previous chapter), there was definitely life in the congregation, and we could use some of this life! The preacher spoke with urgency and passion, and we could use more of this passion! He did state some truth in what he shared. However, he never opened the Bible, and within his words of truth was mixed subtle error—strange fire. While he stated the need to *get holy*, he didn't share what biblical holiness is, nor did he share the need of repentance or turning from a life of sin. The Cross was not mentioned, nor the importance of being rooted in solid biblical doctrine. Rather, he urged that holiness was an *experience* that we receive when we come to the altar. He emphasized the feelings, the sensations, letting it all loose, speaking the language of heaven (tongues[5]), and the supernatural experience of touching a miracle-working God.

It's true that we need a deeper experience spiritually. But what is the basis for the experience we seek? Is it based on the truths of God's Word or on our own feelings and desires? Far too many in the modern church have made the latter their focus. While there is great warmth and excitement during services, and the gospel of grace is dished out like ice cream, all too often everyone returns to their homes to live the same sin-filled, self-filled, *defeated* lives. The biblical truths, which set us free (John 8:32) and set us on fire to witness effectively for God, have been laid aside. The preaching of repentance and turning from sin has become almost non-existent. As a result, the sense of a need for salvation through Christ's death on the cross is obliterated. For many, it's simply all about having a *warm, emotional experience*. But this experience is not preparing us to spend eternity with our Lord.

"Popular revivals are too often carried by appeals to the imagination, by exciting the emotions, by gratifying the love for what is new and startling. Converts thus gained have little desire to listen to Bible truth, little interest in the testimony of prophets and apostles. Unless a religious service has something of a sensational character, it has no attractions for them. A message which appeals to unimpassioned reason awakens no response. The plain warnings of God's word, relating directly to their eternal interests, are unheeded."[6]

Most people experiencing this false revival are not satisfied unless they have an exciting and happy time. They work to get up an excitement of feeling and sensation. But the feelings are not lasting, and when they disappear after the meeting, they sink lower than they were before, because their feelings did not come from God.[7]

Feelings are not bad, but they mustn't lead us, for they easily lead astray. Nowhere in Scripture are we taught to seek feelings or an experience. We are taught to seek Christ. And the message of John the Baptist, Christ, and all His followers has always been: Repent! The kingdom of God is at hand; believe on the Lord Jesus Christ and you shall be saved; turn from your wicked ways; wash yourselves; put away the evil of your doings; be clean; crucify self; and take up your cross and follow Jesus. Following Jesus—not sensations or feelings—was what gave life and power to the early church.[8]

We certainly need a new experience, but the experience we need should be the fruit, not the root, of a genuine biblical revival.

The emergent church: Reinventing the way we do church!

The term *emergent* simply means "newly formed or prominent,"[9] thus the term for the popular thinking now shaping much of modern, or postmodern, Christianity.

The emergent church, as defined, is not a denomination but represents a philosophy affecting all denominations. It doesn't have a formal structure or a formal leader, but it is seeking to rebuild church structure and infiltrate the hearts of all church leaders. Unfortunately, much of what the emergent church philosophy promotes goes against historic Christianity. In essence, it is postmodernism baptized and sanctified with the goal of reaching the masses with the gospel. It says, "We believe the way church has been done in the past is too old-fashioned, too tied to the Bible and to specific doctrines, and thus it's too exclusive of other people in their need to hear the gospel. So let's change our approach and style. We need to be more open and loving and less judgmental of those practices of which we don't approve. Let's mingle more with the people as Jesus did."

While radical revolution, seeking to change the way we do church, and revamping religion for the twenty-first century may seem harmless and noble, the emergent church is built on a faulty, shifting foundation of anything goes; you're good, I'm good, we're all good, let's mesh everything together! This gospel of *self-building fires* promoted by the emergent church is attracting millions because it has no boundaries. There are no more black and white dos and don'ts. It's all about love and acceptance. While more warmth and love is certainly needed within our walls, the problem is that everything has now turned gray. What God really thinks or says no longer matters. It becomes all about us!

While integrating highly creative approaches in worship, music, and drama, and seeking to create a sensational *sensory experience* for worshipers, as well as to change preaching to dialogue and pull everyone into the "group conversation," the tendency is to downplay the Bible and doctrines for the sake of seeking common ground and unity. Endless dialogue and questions (with no concrete answers) and the focus on *subjective experiences above concrete scriptural truth,* is the mode of emergent church evangelism.

Of course, this foundation is extremely dangerous for Bible-believing Protestant Christians such as ourselves. It is dangerous because this interfaith collaboration and focus leads to relativism (no absolute biblical truth or foundation, which we discussed earlier), universalism (the belief that all human beings, regardless of their beliefs or lifestyles, will be saved), and syncretism (ultimate unity with all faiths, even those that appear contradictory). To many, the beauty of the whole philosophy is that with no absolutes and no objective truths, everyone can be right and no one needs to be offended. But is this the gospel that the Bible teaches? Is the purpose of the two-edged sword of God's Word (Hebrews 4:12), rather than cutting and piercing our hearts and convicting us of sin, to be a warm, loving pat on the back?

Two prominent leaders of the modern emergent church movement are Brian McLaren and Leonard Sweet, both of whom publicly promote Roman Catholic mysticism.

Mysticism, in short, is the belief that direct knowledge of God, spiritual truth, and ultimate reality can be attained through *subjective experiences* and vague speculations. It all centers around the ability to tap into an "inner knowing" or "inner voice" for direction.

As author John MacArthur writes, "The mystic disdains rational understanding and seeks truth instead through the feelings, the imagination, personal visions, inner voices, private illumination, or other purely subjective means."[10]

So what do these leading "mystic worshipers" of the emergent church movement actually think? On the cover of his best-selling book *A Generous Orthodoxy,* Brian McLaren describes himself as a missional, evangelical, post/protestant, liberal/conservative, mystical/poetic, biblical, charismatic/contemplative, fundamentalist/Calvinist, Anabaptist/Anglican, Methodist, Catholic, green, incarnational, depressed-yet-hopeful, emergent, unfinished Christian.[11]

As to be expected, McLaren's book is a smorgasbord of ideas proclaimed in the name of Christ. McLaren shares that he has grown tired of the Christian church of today. He wants to *deconstruct* the old, and *reconstruct* a new kind of Christian faith. And his ultimate goal is for *radical theological reformation,* or a new framework for theology. However, many of his ideas are actually forbidden or rejected by Scripture. As one author writes, "Not only are they [McLaren's ideas] not found in the Bible, but they won't work with an intact Bible. In order for the Emerging Church to succeed, the Bible must be looked at through entirely different glasses, and Christianity needs to be open to a new type of faith."[12]

Leonard Sweet's views are equally disconcerting. In his book *Quantum Spirituality,* Sweet positively quotes Jesuit philosopher Karl Rahner, stating, "The Christian of tomorrow will be a mystic, one who has experienced something, or he will be nothing."[13]

While pulling people together from all Christian faiths, Sweet minimizes the importance of the blood of Christ, teaching that all spiritual roads—even those outside Christ—are equally valid and lead to God. Sounds like another twist on "All roads lead to Rome"! But that's not what the Bible teaches. "Neither is there salvation in any other [speaking of Christ]: for there is none other name under heaven given among men, whereby we must be saved" (Acts 4:12).

Dan Kimball, pastor of the Vintage Faith Church in Santa Cruz, California, and another well-known leader in the emergent church movement, wrote the book *The Emerging Church: Vintage Christianity for New Generations.* Kimball's ideas may not seem so dangerous at first glance, but let's look at what Kimball has to say as he considers the world and Christianity of today: "In a post-Christian world, pluralism is the norm. Buddhism, Wicca, Christianity, Islam, Hinduism, or an eclectic [that is, a choice made from many different options] blend—it's all part of the soil."[14]

He further claims that the basis for learning has shifted from logic and the rational to the realm of *experience* and the mystical. Stressing the importance of the multi-sensory experience in worship (candles, incense, props, etc.) and explaining why it's important to turn the lights down, Kimball explains, "In the emerging culture, *darkness represents spirituality.*" He goes on. "We see this in Buddhist temples, as well as Catholic and Orthodox churches. Darkness communicates something serious is happening!"[15]

Something serious *is* happening! But it's not something good! It is important to understand here that Satan is not simply trying to draw people to the dark side of a good-versus-evil conflict. He is trying to eradicate the gap between himself and God and between good and evil *altogether,* and make darkness appear as light.

Howard Peth, in his book *The Dangers of Contemplative Prayer,* sums it up this way. "The Emerging Church has *sold out Christianity* by using high-tech marketing methods to create their 'seeker friendly' congregations with a watered-down gospel—one that de-emphasizes sin and repentance and promotes sensual approaches to a counterfeit 'worship.' . . .

". . . But in reality . . . the only thing they have to peddle is Satan's same OLD poison packaged in NEW bottles!"[16]

Is this the way we really want to do church?

In summary, there are four things that should especially concern us with the emergent church movement. Consider how one Adventist pastor has summed up these dangers.

> First, the [Emergent Church] movement either minimizes
> or ignores the life-and-death importance of believing
> in, humbly submitting to, and fully obeying solid, non-
> negotiable Bible truth, especially the *Three Angel's* [*sic*]

messages. Secondly, even though Christian concepts may be strongly expressed, much of EC teaching is insidiously laced with Roman Catholic mysticism and New Agism, both of which ultimately lead to the greatest peril of all, deadly spiritualism and invasion by evil spirits. Third, under the guise of promoting a deeper experience with God, EC teachings have become one of Satan's subtlest vehicles in his campaign "to deceive, if possible, even the elect" (Matt. 24:24). Fourth, my biggest concern is for Seventh-day Adventists, especially our young people. At all costs, we must avoid these dangers.[17]

Pause! What are we thinking? Although times and cultures may change, God's Word does not change. His truth never changes. It never alters from generation to generation. The emergent church is proffering the idea today that truth is relative and alters just like evolution. And so, therefore, the truth of the Bible needs to be adapted to fit our culture—as we perceive it. That is blasphemy! This is not how truth works. It is not how it has ever worked. Our generation is not a special generation that can take the Word of God and diminish it down to the level of the culture. The level of the culture is supposed to be convicted and brought up again to the convicting truth of the Word of God.

"We are in continual danger of getting above the simplicity of the gospel," Ellen White writes. She continues:

> There is an intense desire on the part of many to startle the world with something original, that shall lift the people into a state of spiritual ecstasy, and change the present order of experience. There is certainly great need of a change in the present order of experience; for the sacredness of present truth is not realized as it should be, *but the change we need is a change of heart,* and can only be obtained by seeking God individually for his blessing, by pleading with him for his power, by fervently praying that his grace may come upon us, and that our characters may

be transformed. This is the change we need today, and for the attainment of *this experience* we should exercise persevering energy and manifest heart-felt earnestness.[18]

For far too long, Adventists have been experts on biblical theology and doctrine without having that personal, intimate, day-by-day walk with Christ. We need heart change. We need a deeper heart experience that is authentic and real—not merely a pretense to protect our respectability! The heart change we need will come by digging deeper in God's Word, and by greater heartfelt surrender to His desires and commands.

Inspiration tells us, "God's workers must gain a *far deeper experience.* If they will surrender all to him, he will work mightily for them. . . .

"When God's servants with consecrated zeal co-operate with divine instrumentalities, the state of things that exists in this world *will be changed,* and soon the earth will with joy receive her King. Then 'they that be wise shall shine as the brightness of the firmament; and they that turn many to righteousness as the stars forever and ever' [Daniel 12:3]."[19]

In the 1960s, they use to say, "If it feels good, do it!" Today the popular message is, "If it feels good, *it must be right*!" Everywhere we turn, we hear, "Follow your heart! Do what feels right to you." However, God's Word tells us, "He that trusteth in his own heart is a fool" (Proverbs 28:26). When we allow our heart and emotions to lead us, we become subservient to our feelings over the facts of God's Word. Rather than cultivating a spirit of surrender, we are encouraged to foster a *spirit of selfishness.* Is this the path to follow if we are to be ready to meet Jesus? I think the answer is obvious—at least if we study our Bibles!

As we move forward, seeking to avoid the dangers of the postmodern emergent church movement, and as we seek to recognize the different forms of counterfeit revival sweeping Christianity today, let us *dare to ask for more;* not more warm fuzzy feelings and sensations, not more endless dialogue with no answered questions, but more wisdom to discern the truth and stand upon God's Word. Only as we stand on the truths of Scripture will we be transformed, and true transformation comes only by the infilling of the Holy Spirit.

Chapter 23

Exploring Dangerous Forms of Prayer and Meditation

Recognizing Counterfeit Revival: Part 3

> *But when ye pray, use not vain repetitions, as the heathen do.*
> —*Matthew 6:7*

*W*hen one wants to learn to recognize a counterfeit, rather than spending his or her primary focus on the counterfeit, he or she focuses on the true. On the United States Secret Service Web site, you can find a section called, "How to Detect Counterfeit Money." This is what it tells us: "Look at the money you receive. Compare a suspect note with a genuine note of the same denomination and series. . . . Look for differences, not similarities."[1]

In order to follow this advice, we must have a genuine piece of money with which to compare. We also must know *the genuine* backward and forward, inside and out. It is reported that a good Secret Service agent in the counterfeit division spends most of his time getting to know the genuine article—not looking at counterfeits. Once he's become an expert of the genuine, detecting the counterfeit is easy.

That's why it's so important that we be rooted and grounded in the Word of God. For this is our standard, this is our *counterfeit detector*. If what we are doing, or what we are hearing, doesn't match up to the genuine Word of God, something is wrong.

Recognizing the true dangers in the spiritual formation movement

Today many are asking, "What's the big kerfuffle over *spiritual formation,* anyway? Don't we need a deeper experience with God?"

To many, the concept of spiritual formation is harmless—even good. It is a loosely defined term that can mean Christian growth and maturity or anything spiritual, and some have used the concept simply to help others recognize their need to foster deeper genuine spiritual growth and transformation. So the term means something different, depending on who is using it.

Answering the question, "Is the concept of *spiritual formation* biblical?" Mark Finley writes, "If we define spiritual formation as being formed into the image of Christ as we meditate upon God's Word, seek Him in prayer, and open our minds to the transforming power of the Holy Spirit, certainly it is biblical. The apostle Paul admonishes believers at Rome 'not [to] be conformed to this world but [to] be transformed by the renewing of your mind' (Rom. 12:2)."[2]

To understand the seriousness of the issue at hand, we must look a little deeper. The "kerfuffle over spiritual formation," as some have called it, is more than just a battle over "bad terminology," for terminology is often changing, especially as certain terms become offensive in Christian circles.

While many spiritual formation practices have been around since the Middle Ages, the term *spiritual formation* originated with a system of spiritual exercises or "disciplines" invented in 1548 by Ignatius Loyola, the Roman Catholic founder of the Jesuit Order.[3] These spiritual disciplines all centered around *evaluation of one's feelings* and recognition of God's voice within. The exercises were designed to teach the young Jesuit priest-in-training to submit his mind to that of his superior. The superior was given the title of "Spiritual Director."

Although this may appear to be innocent spiritual shepherding, in reality it is putting another man in spiritual control of one's own life. It's really about "mind control." While "godly mentoring" is encouraged in the Bible, this "spiritual directorship" is not according to the pattern of Scripture. It's not easy to recognize at first glance, for we find here truth and error mixed in very subtle ways.[4]

While appearing to dedicate themselves to the "greater glory of God" and being seemingly noble on many fronts (Jesuits take three vows—one of poverty, one of chastity, and one of obedience[5]), what many do not realize is that the Jesuit Order was originally founded with the sole aim to secure wealth and power to be devoted to the overthrowing of Protestantism and to the re-establishment of papal supremacy. And it did its job well. In early years, it was known for its open cruelty to those who opposed the Catholic Church traditions, and especially to those who tried to follow *purely biblical doctrines*.

One Christian historian writes:

> "For professing faith contrary to the teachings of the Church of Rome, history records the martyrdom of more than one hundred million people. A million Waldenses and Albigenses [Swiss and French Protestants] perished during a crusade proclaimed by Pope Innocent III in 1208. Beginning from the establishment of the Jesuits in 1540 to 1580, nine hundred thousand were destroyed. One hundred and fifty thousand perished by the Inquisition in thirty years. Within the space of thirty-eight years after the edict of Charles V against the Protestants, fifty thousand persons were hanged, beheaded, or burned alive for heresy. Eighteen thousand more perished during the administration of the Duke of Alva in five and a half years."[6]

One of the most dangerous things about the spiritual formation movement is that many of its spiritual exercises are actually rooted in bold Jesuit pantheistic spirituality.[7] (Pantheism is a worldwide view based on the belief that *God is in all things.* In other words, there's no distinct personal God, but He's in everything: rocks, tadpoles, trees, and even human beings—even those who blaspheme His name.)

For obvious reasons, Christian proponents of the spiritual formation movement often downplay, ignore, or explain away blatant pantheism and mysticism. However, the faulty foundation upon which the mainstream movement stands *still remains.* These philosophies are deceptive and subtle. They are deceptive because the core belief is that Jesus, in His fullness, can be found in every human being and in all of His creation, everywhere. Not only is this belief completely unbiblical, it actually counterfeits the work of the Holy Spirit in our lives. Rather than directing our minds to see Christ as our Intercessor in the heavenly sanctuary (where the Bible states His physical presence is—not inside us), and rather than inspiring us to pray to Christ through the Holy Spirit (which lives inside us as long as we obey God—see Acts 5:32), people are deceived into thinking they can come right into Christ's *actual presence* whenever they choose, communicating with Him directly through "mind stilling" practices such as contemplative prayer, centering prayer, prayer labyrinths, guided imagery, and so on.

Knowing what would someday come, Ellen White writes, "The warnings of the word of God regarding the perils surrounding the Christian church belong to us today. As in the days of the apostles men tried by tradition and philosophy to destroy faith in the Scriptures, so today, by the *pleasing sentiments of higher criticism, evolution, spiritualism, theosophy, and pantheism,* the enemy of righteousness is seeking to lead souls into forbidden paths."[8]

Because of the dangers in pantheistic philosophy, we can better understand why Ellen White and other Adventist pioneers were so concerned about Dr. J. H. Kellogg's book *Living Temple,* which Ellen White said contained "the alpha of deadly heresies."[9]

Without going into great detail or history of what happened, Dr. Kellogg (an influential Adventist doctor and leader of health reform in the church at that time, who later apostatized) was teaching pantheism—boldly and without apology. Through this "alpha apostasy" (so named because it was considered the beginning of apostasies), church leaders saw people being led into a form of spiritualism where the enemy could speak directly to his victims and lead them away from God. Through prophetic visions, Ellen White was warned that at the end of time, the final "omega" apostasy, similar to the alpha, would come.[10] And it appears that these prophecies, given by God Himself, are coming true.

The Bible tells us, "This know also, that in the last days perilous times shall come." Men will be "ever learning, and never able to come to the knowledge of the truth." They "shall wax worse and worse, deceiving, and being deceived." Is this reason for concern? The Bible continues, "For the time will come when they will not endure sound doctrine. . . . And they shall turn away their ears from the truth, and shall be turned unto fables" (2 Timothy 3:1, 7, 13; 4:3, 4).

Over a hundred years ago, we were warned what Satan would try to do in the end of time. Is he not even now beginning to follow this very path? We need to be alert so that we are not deceived; we are told that Satan will deceive the *very elect* if possible. Inspiration tells us, "The enemy is preparing for his last campaign against the church . . . and when he makes another advance move, [many] will not recognize him as their enemy, that old serpent, but they will consider him a friend, one who is doing a good work."[11]

Truly the evil wolf (otherwise known as the devil) has successfully put on sheep's clothing and is even now attempting to lead astray many in the house of God.

Contemplative prayer and centering prayer: Listening to God's voice within

What exactly is contemplative prayer? It begins with a practice called "centering prayer," a meditative technique in which the practitioner focuses on a chosen "sacred word" or "mantra" that he repeats to "still the mind." Another term for this is *"lectio divina,"* which is Latin for "divine reading."

I quote from "Method of Centering Prayer," inspired by the book

Open Mind, Open Heart, by monk and priest Thomas Keating. He states, "Choose a sacred word as the symbol of your intention to consent to God's presence and action within. . . . The sacred word is chosen during a brief period of prayer to the Holy Spirit. Use a word of one or two syllables, such as: God, Jesus, Abba, Father, Mother, Mary, Amen. Other possibilities include: Love, Listen, Peace, Mercy, Let Go, Silence, Stillness, Faith, Trust."[12]

The instructions continue that the sacred word is not to be changed during prayer (because that would be engaging in thought). The "sacred word" is the anchor. If thoughts, feelings, or distractions intrude, the sacred word should be repeated until all is stillness again.

Thomas Merton, an American Catholic writer, mystic, and Trappist monk of the Abbey of Gethsemani in Kentucky in the mid-1900s, describes the goal of centering prayer this way: "At the center of our being is a point of nothingness which is untouched by sin and by illusions, a point of pure truth. . . . This little point . . . is the pure glory of God in us. It is in everybody."[13]

This is the same lie that Satan (posing as the serpent) told Eve in the Garden of Eden. "Just eat the fruit. You are only one step away from discovering the god within you."[14] However, the Bible says that there is "no good thing" within us (Romans 7:18). Even our righteousness is filthy rags (Isaiah 64:6) and we drink iniquity like water (Job 15:16). Thus, no amount of focusing or mind-stilling practices are going to help us connect with an untainted divinity within. *It just ain't happening!* (Forgive my Southern slang!)

The Bible teaches us to walk by faith, not sight, but contemplative prayer encourages feelings and sensations over doctrines and truth. The Bible teaches that our hearts are wicked and that only by accepting Christ's sacrifice on Calvary can we be saved.

God's Old Testament people offered a morning and evening sacrifice. Today, this could be the equivalent of morning and evening devotions as we renew our commitment to Christ and trust in His blood. The practice of centering prayer is encouraged for twenty minutes in the morning and twenty minutes in the evening each day. (Remember, the devil is an expert at counterfeits!) While true biblical meditation is thought-filled and active, the goal of centering prayer is to clear one's mind from all thoughts and concerns until conscious thought ceases (known as entering "the silence") so that one can more clearly hear the voice of God within.

While focusing on Jesus or words in Scripture may appear innocent—after all, aren't we suppose to meditate on Scripture, and don't we want to hear God's voice more clearly?—this popular prayer technique is very dangerous as it provides a relaxed mental state in which a "voice" (internal or external) can begin to speak and mold the mind. While thinking they are hearing God's voice, people are actually being put in touch with the voices of evil spirits.[15]

Unfortunately, this popular prayer discipline is being practiced now in many Christian denominations and prayer circles. Again, it's just Satan's same old poison called "spiritualism" packaged in a new way, for there is *no biblical support* for this type of prayer.

Contemplative prayer, which is just another mystical practice that enables one to enter an altered state of consciousness, originated in the third and fourth centuries by the Desert Fathers, Catholic monks who practiced Eastern mysticism in the Middle East. It was passed on through the centuries and eventually adopted by Ignatius Loyola in the 1500s, who successfully built the foundation upon which it stands today. While Christian advocates may deny this, it's just another form of self-hypnosis, and it parallels popular forms of meditation, as well as many of the practices of Zen Buddhism, Hinduism, and the occult. It's a purely subjective experience that emphasizes feelings over facts.[16]

Interestingly, those who have practiced contemplative prayer and have come out of this movement report that it's like being on a drug. It's addicting and gives you a wonderful emotional high, just like taking LSD. People who practice this type of prayer even report feeling a deep inner peace and enlightenment. Because of this, they think they have reached a *higher level* of spirituality and attainment. However, it's not God's higher level or God's peace. Rather, they have just opened the door wide to the deadly deception of spiritualism.

Referring to this new kind of "spiritualism" embracing the Christian world, Ellen White writes:

It is true that spiritualism is now changing its form and, veiling some of its more objectionable features, is assuming a Christian guise. But its utterances from the platform and the press have been before the public for many years, and in these its real character stands revealed. . . .

. . . While it formerly denounced Christ and the Bible, it now *professes* to accept both. But the Bible is interpreted in a manner that is pleasing to the unrenewed heart, while its solemn and vital truths are made of no effect. Love is dwelt upon as the chief attribute of God, but it is degraded to a weak sentimentalism, making little distinction between good and evil. God's justice, His denunciations of sin, the requirements of His holy law, are all kept out of sight. The people are taught to regard the Decalogue as a dead letter. Pleasing, bewitching fables captivate the senses and lead men to reject the Bible as the foundation of their faith. Christ is as verily denied as before; but Satan has so blinded the eyes of the people that the deception is not discerned. . . .

. . . Nothing but the power of God, granted in answer to the earnest prayer of faith, can deliver these ensnared souls.[17]

Again and again, I must bring it back to the Word! (Have you noticed my relentless emphasis here?) But God's Word is our divine key, not only to opening the storehouse of heaven's blessing in answer to prayer, but to opening the prison doors of deception entrapping millions today! If we don't know the genuine truths of Scripture, we are setting ourselves up for automatic spiritual downfall; we are allowing ourselves to be locked in the prison of error and deception. Only God can deliver us!

Mind control—the key to evangelization of the world?

Pope John Paul II once said, "Since the contemplative life belongs to the fullness of the Church's presence, let it be put into effect everywhere. Religious institutes of the *contemplative and of the active life,* have so far played, and still do play, *the main role in the evangelization of the world.*"[18]

Amazingly, it appears that the late Pope John Paul's dream is coming true, for the world is certainly being evangelized. Today, many institutes teach contemplative prayer and spirituality to thousands of people every year—many of them attended and applauded by Christians and leaders of all protestant denominations, *including Seventh-day Adventist.*

But is this the kind of evangelization we need? We are told, "Little by little [Satan] has prepared the way for his masterpiece of deception in the development of spiritualism. . . . Except those who are kept by the power of God, through faith in His word, the whole world will be swept into the ranks of this delusion."[19]

> During the entire history of the great controversy, Satan's greatest success has always been directly related to his ability to control the minds of those he ensnares *without their awareness.* This is the secret of his success. When he can deceive those under his power into believing that God is working for them, when in truth it is he [Satan], he has won the day. This is the fundamental characteristic of the omega apostasy and is likely the reason it caused Ellen White to "tremble" when she beheld it: many leaders in God's remnant church were carrying on what they perceived as the work of God, while, in fact, they were being directed to the prince of evil.
>
> The more closely Satan can appear Christ-like in both his behavior and his use of the supernatural, the greater is his ability to deceive.[20]

Can you see how Satan might be successful in the future in getting many professing Christians to unite and promote a unified world religion or a unified day of worship, thinking they are doing God service, and be willing to annihilate those who refuse to embrace their new "one world" religion or chosen style of worship? (See 1 Timothy 4:1, 2.) Remember, it's all about mind control and Satan is on it! He knows what he's doing. *But do we?*

In his book *Revive Us Again,* Mark Finley writes, "Satan's concern in the last days is not the unsaved world. He already has them in his grasp. His concern is Christians. By bringing deceptions into the church, he will mislead millions."[21] And it's beginning to happen before our very eyes! *Lord, have mercy on us!*

We've barely touched the surface of this gigantic iceberg that is only getting bigger all the time. But there are several more prayer disciplines that we need to address briefly while we are on this topic.

Listening prayer: What is God telling you?

In some circles, "listening prayer" is just another term for contemplative prayer. However, in this instance, I am referring to something different. Recently, a friend wrote and shared about an "awesome experience" she'd had in prayer. As she described the experience, warning signals began sounding in my mind.

She described a group coming together to pray for one another. But this wasn't the normal let's-surround-you-and-pray-for-you group—which is to be encouraged! Rather, a person who needed prayer was chosen and then instructed to be silent and listen to what God was telling her. During her time of silence, in another room, a small group prayed for her "protection" (from what, I'm not sure) and that she would hear what God was speaking to her. After a few minutes of silence, the person then shared with the group what had come into her mind. *Believing that this was the voice of God speaking to them,* the group then surrounded her and prayed over what God had told her. It could be an emotional wound from the past that had not yet healed or a certain situation in her current life.

While this may not be on the same page as entering an altered level of consciousness, I think warning is due. There is nothing wrong with surrounding each other in prayer as we lift up our burdens; we should do more of this. However, we want to be careful about encouraging people to be "silent" to hear God's voice and *then* (and this is the key) taking whatever thoughts that come into the mind as direct communication from God.

The Bible says, "The heart is deceitful above all things, and desperately wicked: who can know it?" (Jeremiah 17:9). God does speak to us through the Holy Spirit—but this is primarily through His Word. We can't just sit down, be still, and just assume, "OK, now I'm listening and God is going to speak to me." What comes into our minds might be from Him, but it most likely will be either our own thoughts or promptings from *another spirit*.

Interpreting our random thoughts as direct communication from God is walking on dangerous ground. Thus we are encouraged to immerse ourselves in Scripture, knowing that the primary method He uses to speak to us is His Word, not the stillness of our minds or personal thoughts. Meditating on passages of Scripture and asking God what He wants us to learn from these passages or having a group Bible study and asking teammates, "How did God speak to you through this passage?" is perfectly acceptable. The difference is, it's all based on the Word.

Prayer labyrinths: The sacred path to who knows where

A prayer labyrinth is a "sacred path" that leads one, via a single circuitous route, to the center of an intricate design (where you meet God's presence) and then back out again. According to the Veriditas (those at the forefront of the "prayer labyrinth" movement), this journey into and out of the prayer circle involves three stages: purgation (releasing—on the way in), illumination (receiving—experienced in the center and similar to reaching the "silence"), and union (returning). It is used to facilitate prayer, meditation, spiritual transformation, and global unity.[22]

The patterns of the labyrinth are similar to Buddhist mandalas and to the Japanese Zen practice of *kinhin* walking meditation. Jean Houston, in the early 1990s, introduced the Christian world again to the practice of seeking enlightenment through walking the labyrinth when she linked up with Lauren Artress, spiritual leader of Grace Cathedral in San Francisco—to bring people back to their center and allow them to experience "spirit" for themselves. However, rather than being another positive form of Christian spirituality, the practice of walking prayer labyrinths is decidedly pagan in origin and function, even if all the steps associated with its intended use are not followed.

When we do a little research, we find that prayer labyrinths have been used by a variety of pagan cultures for thousands of years, in goddess worship, in ritualistic dances and ceremonies, and by ancient Indian tribes in occultist practices. We find evidence of ancient labyrinths in Egypt, Italy, Scandinavia, and even in North America. Also, the Catholic Church has incorporated prayer labyrinths into its buildings and architecture for centuries now, embracing and baptizing the heathen-based practice for their own Christian purposes.

The Catholic Church is not alone in embracing these pagan practices from the past. Prayer labyrinths (and other mystical practices) have been embraced and lauded by many faiths for years. Recently, we have seen a resurgence of their popularity and appeal, especially within the emergent church, among New Age groups, and with neo-pagans. However, while prayer labyrinths may seem innocent enough, they represent another form of *counterfeit fire,* and should be avoided at all cost.

The prayer room: Creating a place to meet with God

Prayer rooms are popping up all over the place—in churches, Christian schools, universities, and hospitals. My friends and I even discovered three prayer rooms right next to each other in an airport in Frankfurt, Germany—one decorated for Christians, one for Jews, and one for Muslims.

Prayer rooms in and of themselves are not evil! To create a quiet place where someone could step away from his or her studies or work to take time for prayer is not a bad idea. Incidentally, I have staffed prayer rooms for various schools, universities, and official church functions around the United States and internationally for several years now. I've also seen much spiritual healing take place in prayer rooms, as people join together in sincere, earnest prayer, claiming the promises of God. I believe in the importance and benefit of prayer rooms.

However, this is my word of caution and this is why I'm even mentioning this here: While creating a "prayer journey" or having a room decorated for prayer may make the environment more peaceful and welcoming, we need to guard against thinking that we have to *create the right physical environment* with which to meet or experience God. I'm not talking about a worship environment here; I'm talking about a place to pray. The point is that we could have the most elaborate and beautiful prayer room this side of heaven—and still not find His presence if our hearts are not humble and repentant. Humility and repentance compose the environment where He truly meets us (Psalms 66:18; 51:17; and Isaiah 57:15). In this genuine, biblical environment, any place can become a sanctuary, whether a lonely prison cell or a prayer room full of believers.[23]

So wherever we are—driving to work, in our private prayer closet, in a special prayer room with friends—rather than "looking to physical props" to help create the environment, let us remember that only God's presence through the Holy Spirit can make our room (or anywhere) a truly sacred place. *His Spirit is what we most need, and it comes only to those who are broken and humble in heart!*

Visions and dreams: Can we trust them?

At an increasing rate, people all over the world, even Christians, are having visions, dreams, and out-of-body experiences, stating that they have seen God or dead loved ones alive in heaven, or that they were taken to hell where people are being tortured.

While the Bible tells us that God will speak to His people through visions and dreams in the end of time, if these experiences contradict the plain teachings of Scripture, they cannot be attributed as coming from God. Many are so overwhelmed—as Satan would have it—by these supernatural experiences that as they breathlessly share their stories with friends and loved ones, scriptural truth is left by the wayside.

Such an experience happened a few years ago to a neurosurgeon who, having suffered a tragic accident, was pronounced brain dead. He was not a Christian before his accident; however, during the operation, as they were trying to save his life, he experienced an out-of-body experience and journeyed with an angel to heaven and then to hell.

His brain function restored, he awoke from the operation to tell his amazing story. He has now written a *New York Times* bestseller on the afterlife, which is selling hundreds of thousands of copies—even today. The problem is that the truths about heaven and hell that he received in his out-of-body experience do not line up with the Word of God. But because of the supernatural, miraculous phenomenon he experienced, and because he was obviously healed from being brain dead, many are taking his visions and revelations as gospel truth—above the Word of God.

Another recent experience by a young boy has also caught the attention of thousands, if not millions, of unsuspecting Christians, and has just been released as a Hollywood movie titled *Heaven Is for Real.*

According to the story, four-year-old Colton, the son of a Nebraska pastor, while on the operating table for a ruptured appendix, had a near-death experience, went to heaven, and met his older sister who had died in a miscarriage and his great-grandfather who had passed away thirty years prior. After surgery, Colton revealed to his stunned parents "impossible-to-know" details and heavenly insights, all supposedly learned from these two family members in heaven.

As astounding as Colton's revelations seem, they directly contradict God's Word.

The Bible clearly states that "the dead know not any thing, . . . neither have they any more a portion for ever in any thing that is done under the sun" (Ecclesiastes 9:5, 6). The Bible also teaches that immortality comes not at death, but at the resurrection at the end of time (1 Corinthians 15:52).

Nevertheless, most Christians today have been taught to believe that the soul is immortal and that a person goes immediately to heaven or hell when they die. What these unsuspecting people don't realize is that this belief is setting them up to fall for Satan's next powerful delusion. That's why stories like these are so dangerous.

While God does at times still work in the supernatural (and we will see more of His supernatural manifestations in the future), we must not forget that the devil can work miracles and give supernatural manifestations, as well. That's why these things, including visions and out-of-body experiences, cannot be the test for truth or doctrine. No matter how spectacular the story or how much our sensations are pulled, if something contradicts the plain teachings of Scripture, we cannot accept it. *Period!* The Bible will never—I repeat—*never* be superseded by miraculous manifestations.[24] We must cling to the Word at all cost! We do or we die!

"The last great delusion is soon to open before us. Antichrist is to perform his marvelous works in our sight. So closely will the counterfeit resemble the true that it will be impossible to distinguish between them except by the Holy Scriptures. By their testimony every statement and every miracle must be tested."[25]

Satan has an agenda and his time is running out. He knows that if he can get Christians to embrace the supernatural and the sensational, at the expense of biblical truth, they will be ready for his last great deception when he finally reveals himself to humanity pretending to be Christ. But Christ tells us what it will be like when He returns (Revelation 1:7; Matthew 24:24–27). With the Bible before us, we have no reason to be deceived.

Our call to true prayer and biblical meditation

As we close this chapter, let's remember that the goal of true, biblical meditation and prayer is not met by emptying the mind or looking to "divinity within." Rather, it is met by filling the mind with the Word and works of God. All throughout Scripture, we are told that prayer is to be an active, thought-filled activity. It's an actual communication with God, via the Holy Spirit, made up of specific thoughts and words. Not once is there an example of prayer repeating a "sacred word" or "mantra." Christ warned against this specifically when He said, "But when ye pray, *use not vain repetitions,* as the heathen do" (Matthew 6:7; emphasis added). It's also important to note that in Bible times, men and women *never chose when* God would speak to them. The timing was always in God's control, and they were often shocked and afraid when they heard His voice.

Mark Finley writes, "The New Testament believers did not 'turn the world upside down' with a gospel that blended Eastern philosophy with Christian doctrine. Neither should we. The New Testament believers did not seek to get 'in touch' with the divine presence within. They looked to their crucified, resurrected, and returning Lord, and their lives were transformed."[26]

Bible meditation and contemplation are key to growing our walk with Christ. Ellen White used the terms "meditate" and "meditation"

569 times in her writings. She also used the word "contemplation" 580 times.[27] In using these words, she was speaking of meditating on and contemplating God's Word, God's works, and God's providence. She encouraged us "to spend a thoughtful hour each day in contemplation of the life of Christ," to let our "imagination grasp each scene, especially the closing ones."[28] As we picture more clearly what took place on Calvary, our confidence in God will grow and we will receive more of His Spirit. This is crucial, for we are told, "If we would be saved at last, we must learn the lesson of penitence and humiliation at the foot of the cross."[29]

I have been discussing different forms of strange fire to avoid in the counterfeit revival movements sweeping Christianity today. There is another danger—the danger of quenching the true Holy Spirit fire in times of genuine revival. In the next few chapters, I will address this danger and how we can avoid it. So keep reading and keep daring to ask for more—not more warm sensations or mystical experiences, but a deeper foundation built upon God and His unchanging Word!

Chapter 24

How to Avoid Quenching the Holy Spirit

Embracing Biblical Revival

> *Quench not the Spirit. . . . Prove all things;*
> *hold fast that which is good.*
>
> *—1 Thessalonians 5:19, 21*

*D*o you know someone with so many miracles happening in his or her life that you wonder if they are for real? These people are rare, but they do still exist. I know of such a man. Jeremiah[1] experienced so many miracles that some people in the church decided all his power couldn't possibly be from God, and they tried to prohibit his work. Let me share his story.

Jeremiah was a district pastor in Africa. As a district pastor, he was very busy. He worked hard and, although it was a difficult area, he began to experience amazing church growth. Miracles accompanied his work, power attended his preaching, and many souls were coming to the Lord.

His success made the devil very unhappy, and the enemy began to stir up problems. What was happening in his life and ministry was so unusual that some people in the church began to question if it was a *counterfeit power.*

One week during prayer meeting, two men came in. As if a prophet, Pastor Jeremiah spoke up. "These two men are not here to pray but to steal. They have weapons on them." The congregation thought his words were strange, but they took the two men to the police station and discovered that Pastor Jeremiah's words were true. Everyone was amazed. "How could he know these things?" they questioned. "This is not normal!" As a result, they were somewhat afraid. But the devil was more afraid.

Another time, a girl was possessed by demons and those surrounding her did not know what to do. So they said, "Let's call Pastor Jeremiah to pray that the demons will leave." At this suggestion, the demons quickly spoke up. "No, no, no! Do not call Pastor Jeremiah. We are leaving now!" And the girl was healed right then and there, without Pastor Jeremiah even coming to pray.

As the time for his ordination drew near, the church decided *not* to ordain him. He hadn't done anything wrong, but they felt that he was not operating as a normal pastor should. It was obvious to all that he had a lot of power, but they were seriously concerned that this power was not from God but was black magic or some other occultist practice to influence the people.

To confirm their suspicions, the ministerial directors decided to conduct a special investigation. While Pastor Jeremiah was away from home one day, they came and searched his house. But nothing was out of the ordinary and there were no signs of black magic or the occult. They then interviewed his wife. "What does your husband do when he's at home? Is there any strange behavior? What are his habits?"

"He's a good husband," she replied. "He's kind to his family. He doesn't really do anything strange. But there is something he does every day that probably most people don't do. He's up at three in the morning every day, praying and studying his Bible. And two days a week, he asks me *not* to prepare food for him, because he fasts and prays."

Speechless, they had no more questions. In glad amazement, they shook their heads and went home. Finally, convinced that the power they saw in Pastor Jeremiah's life was indeed from God and not from Satan, they decided to ordain him.

Not long after his ordination, they made him the evangelist of one of the largest conferences in their region. The Lord continued to bless his ministry as he spoke boldly condemning sin and calling people to repentance. Many more souls were won to the Lord, and as a result, the church elders came to respect him more and more. Then they promoted him to union evangelist. God blessed more as he labored tirelessly. Next, they promoted him to conference president. Today, he is union secretary in the region, and God is continuing to bless his ministry.

The reason I share this story is because Pastor Jeremiah's testimony illustrates an important point. Although we talk about the power of God, we are not used to seeing it in daily life. So all too often, if such power is seen, we might be tempted to doubt and think that it is a counterfeit. By doing this, if we aren't careful, we can grieve the Holy Spirit.

I am not suggesting that we accept all miracles and supernatural occurrences as of God. They must all be tested and measured by Scripture. But before we discourage the genuine work of God and cast needless roadblocks across someone's path, we need to ask, "How does this measure up with the Word? What is the fruit?" If people are being won to the Lord and genuinely turning away from their sins, it's most likely *not* the devil's working; for he does not convict people to repent and turn from their sins.

Mistaking the genuine for the counterfeit

Genuine revival always includes genuine *reformation*. Counterfeit revival may be exciting, and it may make people feel warm and fuzzy inside, but there is no deep heart searching, there is no deep reformation and turning from sin. Rather, people are embraced in their sins, forgiven in their sins, and empowered to continue their lives *still in sin*.

Mistaking the genuine work of God for the counterfeit is not something that happens just today. It happened in Bible times too. Consider the following:

Hannah. While weeping in great surrender and making a vow to

God as she requested a son, the priest Eli accused this meek woman of being drunk (1 Samuel 1:13–15). You would think that he, of all people, should have recognized someone experiencing true heart repentance and spiritual revival. But he didn't! However, God did, and the next year, her repentant, broken prayers were answered, and she gave birth to a baby named Samuel who became the next prophet of Israel.

Christ's disciples. After Pentecost, the disciples were so overcome with the Holy Spirit that they were actually able to share the gospel in other languages—and were understood. This had never happened before and the people were so startled that some mocked them, saying that they were full of new wine. Some of those who witnessed these things began to yell, "Beware! Beware! Great things may be happening here, but it's not a true revival—it's a counterfeit!" But was it a counterfeit? No! Peter went on to preach the gospel in power, and about three thousand people became believers that day and turned from their lives of sin. (You can read more about this in Acts 2.)

Christ Himself. The most startling illustration comes from the life of Christ Himself. After casting out a demon and healing a man who had been dumb and blind, the Pharisees immediately yelled, "This isn't the work of God! This man is casting out devils by the power of Beelzebub, the prince of devils." (See Matthew 12:22–24 for more of the story.) They saw the work, they saw the revival and reformation in this man's life, but rather than giving glory to God, they actually accused Christ of doing the work of Satan. How much further from the truth could they have been? The spiritual leaders of Israel did not recognize Jesus for who He actually was when He came to earth. Although they knew the prophecies, they knew the Bible doctrines, and they rigorously obeyed the commandments (at least when it was to their advantage), their hearts were shut to the power of the Holy Spirit. So how could they recognize the Spirit at work? They were blind, just as many today still are.

Inspiration gives us a somber warning:

> The baptism of the Holy Ghost as on the day of Pentecost will lead to a revival of true religion and to the performance of many wonderful works. Heavenly intelligences

will come among us, and men will speak as they are moved upon by the Holy Spirit of God. But should the Lord work upon men as He did on and after the day of Pentecost, *many who now claim to believe the truth* would know so very little of the operation of the Holy Spirit that they would cry, "Beware of fanaticism." They would say of those who were filled with the Spirit, "These men are full of new wine" (Acts 2:13). . . .

. . . The great sin of those who profess to be Christians is that they do not open the heart to receive the Holy Spirit. When souls long after Christ and seek to become one with Him, then those who are content with *a form of godliness* exclaim, "Be careful, do not go to extremes." . . .

. . . But while we should be careful not to go into human excitement, we should not be among those who will raise inquiries and cherish doubts in reference to the work of the Spirit of God.[2]

To illustrate, let's review an incident that took place in California in the mid-1880s. Healdsburg College—later to become Pacific Union College—was just beginning, and during this time a genuine revival among the students broke out. However, some unconverted, fanatical ones pushed their way into the work, and as a result the leadership at the college shut the revival down. Here is what Ellen White had to say about the incident:

I wish to say some things in reference to the revival at Healdsburg.

I wish to say I am not in harmony with your treatment of this matter. That there were fanatical ones who pressed into that work I would not deny. But if you move in the future as you have done in this matter, you may be assured of one thing, you will condemn the work of the latter rain when it shall come. For you will see at that time far greater evidences of fanaticism.

I believe the work at Healdsburg to be genuine. I believe there were the deep movings of the Spirit of God. I believe unconsecrated, unconverted ones urged themselves to the front. The enemy always works through those of unbalanced minds and imperfect characters. I do not believe that Elder E. P. Daniels moved wisely in all things, and it would be a new chapter in the experience of workers if there was not a mistake made in some things.

Has not God presented before you the defects and want of wisdom in your ways and in your management? If Elder Daniels erred in some things, who of you dared to tell him to preach no more? Who of you dared to stop the work because in your finite judgment everything did not appear to meet your ideas? Every time I think of this matter I am so pained I try to put it out of my mind at once.

When an effort shall be made in the work of God, Satan will be on the ground to urge himself to notice, but shall it be the work of ministers to stretch out the hand and say, This must go no farther, for it is not the work of God? I believe that God was giving the people in Healdsburg a warning and I believe that some would have taken hold of the truth; and I believe you had no right whatever to lay your hand on that work, but should have joined yourself to it. If you saw errors—as there must have been errors—then you should have corrected them in as private a manner as possible and put no arguments or excuses in the minds of the opposers of truth, to resist the truth.

I wish you could see what a delicate, dangerous matter it is to meddle with the work of God unless you have light from heaven to guide you in your decisions. . . . I fear you have grieved the Spirit of God. . . .

. . . If this is the way you manage when God sends good, be assured the revivals will be rare. When the Spirit of God comes it will be called fanaticism, as on the day of Pentecost. "These men are filled with new wine," was the saying of those who took no decided interest in the work.[3]

We want to be very careful not to plant seeds of doubt or speak against a work that the Holy Spirit is doing by calling it evil or fanatical. While we should ask God for wisdom on how to respond when unconsecrated ones rise up and detract from the work, we do not want to cast shadows upon or shut down a true work of God.

As humans, we tend to run from one extreme to the other, and this is as Satan would have it. His chief goal is to get us to embrace fanaticism on one hand or cold formalism on the other. Either way, we will not recognize his delusions. Most assume that fanaticism is the biggest danger. However, cold formalism can be just as disastrous. While cold formalism may pride itself on not getting caught up in the delusions of this new age, it could very well keep us from recognizing the outpouring of the Holy Spirit when it comes. This is dangerous! We don't want to be in either ditch spiritually. We want to be on that straight and narrow path, holding tightly to God's hand, daily receiving fresh oil from His throne room.

The root and fruit test

It's important to remember that a powerful *counterfeit* is an imitation of an even more powerful *genuine,* with only slight differences. Rather than being quick to dismiss a genuine revival because of its similarities to nonbiblical movements, or mistakenly embracing a false revival because it seems genuine and promotes Christ, we need to be looking for the differences—the differences that show the true heart of the movement. In many ways, the true and the false can appear almost identical. Ellen White writes, "The track of truth lies close beside the track of error, and both tracks may seem to be one to minds which are not worked by the Holy Spirit, and which, therefore, are not quick to discern the difference between truth and error."[4]

In the Adventist pioneer days, a great spiritual awakening was taking place. God was working in a mighty way upon many hearts, and the work was going forward with Holy Spirit blessing and power. However, there were some fanatical individuals who tried to disrupt the work.

Speaking to this, Ellen White wrote, "Many are fanatics. They are consumed by a fiery zeal which is mistaken for religion, but *character is the true test of discipleship.* Have they the meekness of Christ? have they His humility and sweet benevolence? Is the soul-temple emptied of pride, arrogance, selfishness, and censoriousness? If not, they know not what manner of spirit they are of. They do not realize that true Christianity consists in bearing much fruit to the glory of God."[5]

We must remember that to truly understand the difference between a false revival and the true genuine work of God—which we want to embrace—we need to do a "root and fruit" test. In other words, we need to ask, "On what foundation does the movement take its root, and what is the fruit of its profession?"

There are many noble-sounding revival movements occurring throughout Christianity today. Though they may look good at first glance, make sure they are firmly rooted in biblical truth. Be wary of any movement that claims to be "all about Jesus" if it has the tendency to create skepticism and doubt towards God's Word or to minimize distinct biblical doctrines and truth for the sake of greater unity and love.

Ellen White writes, "The present truth, the special message given to our world, even the third angel's message, comprehends a vast field, containing heavenly treasures. No one can be excusable who says, 'I will no longer have anything to do with these special messages; I will preach Christ.' No one can preach Christ, and present the truth as it is in Jesus, unless he presents the truths that are to come before the people at the present time, when such important developments are taking place."[6]

Any movement that claims to lift up Jesus while diminishing the truths He taught is not built on the Word. Our doctrines center on Jesus—He is the most important part—and we often forget Him if our focus is on our own works rather than on His righteousness. However, it is a deceptively neutralizing gospel that waters down the doctrines that Jesus has called us to embrace and uphold just so we can reach more people. Consider the following:

> In the truths of His word, God has given to men a
> revelation of Himself; and to all who accept them they are

a shield against the deceptions of Satan. It is a neglect of these truths that has opened the door to the evils which are now becoming so widespread in the religious world. The nature and the importance of the law of God have been, to a great extent, lost sight of. A wrong conception of the character, the perpetuity, and the obligation of the divine law has led to errors in relation to conversion and sanctification, and has resulted in lowering the standard of piety in the church. *Here is to be found the secret of the lack of the Spirit and power of God in the revivals of our time.*[7]

Did you catch that? The lack of God's Spirit and power is often because we don't understand His character and we've minimized His divine law. This is key! The Bible tells us, "All scripture is given by inspiration of God, and is profitable for doctrine, for reproof, for correction, for instruction in righteousness: That the man of God may be perfect, thoroughly furnished unto all good works" (2 Timothy 3:16, 17).

While writing this chapter, I heard a powerful series of messages by my friend Pastor Benjamin Orian from the Rocky Mountain Conference. He spoke of many people today getting caught up arguing over the validity of the Bible or its relevance for today's culture. As a result, they miss the whole purpose and goal of its message. And this is exactly as Satan would have it. I think this must be why Ellen White wrote, "Brethren, cling to your Bible, as it reads, and stop your criticisms in regard to its validity, and obey the Word, and not one of you will be lost."[8]

We would do well to heed this advice! In another place, she writes, "Obedience is the test of discipleship. It is the keeping of the commandments that proves the sincerity of our professions of love. When the doctrine we accept kills sin in the heart, purifies the soul from defilement, bears fruit unto holiness, we may know that it is the truth of God."[9]

Remember, Christ is the root, and obedience is the fruit!

Let's not quench the Spirit through unbelief

In the previous chapter, I talked about the dangers of mind-stilling practices such as centering prayer and looking for silence or that voice in the inner soul. Don't allow this fear to quench the true inner working of the Holy Spirit in your heart! If you are truly aligning your life with Scripture, you don't need to be worried that Satan might be the one speaking to you—unless what you hear goes contrary to God's Word. (If in doubt, review chapter 12, "Dangerous Truth Distortions.")

In a letter written to Brother and Sister McCullagh in March of 1896 about how to be more effective in ministry, Ellen White encouraged, "Do not lightly esteem the voice of the Holy Spirit. God wants you to have liberty in Him, and by placing yourself in His hands you may abound in every good work, and represent Him to the world."[10]

As we pray according to the pattern of Scripture, humbling ourselves before God's throne and acknowledging that within us is no good thing, the Holy Spirit will speak to us day by day. The Holy Spirit working upon our hearts and minds is what draws us to God in the first place. We have no yearnings after holiness within ourselves. The Holy Spirit gives us these yearnings (Philippians 2:13). He is our Companion day by day, prompting us in the way we should go and convicting us of sin.

I can't tell you how many times I've prayed and asked God to give me wisdom or to show me how to move forward in ministry, and as I've reflected upon His Word, slowly some thought or idea would come to my mind that I'd never considered before. It turned out to be the exact wisdom or direction I needed! At those times, I knew without a doubt that God was speaking to me through His Spirit. And His Spirit continues to speak to me day by day as I continue to yield my heart and life to Him. While invisible, the Holy Spirit's presence is always felt in the hearts of true believers. God's Spirit not only brings conviction about things we need to make right in our life, but also prompts us when to speak, what to say, and how to reach out to those around us. As I've followed these promptings, often in faith, they have been exactly what I needed in specific situations. There's nothing more wonderful than knowing you are indeed in tune with the Holy Spirit's voice.

Ellen White writes, "To effect the salvation of men, God employs various agencies. He speaks to them by His word and by His ministers, and He sends by the Holy Spirit messages of warning, reproof, and instruction. These means are designed to enlighten the understanding of the people, to reveal to them their duty and their sins, and the blessings which they may receive, to awaken in them a sense of spiritual want, that they may go to Christ and find in Him the grace they need."[11]

Over a hundred years ago, the church was warned:

> There is at the present time almost a universal state of un-belief in regard to the operations of the Holy Spirit, especially in the manifestation of the gifts. Unbelief shuts the Spirit of God away from the mind. It quenches the Spirit, and leaves the masses exposed to the delusions of these last days.
>
> Again, those who by unbelief quench the Spirit in these last days will be ill prepared to share in the great blessings which God promises by the prophet Joel, quoted by Peter [Acts 2:17, 18]. . . . Take care, dear reader, lest unbelief in you quench the Spirit, and shut you away from this great blessing designed for "them that believe."[12]

Remember that even Jesus, in His own country, "did not many mighty works" because of the unbelief of His people (Matthew 13:58). Might we still be limiting His work today by our unbelief?

As I bring this chapter to a close, let's remember that "a revival of true godliness among us is the greatest and most urgent of all our needs. To seek this should be our first work. . . . [However, this] revival need be expected only in answer to prayer."[13] Only those who walk by faith and stand upon the promises of His Word—refusing to let go without a blessing—only those who are pleading for more and more of the Holy Spirit will indeed receive the fullness of what God longs to give (see Ephesians 3:14–19).

Are you, dear friend, willing to hold on and not let go until you receive God's blessing? I challenge you to search the Scriptures, test and prove all things, and once you know you are firmly rooted upon the Solid Rock, I challenge you to hold on with a tenacity that will not let go! Keep daring to ask for more, because God has much more He is longing to do in your life and ministry. You think you've seen it all? God has infinity beyond! I believe we have yet to discover the full potential of this *amazing and divine gift called prayer*!

Chapter 25

Understanding the Heart of United Prayer

Embracing True Prayer Revival

> For the eyes of the LORD run to and fro throughout the whole earth,
> to shew himself strong in the behalf of them
> whose heart is perfect toward him.
>
> —*2 Chronicles 16:9*

A few summers ago, our ARME Ministries prayer team was asked to hold a prayer room on the campus of the Adventist University of the Philippines. Here, for a number of days, we did little more than pray with students and faculty. While the hours were long, it was very rewarding as our team watched the lives of lukewarm, Christian young people being revived, energized, and transformed. Many who had never before been interested in spiritual things gave their lives to Christ and were decidedly changed. And many of the young people would stay in the prayer room for hours.

One day, a girl named Kristin, compelled by the invitations of a friend, came to see what was so special about this time of united prayer. Kristin had never prayed with others before and didn't really have a close relationship with God. But compelled by the Holy Spirit, she began to weep as she prayed with our team, asking God to forgive her of her sins and to give her a new heart.

Afterward, she told us with tears in her eyes, "God has given me such peace—like I've never experienced before. Thank you for praying with me." Then she continued, "This may sound strange, but during the united prayer, I saw a circle of evil angels trying to break into our prayer circle to stop the praying. But they could not get into our circle, for holding them back was a stronger circle of angels of light!" She paused. "I can see that God is really with you and protecting you all as you pray."

While seeing angels is not the norm for our prayer circles, we know that as Bible-believing Christians, we are engaged in a very real spiritual battle between the powers of darkness and the power of Light. For some reason, God allowed Kristin to catch a glimpse of this battle to remind us of the seriousness of our work and to encourage us to press forward in prayer. As Psalm 34:7 says, "The angel of the LORD encampeth round about them that fear him, and delivereth them." What an amazing promise, and what a gift to see this in reality!

As I have traveled around the world the last few years speaking about the power of prayer and encouraging churches to unite in prayer, I have seen miracle after miracle as God's Spirit has been poured out, bringing indifferent Laodiceans back to life. I've seen small united prayer groups springing up everywhere. However, the enemy is not happy and has gone to great lengths to shut down or otherwise hinder the work, for we know that prayer—especially united prayer—is the most hurtful weapon against his forces.

Surprisingly, some of those who have tried to stop the united prayer movement are actually fellow believers—believers who are afraid of being swept up in a counterfeit revival. While I think these believers are sincere in their motives, I know the Holy Spirit has been grieved at how the genuine prayer revival has been held back by their words and actions.

This is why we need to press together in *even more prayer,* that God's genuine prayer movement would not be held back, even by friendly fire!

"There is need of a strong and united influence to co-operate with the Captain of our salvation in taking the spoil from the power of the enemy, and making men and women free in Christ. Shall we not every one seek to stimulate others to work for fallen man? *Pray earnestly, unitedly, perseveringly, for spiritual power.* The fountain of grace and knowledge is ever flowing. It is inexhaustible. It is from this abundant fulness that we are supplied."[1]

When we pray together, we aren't just doubling the power, for God works in the business of multiplication, not addition. When we pray together, we can claim God's promise that if we are filled with His power and standing upon His Rock, one of us can chase a thousand, and two can put ten thousand to flight (Deuteronomy 32:30). Another passage tells us, "And five of you shall chase an hundred, and an hundred of you shall put ten thousand to flight" (Leviticus 26:8). While there's a lot of power in secret prayer, there's even more power when two or more are praying together.

This is why Satan is so keen on keeping us from praying together. This is also why I think we need to briefly address a few issues. If we don't understand the heart of genuine, biblically based, united prayer, it *is possible* that we could be swept away with a counterfeit prayer movement—or worse still, hinder a genuine prayer movement. We don't want either!

Does following a leader or praying themes prohibit the leading of the Holy Spirit?

God's kingdom is a kingdom of law and order; it shows no confusion or chaos. The Bible tells us, "Let all things be done decently and in order" (1 Corinthians 14:40). Ellen White writes, "I have seen that confusion is displeasing to God, and that there should be order in singing, and order in praying."[2]

In a large group, if no one took charge, all would be chaos. We would not know whether we were coming or going, and we would be prone to follow the unbalanced, fanatical, or more domineering among us. To keep dignity and order, we believe that every prayer meeting, whether following the united prayer format or just a general time of brief prayer, should have a *designated leader*. This leader can be anyone who displays evidence of the Holy Spirit working in his or her life—it would be foolish to allow otherwise. Keep in mind that this designated prayer leader (whether a pastor, elder, or anyone else) is by no means to be compared with a "spiritual director" or "prayer guide" as is often used in the spiritual formation movement. This is just an individual who helps lead out and safeguard order and balance in the prayer meeting. With united prayer, this leader may at times take a more active role by opening and closing the prayer, by introducing each new prayer theme by reading Scripture, or by leading a short song. But there is no mystical mind control or "spirit guiding" involved. It's just a way to keep order from turning into chaos when multiple people pray.

Although unity in prayer can be accomplished many ways, my friend Janet Page and I put an outline together for united prayer in our small booklet titled *Praying for Rain: A Mini-Handbook for United Prayer.*[3] It's important to remember, though, that there is not *one* prayer method to end all methods.

While we do not feel that united prayer *always* has to follow a certain pattern or theme, the primary reason we encourage the sanctuary model in prayer (thanksgiving followed by confession, then supplication, and ending with worship) is simply because in the church today most people focus only on supplication. We are best at that! We all have lots of needs and we know how to ask God for them, just like most children know how to beg for good things from their parents. But sadly, our prayers have become quite self-centered and stale. We have forgotten to take time to worship God, to praise God, and most importantly, to humble our hearts and make things right with Him. To counteract this, we are seeking to turn people's minds back to the prayers modeled in Scripture, such as the prayers of Nehemiah (Nehemiah 1:5–11), of Daniel (Daniel 9:3–20), of Jesus (the Lord's Prayer in Matthew 6:9–13), and of others. Just because we have prayer themes doesn't mean we are stuck in a rut. No! It just gives us a place to start.

Remember, not united prayer, nor the Lord's Prayer, nor any other prayer model is to be repeated as a mere form. These prayers are only illustrations and examples of what our prayers should be like—simple, earnest, and *comprehensive*.[4]

What about long prayers?

We've all been in that prayer meeting where one person prays on and on and on. Talk about wearing out the saints! Everyone is about to fall asleep and we are wishing with all our heart that the one praying would end the prayer so we could have a turn. Over and over we find references throughout the Spirit of Prophecy encouraging that public prayers should be kept short. Ellen White always wrote these words in the context of keeping prayer meetings interesting. "Make short prayers in meetings, and lengthy prayers when you talk and commune with God in your closet."[5] "Learn to pray short, and right to the point, asking for just what you need,"[6] she exhorted again and again.

Her words of counsel more often than not refer to the length of individual prayers, not necessarily to the length of the prayer meeting itself. In Adventist pioneer days, prayer meetings often went on for quite some time, even into the night. Ellen White would probably be quite distressed if she felt her words limited God's remnant from praying for more than ten minutes at a prayer meeting today. It would certainly go against how God has worked in the past down through history.

This is not to say that every meeting needs to include a time of lengthy prayer. We don't want to make our meetings wearisome and tedious. Even Christ, when He taught the people, did not force upon them—as did the Pharisees—long, tedious ceremonies and prayers. We must remember that the value of our prayers is not necessarily in proportion to the time we spend on our knees, but rather to the heart and motive behind the prayer. However, encouraging specific time for more unhindered group prayer would actually be beneficial and would bring dry, stale churches into much greater spiritual life and unity.

In general, we encourage brief prayers that are two to three sentences or one complete thought. Inspiration tells us, "A prayer with one half the number of words" is adequate.[7]

The beauty of united prayer in large groups is that, because each prayer is kept short and concise, many people can pray. Even children, no longer intimidated by the usual lengthy prayers of the adults, eagerly jump right in, and their prayers often convict to tears the hearts of their elders.

In smaller group settings, and when it's obvious everyone wants to pray, it's not as important to keep individual prayers brief. Inspired by the Holy Spirit's promptings, we usually pray longer prayers in these instances. But again, if an extended time for prayer is taken, it's important that everyone be unified in the desire to pray. If one or two people are being resistant and wanting to see the prayer service end, it's best not to continue long, for the lack of unity will prohibit God's blessing.

While we are told that one or two minutes is long enough for a normal, individual public prayer, we are also told, "There may be instances where prayer is in a special manner indited by the Spirit of God, [and] where supplication is made in the Spirit. The yearning soul becomes agonized and groans after God. The Spirit wrestles as did Jacob and will not be at rest without special manifestations of the power of God. *This is as God would have it.*"[8]

If God's children were praying more in private, they probably wouldn't be raising objections to praying more in public, for this would be the fulfillment of their true heart's desire. However, most of us aren't praying in private, at least not as we should be. As a result, true prayer, earnestness, and Holy Spirit–inspired praying in group settings can be quite uncomfortable and disconcerting. This is because our own hearts have become dry and cold.

A survey taken a number of years ago on the devotional life of pastors found that 80 percent of pastors pray less than fifteen minutes a day. Seventy percent said they prepare for sermons by studying the Word only.[9] I wonder what such a survey would reveal today?

What about prayer walking—is this biblical?

Prayer walking is a relatively new phenomenon, the origin of which is not completely clear. There is no solid biblical model for prayer walking, although some use the story of the children of Israel walking around Jericho as support. However, to say that certain prayers offered in one setting or while in one position are more effective than those offered at another time or in another manner *is simply not scriptural.* While we may feel we need to be physically close to a location or situation to pray more effectively, remember that our heavenly Father, who is not only omniscient (all knowing) but omnipresent (can be everywhere at the same time), knows exactly what our needs are, and He will respond to them in His own perfect will and timing, no matter where we pray.

Having stated this, we know that those in Bible times walked the majority of the time, and it's no doubt they also prayed while they walked. Furthermore, the Bible tells us to "pray without ceasing" (1 Thessalonians 5:17), and since walking is something we do daily, surely part of praying without ceasing is praying while walking—whether at our home, work, or church.

I live in the country and one of my favorite pastimes is to walk and pray aloud out in nature where only God sees and hears. I often carry my Bible with me, and while I'm praying, I will hold it up to God as I humbly remind Him of His promises. The Bible tells us that His Word does not return unto Him void (Isaiah 55:11) and I believe He is honored when we claim it by faith. Some of my best conversations with God have been during these prayer walks out in nature.

In addition to my own private prayer walks, I also have seen God work miracles as friends and I have been convicted to dedicate specific time to actual prayer walking through our church headquarters during important meetings. In 1 Timothy 2:1–8, we are encouraged to pray for kings and those in authority (this includes our church leaders). Recognizing the spiritual battle we face today as a church, I think it's important that we uphold the arms of our pastors and church leaders in prayer, just as Aaron and Hur upheld the arms of Moses when he was interceding for Israel (Exodus 17:12). We must keep in mind that all those in *higher power* are ordained of God (Romans 13:1), and as such, especially deserve our prayers and intercession, whether or not we agree with what they do.

Most of us can't travel to Silver Spring, Maryland, and spend weeks praying for our leaders at the General Conference headquarters, but we can pray in our local communities where we live. Just imagine what might happen, the difficulties that might be overcome, the growth that might be achieved, the backslidden members who might be brought back, if we as church members, laypeople, and leaders alike, would band together, shoulder-to-shoulder, consistently praying for spiritual breakthrough and Holy Spirit blessing!

It's true that we can pray these prayers from the privacy of our own homes rather than on the front steps of our church or walking through a meeting hall or conference building. But I've discovered that *meeting together* and *praying on location* carries an added blessing. Not only do we experience greater unity as a prayer team, but being on location also helps us realize the seriousness of the spiritual battle at hand—thus our prayers are more in earnest. And God answers earnest prayers!

Of note, Ellen White wrote that Enoch walked with God in prayer. She wrote, "I wish I could impress upon every worker in God's cause, the great need of continual, *earnest prayer.* They cannot be constantly upon their knees, but they can be uplifting their hearts to God. This is the way that Enoch walked with God."[10]

Thankfully, God hears all prayers offered by those who abide in Christ (John 15:7), regardless of time, place, or position. However, anything that prompts us to pray more earnestly is worthy of consideration.

> We would not discourage prayer, for there is far too little praying and watching thereunto. And there is still less praying with the Spirit and the understanding also. Fervent and effectual prayer is always in place, and will never weary. Such prayer interests and refreshes all who have a love for devotion. . . .
>
> . . . If Christians would take home the teachings of Christ in regard to watching and praying, they would become more intelligent in their worship of God.[11]

Again, it's significant to note that there are not a lot of specifics given in Scripture on how to pray as a group unitedly. We are instructed that praying together is necessary, and we are told what should be included in these times of prayer, but we don't have a lot of dos and don'ts. Maybe the silence on this topic speaks for itself. If Christ had taught people a specific way to unite in prayer, that's all we would be doing—and it would be more likely to turn into a mere form. Let us be ever mindful, ever on guard, testing and proving all things by the Word of God. But let us not be among those who will cast doubt upon God's true work.

What about corporate confession? What is and is not appropriate?

This is one of the most common questions I am asked. It is an important question and worthy of comment, as many are afraid or uncomfortable of where corporate confession might lead.

We know that God is the only One who can forgive sins. Confession of sins before our fellow man holds no merit. What matters is what God hears and sees, and He reads the motives of our hearts. Having stated that, there is need of public confession for many reasons. In the Spirit of Prophecy, we find the following principles, which I have paraphrased for simplicity:

- Public confession is humbling to our souls! We need to be humbled![12]
- Public confession is a witness to others who need to humble themselves.[13]
- Public confession is taking responsibility for what we have done wrong against God or others and seeking to make it right. When we do this, there is healing![14]
- Public confession fosters unity and love as we pray for one another and bear each other's burdens.[15]
- Public confession of sins like selfishness, over-reaching, dishonesty toward God and our neighbor, pride, prayerlessness, sins in the family, and many other such sins that have brought the frown of God upon His people need to be acknowledged. These are appropriate to be shared in public, for we all bear responsibility![16]
- Public confession is often urged by the Holy Spirit, and we need to obey. Of course, what is private to some may not be private to another, but if the Holy Spirit prompts us to confess, we must not refuse that call.[17]

Ellen White also writes:

> Confession of sin, whether public or private, should be heartfelt and freely expressed. It is not to be urged from the sinner. It is not to be made in a flippant and careless way or forced from those who have no realizing sense of the abhorrent character of sin. The confession that is mingled with tears and sorrow, that is the outpouring of the inmost soul, finds its way to the God of infinite pity. Says the psalmist: "The Lord is nigh unto them that are of a broken heart; and saveth such as be of a contrite spirit."[18]

Oh, how beautiful is the heart of a truly repentant soul!

Unfortunately, the devil likes to take us to one extreme or the other. His goal is to get us to either shun confession and keep things generic (which protects pride and keeps self intact) or spill all the ungodliness of our heart, which in turn can lead others' minds astray.

While Ellen White encouraged corporate and public confession and the need for greater brokenness, she also emphatically shared that there are many confessions that should not be spoken in the hearing of others. She is almost always speaking of sins of a sexual nature or "thought sins" such as lust, jealousy, evil surmising, or emotional adultery. Of course, we need to confess these sins, but they should always be confessed to God alone and optionally shared with only a mature few who can help us gain the victory—if victory is still needed. However, it is dangerous to confess these types of sins publicly—especially sins of a sexual nature—because they can neutralize the witness we have for Christ and plant seeds in the hearts of other Christians that will spring up and bear fruit when they fall under similar temptations. "These sins cannot be so very grievous; for did not those who have made confession, Christians of long standing, do these very things?"[19]

We need to ask God what we should and should not speak of publicly. However, one thing is quite clear. *Much more public confession should be happening than is currently happening!* All known sin needs to be specifically confessed and put away. That always means making things right with God in our prayer closet, but it often also means individual confession to a brother or sister whom we have injured, and sometimes it may mean taking responsibility for our sins before our whole church family.

"Fall on the Rock and be broken," Sister White urges, "and Christ will give you the true and heavenly dignity. Let not pride, self-esteem, or self-righteousness keep anyone from confessing his sin that he may claim the promise. 'He that covereth his sins shall not prosper: but whoso confesseth and forsaketh them shall have mercy' (Prov. 28:13). Keep nothing back from God, and neglect not the confession of your faults to your brethren."[20]

The goal of biblically inspired united prayer

As we close this chapter, let's remember once again that the goal of true, biblically inspired united prayer is not about pushing a specific agenda or about experiencing warm and fuzzy feelings. The goal of united prayer is to come into *greater unity in the truth,* that God's agenda and His desires may be fulfilled.

Ellen White writes:

> Great importance is attached to united prayer, the union of purpose. God hears the prayers of individuals, but on this occasion [referring to Matthew 18:19] Jesus was giving especial and important lessons that were to have a special bearing upon His newly organized church on the earth. There must be agreement in the things which they desire and for which they pray. It was not merely the thoughts and exercises of one mind, liable to deception; but the petition was to be the earnest desire of several minds centered on the same point.[21]

On what point should we center our prayers? That the Holy Spirit would be poured out, that the gospel would be preached, and that God's glory would be revealed to the world so that He can return to claim His bride.

Satan knows the seriousness of our great commission, and thus he seeks to keep us away from our true source of power. However, while the battle over prayer may continue, let's make sure we are on the right side of this spiritual battle, otherwise Satan will be victorious. Let us shun the false and embrace the true as we move forward on our knees, asking for God's will to be accomplished, and for His Spirit to be poured out. He has more He's waiting to do, but He's waiting for more of us to pray!

Chapter 26

The Power of Genuine Humility

What Might Have Been, Can Be

> *Verily I say unto you, Except ye be converted, and become as little children, ye shall not enter into the kingdom of heaven.*
> —Matthew 18:3

Have you ever noticed how forthright little children are? They don't waste time with long speeches and they don't beat around the bush. They get right to the point of what they want. And they ask *a lot* of questions. Why? Because they want answers.

All too often in our adult years, when we come to God with questions, we already think we know the answers and it's more about trying to convince Him to follow our wisdom than being teachable and pliable to His wisdom. But true humility bows to the wisdom that is higher than our own. True humility recognizes that we have no strength or wisdom of our own. We must rely upon God, just as a young child relies upon his or her parent.

Children are also known for their blunt honesty. I have been with groups of children as they honestly and forthrightly asked God for forgiveness of their sins, and then made wrongs right between each other. Their humble example brought tears to their parents' eyes and convicted my own heart of its great need. Indeed, we have a lot to learn from children.

Christ tells us, "Except ye be converted, and become as little children, ye shall not enter into the kingdom of heaven" (Matthew 18:3). This was a statement of profound meaning in Christ's day. Yet, we know that it was a shock to Christ's disciples and all those listening, for it was the reverse of what their culture taught.

Even today, in our human way of thinking, it doesn't make sense to become a child again. The logical progression is that we advance in our thinking; that we become more astute, more knowledgeable, more biblically studied, more mature, *not more childlike*. So what could Christ have possibly meant? Let's keep reading: "Whosoever therefore shall humble himself as this little child, the same is greatest in the kingdom of heaven" (verse 4).

Ah, humility! Of course, we all know about humility. Many of us take pride in our humility. When people speak of us and say things such as, "He is such a humble person," our heart glows. When someone asks how we accomplished something, we'll glibly reply, "It wasn't me; it was Him! I don't deserve the credit." But all too often our hearts are whispering, "Yeah, but you did do a lot of work on the project. God couldn't have done it without you!" True humility that does not take pride in itself is a rare gift and one that only God can give. But it is this Christ-centered humility that we desperately need.

As one Christian profoundly put it: "The Christian life can be explained only in terms of Jesus Christ, and if your life as a Christian can still be explained in terms of you—your personality, your willpower, your gift, your talent, your money, your courage, your scholarship, your dedication, your sacrifice, or your anything—then although you may have the Christian life, you are not yet living it."[1]

Back in 1902, the Seventh-day Adventist Church was beginning to expand rapidly. Great things were happening on many fronts as the work was going forward. Yet one thing was lacking. This one thing, if experienced, would have brought all other blessings in its wake, and the work would have been finished. Referring to this lack, Ellen White sadly recounts a vision she received:

> One day at noon I was writing of the work that might have been done at the last General Conference if the men in positions of trust had followed the will and way of God. Those who have had great light have not walked in the light. The meeting was closed, and the break was not made. Men did not humble themselves before the Lord as they should have done, and the Holy Spirit was not imparted.
>
> I had written thus far when I lost consciousness, and I seemed to be witnessing a scene in Battle Creek.
>
> We were assembled in the auditorium of the Tabernacle. Prayer was offered, a hymn was sung, and prayer was again offered. Most earnest supplication was made to God. The meeting was marked by the presence of the Holy Spirit. The work went deep, and some present were weeping aloud.
>
> One arose from his bowed position and said that in the past he had not been in union with certain ones and had felt no love for them, but that now he saw himself as he was. With great solemnity he repeated the message to the Laodicean church: " 'Because thou sayest, I am rich, and increased with goods, and have need of nothing.' In my self-sufficiency this is just the way I felt," he said. " 'And knowest not that thou art wretched, and miserable, and poor, and blind, and naked.' I now see that this is my condition. My eyes are opened. My spirit has been hard and unjust. I thought myself righteous, but my heart is broken, and I see my need of the precious counsel of the One who has searched me through and through. Oh, how gracious and compassionate and loving are the words, 'I

counsel thee to buy of Me gold tried in the fire, that thou mayest be rich; and white raiment, that thou mayest be clothed, and that the shame of thy nakedness do not appear; and anoint thine eyes with eyesalve, that thou mayest see.' " Revelation 3:17, 18.

The speaker turned to those who had been praying, and said: "We have something to do. We must confess our sins, and humble our hearts before God." He made heartbroken confessions and then stepped up to several of the brethren, one after another, and extended his hand, asking forgiveness. Those to whom he spoke sprang to their feet, making confession and asking forgiveness, and they fell upon one another's necks, weeping. The spirit of confession spread through the entire congregation. It was a Pentecostal season. God's praises were sung, and far into the night, until nearly morning, the work was carried on.

The following words were often repeated, with clear distinctness: "As many as I love, I rebuke and chasten: be zealous therefore, and repent. Behold, I stand at the door, and knock: if any man hear My voice, and open the door, I will come in to him, and will sup with him, and he with Me." Verses 19, 20.

No one seemed to be too proud to make heartfelt confession, and those who led in this work were the ones who had influence, but had not before had courage to confess their sins.

There was rejoicing such as never before had been heard in the Tabernacle.

Then I aroused from my unconsciousness, and for a while could not think where I was. My pen was still in my hand. The words were spoken to me: "*This might have been. All this the Lord was waiting to do for His people. All heaven was waiting to be gracious.*" I thought of where we might have been had thorough work been done at the last General Conference, and agony of disappointment came over me as I realized that what I had witnessed was not a reality.[2]

What "might have been" may not have happened in 1902, but *it could happen today*! The Bible tells us: "Draw nigh to God, and he will draw nigh to you. Cleanse your hands, ye sinners; and purify your hearts, ye double minded. Be afflicted, and mourn, and weep: let your laughter be turned to mourning, and your joy to heaviness. Humble yourselves in the sight of the Lord, and he shall lift you up" (James 4:8–10).

As one author wrote:

> It is easy to think we humble ourselves before God: [but] humility towards men will be the only sufficient proof that our humility before God is real. . . .
>
> The humble man feels no jealousy or envy. He can praise God when others are preferred and blessed before him. He can bear to hear others praised and himself forgotten, because in God's presence he has learnt to say with Paul, "I am nothing." He has received the spirit of Jesus, who pleased not himself, and sought not his own honor, as the spirit of his life.[3]

The pastors retreat that changed lives

Not long ago, a group of pastors came together for a three-day retreat in the Romanian North Transylvania Conference. Initially, the program went according to plan, but then, on day two, something unexpected happened.

Pastor Ioan Campian-Tatar, the Romanian Union General Secretary and Ministerial Secretary, presented a late afternoon devotional on the ministry of the Old Testament prophet Nehemiah. The devotional was scheduled as part of the retreat program. Initially, the pastors began discussing the need to repair and restore "the walls," following the pattern of Nehemiah. During the early part of this discussion, one pastor said that he had come to the retreat to pray, but since arriving, he felt he needed to do more. He then began to confess and seek the forgiveness of his colleagues for being critical of them—particularly of the conference administration.

As a result, one pastor after another began to confess his sins, seeking the forgiveness of his colleagues for the pain and wrongs he had specifically caused one another. Those in attendance said they felt the Holy Spirit in a powerful way as the spirit of humility and reconciliation continued for more than two hours.

Not only did the pastors ask forgiveness for their wrongs to one another, but they also publicly confessed their failures toward God for flawed priorities. The majority of those in the meeting were moved to tears. As a result of the pastors being willing to be open and honest with each other, the "masks" were removed and much healing took place. This experience led to a complete change of priorities for many of the pastors.[4]

So how do we obtain true humility? How do we humble ourselves in such a way that God's Spirit can truly be poured out? This is something that I have been praying about for quite some time. The older and more experienced we become in ministry, the harder it often is to humble ourselves and acknowledge our weaknesses to one another and to God. In the book *Pastoral Ministry*, we find the following:

> I have been shown that many are in the greatest danger of failing to perfect holiness in the fear of the Lord. . . . There is with nearly all a neglect of self-examination. . . .
>
> . . . You will receive more strength by spending one hour each day in meditation, and mourning over your failings and heart-corruptions, and pleading for God's pardoning love, and the assurance of sins forgiven, than you would by spending many hours and days . . . making yourself acquainted with every objection to our faith, and the most powerful evidences in favor of our faith.[5]

The context of this statement was that one pastor, while being well-studied in all the doctrines, was not allowing the Holy Spirit to break his heart. While we should know the Bible inside and out and be fortified in correct biblical doctrine, the more important thing is that we allow God to break our hearts.

Ellen White pleads:

> Let the proud spirit bow in humiliation. Let the hard heart be broken. No longer pet and pity and exalt self. Look, oh look upon Him whom our sins have pierced. See Him descending step by step the path of humiliation to lift us up; abasing Himself till He could go no lower, and all to save us who were fallen by sin! Why will we be so indifferent, so cold, so formal, so proud, so self-sufficient?
>
> Who of us is faithfully following the Pattern? Who of us has instituted and continued the warfare against pride of heart? Who of us has, in good earnest, brought himself to wrestle with selfishness until it should no longer dwell in the heart and be revealed in the life?[6]

We need a deeper experience!

Earlier, I spoke of the dangers of basing our faith *purely on experience.* This is where many get swept away with error because their quest for an *emotional experience* is what leads them. However, while we must make sure we are rooted and grounded in God's Word, we must also remember that we are emotional beings, and as such, we need more than just intellectual knowledge. *We need a heart experience.*

When it comes to the spiritual walk, many people have the intellectual knowledge—they've made the decision to believe in God—but what is missing is the *heart experience* with God. They don't know Him personally; they haven't genuinely *experienced* what it is to walk in harmony with Him daily.

Speaking of our need for a deeper living experience, Sister White writes the following: "We all need to gain a much *deeper experience* in the things of God than we have gained. Self is to die, and Christ is to take possession of the soul temple."[7] She adds: "Faith and prayer are necessary in order that we may behold the deep things of God. Our minds are so bound about with narrow ideas, that we catch but *limited views of the experience* it is our privilege to have."[8]

I have a dear friend named Phyllis who brings conviction to my heart every time I hear her talk and pray. She is a mature Christian, a leader in her church, and even teaches her own Bible study group in our community. She's level-headed, emotionally stable, and is always looking out for others. Yet, when she talks of the things of God, of how she sees Him changing someone's life, or of something that He has taught her through His Word, tears often come to her eyes. When she prays during church or Bible study, she often gets choked up with emotion as she pours out her love and adoration for God, and her thankfulness for His tender mercies. What a convicting testimony this has been to me.

Some people might frown upon this expression of emotion as being a bit overly sentimental, but I see in Phyllis someone who has truly come to recognize what Christ has done for her. And she understands what it means to have an abiding experience in Christ. Religion is not just a profession for Phyllis, for Christ has touched the very core of her being, and it shows—not just in her public prayers or testimony, but in the practical outflow of her daily life. More of us need this type of *heart experience,* an experience that brings us to tears by the goodness of God's love.

Remember that the presence of emotions doesn't mean something is fanaticism. We are told to love the Lord our God with all our heart, mind, soul, and strength, and to love our neighbor as ourselves (Mark 12:30). Love involves emotions and feelings, and the more we love God, the more our feelings will grow, and the deeper our personal *experience* of closeness with God will become.

In a genuine revival, emotions of love, brokenness, repentance, and a greater appreciation of God's love and sacrifice will often be present. Emotions per se aren't what we seek, nor are they necessary for revival. While each of us responds differently to the Spirit's working, we shouldn't shun these emotions when they are followed by deeper consecration.

We need a deeper—much deeper—experience than we have yet even imagined possible. We need to keep being converted daily, for Inspiration tells us, "To follow Jesus requires wholehearted conversion at the start, and a repetition of this conversion every day."[9] This is the key!

Lessons from the Welsh Revival

After years of private prayer, begging for a deeper filling of the Holy Spirit, humbling his heart before God, putting away sin, and denying himself selfish pleasures, an unknown youth suddenly rose out of obscurity to almost instant fame across the land of Wales. The young man's name was Evan Roberts, the young college student instrumental in bringing about the Welsh Revival of 1904. This revival, which originated in Loughor, was reported to be the greatest global revival the church had seen in over two hundred years.[10]

At Roberts's first meeting, seventeen people gave their lives to Christ, but soon the entire village of Loughor, as well as those from other towns and villages nearby, were filling the streets around the chapel where he spoke, begging an entrance. Meetings often went all night, and even when dismissed, the people did not want to leave. While there was no fancy program, people continued to come night after night, drawn by the power of the Holy Spirit.

Evan Roberts was not a mighty preacher. In actuality, his message was very simple: First, we must confess any known sin to God and make right any wrong done to others! Second, we must put away any doubtful habit! (We need to let go of sinful habits or lifestyles!) Third, we must obey the Spirit promptly! (We can't procrastinate!) And fourth, we must confess our faith in Christ publicly! (See Matthew 10:32 and Luke 12:8.)[11] As a result of this simple message, a deep sense of Holy Spirit awe and conviction of sin came upon everyone, including those who had come to criticize or condemn the prayer meetings. And God's work, evidenced by changed hearts and reformed lives, went deeper and deeper. Roberts urged his listeners, "We must rid the churches of all bad feeling—all malice, envy, prejudice, and misunderstandings. Bow not in prayer until all offenses have been forgiven: but if you feel you cannot forgive, bend to the dust, and ask for a forgiving spirit. You shall get it then."[12]

As a result of following his four simple principles, powerful prayer groups began to spring up everywhere, and church prayer meetings were revitalized around the countryside. In many churches, the all-night

prayer meeting was restored, or introduced for the first time, resulting in the real movings of the Spirit of God in conviction of sin, confession, and re-consecration—for both ministers and congregation. In
some areas, churches held citywide all-night prayer meetings as they
interceded before God for the whole community. Godly ministers, bur-
dened for real revival, sought God in fasting and prayer on behalf of
their churches, and many witnessed gracious manifestations of the Holy
Spirit's working such as they had never seen before.[13]

Speaking of this movement, which spread all over Wales, Pastor Ron
Clouzet summarizes:

> The Spirit of God took hold of Wales by storm. In five
> months, half a million people became Christians. Taverns
> went bankrupt for lack of patronage. Unwed pregnancies
> practically disappeared. Judges were given white gloves:
> not a case to try—no robberies, no burglaries, no rapes,
> no murders, and no embezzlements. Crime had simply
> stopped. District counsels held emergency meetings to
> decide what to do with so many police with nothing to
> do! Some got creative; instead of patrolling football (soc-
> cer) games or the pubs at night, they began singing in the
> churches. So many coal miners turned their lives over to
> Jesus and stopped using foul language that the horses used
> in the mines slowed down production, not knowing what
> was being said to them![14]

This revival continued to affect the world noticeably for the next forty
years and its impact spread to all English-speaking countries, including
the United States, northern and central Europe, India, Japan, China,
Korea, Indonesia, and Latin America. It is estimated that this Holy
Spirit outpouring may have exceeded any previous spiritual awakening
in Christian history, and it birthed many of the Christian churches,
ministries, and charitable organizations that still thrive today.[15]

What God did in Wales and in other revivals throughout history
pales in comparison with what He's going to do in the future. But as long

as we continue to hold on to our sins and grievances, as long as we continue to nurse our hurt feelings and build walls instead of bridges in our churches and congregations, this outpouring cannot occur.

In *Gospel Workers,* Ellen White admonishes:

> My brethren, there should be a different kind of labor from what we too often see in our camp-meetings. *There should be more prayer and weeping, and more confession of sin to God and to one another.* Let the indifference be broken up, let the complaining and faultfinding cease, and the time heretofore worse than wasted in this manner be spent in prayers of living faith for the refreshing from the presence of the Lord. Let us arouse as one man, and unitedly call upon God to send down his grace upon the souls of his people, and to revive his work in the midst of the years.[16]

Where are men like Evan Roberts today? Where are the women willing to give God's straight testimony of repentance? Maybe the greater question to ask is, Where are the people willing to humble their hearts and follow this testimony, were it to be given today? We need a thorough revival; we need a converted ministry.

The result of true humility

Inspiration promises us:

> There is nothing that Satan fears so much as that the people of God shall clear the way by removing every hindrance, so that the Lord can pour out His Spirit upon a languishing church and an impenitent congregation. If Satan had his way, there would never be another awakening, great or small, to the end of time. But we are not ignorant of his devices. It is possible to resist his power. When the way is prepared for the Spirit of God, the blessing will come. Satan can no more hinder a shower of blessing from

descending upon God's people than he can close the windows of heaven that rain cannot come upon the earth. Wicked men and devils cannot hinder the work of God, or shut out His presence from the assemblies of His people, if they will, with subdued, contrite hearts, confess and put away their sins, and in faith claim His promises.[17]

Just imagine how different we would be as Christians today, as churches, as ministries, as leaders in God's work, if we truly allowed the Lord to search our hearts and break us of all pride and selfishness! What "might have been" would no longer be just a dream. It would be reality! And God's Spirit would be poured out and the work would be completed.

Time is short, brothers and sisters. Let us humble our hearts as little children before the Lord. Let us press together unitedly, putting away wrongs and pleading for the outpouring of the Holy Spirit upon our lives and church. Let us seek for divine guidance, for we are told, "To those who in humility of heart seek for divine guidance, angels of God draw near."[18]

Do you ever feel that your prayers for the Holy Spirit have been in vain? Have faith; the outpouring is coming! Soon, we are told, "The revenue of glory [that] has been accumulating for this closing work of the Third Angel's Message" will "overflow and pour forth a healing flood of heavenly influence and accumulated light all over the world." Not one prayer we've prayed for this gift has been lost. Each prayer has been heard and is adding up, and soon the reward will spill forth.[19] But we must be humbled; we must be broken of all pride if we are to receive this great gift.

Let us search our hearts today. Let us humble ourselves before His throne. Let us dare to look up in simple, childlike earnestness and faith, and let us continue *daring to ask for more*!

Chapter 27

The Book of Acts to Be Continued

Learning to Agonize and Organize

> *Not by might, nor by power, but by my spirit,
> saith the LORD of hosts.*
>
> —Zechariah 4:6

ruly, *the sky is not the limit* to God's amazing power, and we've only begun to touch the endless frontier of spiritual possibilities that lay before us as we pray in faith. However, while we may have experienced a glimpse of God's amazing power, He is ever longing to do more. Thus, our prayers should always be for more of the Holy Spirit—much more, more of the character of Christ; much more, more of self-sacrificing love and faith; much more, and more of courageous witness—much more.[1] If we keep asking for more, God will keep giving us *more*!

In the book of Acts, we see the results of the great Pentecostal outpouring. I don't know about you, but I long for what happened at

Pentecost to happen again in our day. Not only were the disciples able to communicate effectively in other tongues,[2] but three thousand were converted in one day (Acts 2:41) and five thousand not long after (Acts 4:4)! People were miraculously healed, just as when Jesus had walked among them.

While the challenges were great, Christ's apostles and other followers were continually in prayer—not halfhearted, superficial prayers prayed out of Christian duty, but agonizing prayers, prayers for victory. And their prayers brought answers! Business meetings turned into prayer meetings. Prison meetings were turned into praise meetings, and God's Spirit was poured out, bringing many new believers into the fold *daily*.

We know that the final great outpouring during the last days will be even greater than what happened at Pentecost. Revelation 18:1 talks about this time—a coming time when the whole earth will be ablaze with God's glory. "The outpouring of the Spirit in the days of the apostles was the 'former rain;' and glorious was the result. But the 'latter rain' will be still more abundant."[3]

Have you noticed that when we pray for the Holy Spirit, our prayers often turn into merely a repetition of the same request over and over again? "Please send us Your Spirit! Lord, we need Your Spirit!" We need to pray this prayer, but we need to pray it intelligently. Praying intelligently means that we are praying that the Spirit will have *free rein* in our lives. Praying intelligently means asking for the Holy Spirit to change us: our hearts, thoughts, attitudes, habits—in short, *our whole lives,* just as the disciples prayed in the upper room!

When our sinful, selfish, prideful human hearts and minds are made into something completely new—lives that can fully manifest the power of God's love, the greatest evidence of Holy Spirit filling has just occurred! But this is the experience we need *as a church collectively*. When we have this experience as a church, the latter rain will fall, and what a work will then take place! Speaking of this coming outpouring, Ellen White writes:

> In visions of the night representations passed before
> me of a great reformatory movement among God's people.

Many were praising God. The sick were healed and other miracles were wrought. *A spirit of intercession was seen, even as was manifested before the great day of Pentecost.* Hundreds and thousands were seen visiting families and opening before them the word of God. Hearts were convicted by the power of the Holy Spirit, and a *spirit of genuine conversion* was manifest. On every side doors were thrown open to the proclamation of the truth. The world seemed lightened with the heavenly influence. Great blessings were received by the true and humble people of God. I heard voices of thanksgiving and praise, and there seemed to be a reformation such as we witnessed in 1844.[4]

I want to be part of this final revival and reformation. How about you? It is possible!

We need the fire!

Back in the mid-1800s, there was a party of explorers in central Africa that had set out to make maps of their territory. Each day they would explore and then come back to camp, gather sticks, build their fires, cook their meals, and go to bed. After following this routine for several days, they returned from exploring one evening to discover little stacks of wood arranged like miniature teepees all around their camp. Perplexed, they asked each other, "Where did all these little stacks of wood come from?"

Upon finding *even more* stacks of wood another evening, they looked up in the trees to see monkeys excitedly chattering away. Then they realized what had been happening. Each day the monkeys had watched the men build their fires and, intrigued by this process, had set out to do the same. They had done a great job, but they had one significant problem. While they put the sticks all together in perfect order, just like the men had done, no matter how hard they worked, and no matter how big their pile of sticks, they still couldn't start a fire.

We may laugh, but how often have we been just like those monkeys—great at building forms and models, but seriously lacking in Holy Spirit fire?

Carl Bates, one-time president of the Southern Baptist Convention, made a sobering statement that should cause us to search our hearts and pray as never before. He wrote, " 'If God were to take the Holy Spirit out of our midst today, about ninety-five percent of what we are doing in our churches would go on, and we would not know the difference. Yet if God had taken the Holy Spirit out of the midst of the first Christian community, about ninety-five percent of what they were doing would have ceased immediately.' "[5]

In Ezekiel 37, we find a valley of dry bones, *very dry bones,* representing the house of Israel. As the prophet Ezekiel, in vision, looked over this valley of dry bones, all hope of life seemed forever gone. However, God instructed Ezekiel to prophesy—to speak His Word to the dry bones. As he obeyed, God's Spirit entered the dry bones. They not only came together with flesh and muscle, but when God's breath entered into them, they rose up as an exceeding great army. This is the army God needs today—not a man-made army with physical weapons or artillery, but a Holy Spirit–filled army with God's spiritual artillery (see Ephesians 6).

Pleading for the backslidden, sleeping members of God's army, Ellen White writes, "The end is near, stealing upon us so stealthily, so imperceptibly, so noiselessly, like the muffled tread of the thief in the night to surprise the sleepers off guard and unready. May the Lord grant to bring his Holy Spirit upon hearts that are now at ease, that they may no longer sleep as do others, but watch and be sober."[6]

It is evident that God is working in His church today! Millions are coming to the truth, yet there are many more millions unreached with the gospel—millions locked behind closed doors, locked in tall skyscrapers, or locked in heathen lands hostile to Christianity. The task before us is really quite impossible by human standards. However, it's not up to human standards to complete it, for it will be completed by the power of the Holy Spirit.

Thankfully, we serve the God of endless possibilities—our "inexhaustible storehouse."[7] But how do we access this *inexhaustible storehouse*? It is through prayer—much prayer, agonizing prayer, persistent prayer, faith-filled prayer, united prayer, daring prayer, prayers based upon the Word, and prayers based on a *personal relationship* with Christ!

"The gospel still possesses the same power, and why should we not today witness the same results?"[8]

Are you willing to agonize and organize?

There are plenty of organizers in our church today—those who know how to make things happen and get amazing tasks accomplished. But where are the *agonizers*? Where are those who will pray through the night for the salvation of souls? Where are those who will wrestle like Jacob until the breaking of the day? Inspiration tells us, "We must look to Christ; we must resist as He resisted; we must pray as He prayed; we must agonize as He agonized, if we would conquer as He conquered."[9]

Of course, agonizing doesn't come without working! We are told that there are three *key watchwords* that must be heeded in our lives today if Satan is not to gain the advantage over us. These watchwords are "Watch, Pray, Work."[10] Not surprisingly, these three watchwords are what characterized the daily lives of Christ and His disciples. They expected much, therefore they attempted much. And so it should be with us. If we truly pray in faith, and if we truly desire to see our prayers answered, *earnest labor* will accompany our prayers. The danger today is that, as we experience success in ministry, we will keep *organizing* but stop *agonizing*.

> As activity increases and men become successful in doing any work for God, there is danger of trusting to human plans and methods. There is a tendency to pray less, and to have less faith. Like the disciples, we are in danger of losing sight of our dependence on God, and seeking to make a savior of our activity. We need to look constantly to Jesus, realizing that it is His power which does the work. While we are to labor earnestly for the salvation of the lost, we must also *take time* for meditation, for prayer, and for the study of the word of God. *Only the work accomplished with much prayer, and sanctified by the merit of Christ, will in the end prove to have been efficient for good.*[11]

As believing Adventist Christians, we profess to be people of the Bible looking for our Lord's soon coming. If this is true, we can no longer do business as usual. We can no longer do ministry as usual. We can no longer live our lives and build our careers as usual. We can no longer pray and study our Sabbath School lessons each week as usual. We cannot plan to be here for another generation as others do. We are not here on earth just to work, but to *finish God's work.*

You know, there is a difference. When many people work, they often don't worry if the work is finished or not. They are on the job to put in their hours and then clock out and go home. But when our goal is to *finish the work,* we have a specific target. And everything we have in life is put on the line for the accomplishment of this goal. With or without a paycheck, we are here to see the task completed.

Remember, for Christ's disciples, as well as for the Advent pioneers, giving the gospel to the world was not a nine-to-five job. Every opportunity found them boldly sharing the truth. It was a lifestyle, a way of life. And it should be our way of life, as well. Inspiration challenges us: "Greater light shines upon us than shone upon our fathers. We cannot be accepted or honored of God in rendering the same service, or doing the same works, that our fathers did. In order to be accepted and blessed of God as they were, we must imitate their faithfulness and zeal, improve our light as they improved theirs, and *do as they would have done had they lived in our day.* We must walk in the light which shines upon us, otherwise that light will become darkness."[12]

When I read this passage, it made me stop and think hard. Can you imagine if William Miller or James and Ellen White had what we have today? Can you imagine what Martin Luther or the other Reformers would have done with our modern technology? What about the disciples? What would they have accomplished if they had cell phones, computers, the Internet, or the ability to fly? We have all the gadgets and time-saving devices of the modern age, and yet we are so distracted, losing time, and going in circles faster than ever before. Think of it! We can communicate instantly, travel to another part of the globe in a matter of hours, and speak to millions via television and satellite, and yet the work is still not done. What is wrong?

I believe the problem is that as a body of believers, we haven't truly surrendered our all for the sake of the gospel. We aren't willing to *spend and be spent* as the disciples were, and because of this the latter rain can't fall. We are holding back when God is calling us to go all the way.

Ellen White exclaims that "the Lord can do more in one hour than we can do in a whole lifetime, and when He sees that His people are fully consecrated, let me tell you, a great work will be done in a short time, and the message of truth is to be carried into the dark places of the earth, where it has never been proclaimed. . . ."[13]

The final call

The Duke of Wellington was listening to a group of Christian men talk as they discussed the possibility of success in missionary efforts among the unsaved. They turned to the duke and asked whether, in his judgment, such efforts were likely to prove a success in comparison to the expenditure and cost. The old soldier replied, " 'Gentlemen, what are your marching orders? Success is not the question for you to discuss. If I read your orders aright, they run thus, "Go ye into all the world, and preach the gospel to every creature." Gentlemen, obey your marching orders.' "[14]

The question to ask as we work in the final days of earth's history is not, "Do we have enough resources?" or "Will our efforts be successful?" The question is rather, "Are we willing to be faithful to God's call regardless of the outcome, regardless of the sacrifice?"

Paris Reidhead, a missionary from the mid-1900s, tells the story of two young Moravians who heard of an island in the West Indies where an atheist British slave trader had two thousand to three thousand slaves. No preachers or clergy were ever allowed on the island, as he didn't want his slaves to learn about Christ. However, the thought that all these slaves might live and die without ever knowing the gospel was too much for these young Moravian men.

So they thought of a plan. They decided to sell themselves to the British slave trader. This they did, then they used the money from the sale to pay their passage to the island where they were committing their lives to his service.

As the ship that would carry the young men to their destination left the pier in Hamburg, Germany, many of the Moravians came to see these two lads off. The families were weeping for they knew they'd never see these boys again. Some wondered why they were going and questioned the wisdom of it. The boys were in their early twenties with their whole lives ahead of them. For them, this wasn't a four-year term of mission service. They'd sold themselves into lifelong slavery, simply that as slaves they could be as Christians where these other slaves were.

As the gap widened between the dock and the ship, one lad with his arm linked through the arm of his fellow raised his hand high in the air and shouted across the water the last words that were ever heard from them. They were these: " 'May the Lamb that was slain receive the reward of His suffering.' "[15] From then on, this became the call of the Moravian missionaries!

God is looking for faithful men and women—men and women who will pick up the torch, not worried about applause, not worried about the wages they will or won't receive, and not worried about the sacrifices they will endure. God is looking for faithful men and women who will recognize the urgency of the times and be willing to *agonize and organize,* realizing that the success of their mission lies only in their steadfast dependence upon Him. He's waiting for men and woman who will carry His torch over the finish line so we can go home.

Will you be this man or woman? Will you answer His call? Will you join other Seventh-day Adventist members from around the world in seeking for the mighty outpouring of the Holy Spirit? Will you join us in crying out to God for heaven's fullness? Will you seek God with your Division, Union, Conference, Mission, local church, or ministry? Will you petition God in prayer bands, with your families, in your homes, with your colleagues, and with other members in your local church, so that every church can become a house of prayer?

God is calling us to a deeper commitment in these critical hours of earth's history—deeper than ever before! There is no more time to play church. The games are over. This is the last, urgent call for total surrender and utter abandonment to Christ and to the fulfilling of His great commission. Everything we have in life must be put on the line for the fulfillment of this task.

Let us not be content with a half-work any longer, for *half-surrender equals no surrender*. Let us not be satisfied to be spiritual dwarfs another moment. Let us not be content with a superficial, wilderness spirituality, where we live three inches below the water-line gasping for breath and just trying to survive. Let us not be content with superficial praying, nor with mere superficial blessings. God has much more He longs to give. All heaven is waiting to be poured out. *But it's waiting for us to pray!*

This book is coming to an end, but our amazing journey with God is only beginning. We've only begun to see the endless possibilities of what He can do as we go deeper and deeper in our walk with Him. So let us dare to move forward on our knees, humbly continuing to ask for more until the final chapter of Acts is completed. The call has been given. Let's answer God's call and get ready to go home.

Now unto him that is able to do exceeding abundantly above all that we ask or think, according to the power that worketh in us, unto him be glory in the church by Christ Jesus throughout all ages, world without end. Amen.

—*Ephesians 3:20, 21*

Endnotes

Foreword

1. This is the yearly fall meetings at the General Conference headquarters in Maryland, where all the leaders from the worldwide Seventh-day Adventist Church meet each year to make plans for the coming year.

2. Ellen G. White, *Last Day Events* (Nampa, Idaho: Pacific Press® Publishing Association, 1992), 189; emphasis added.

3. Ellen G. White, *Testimonies to Southern Africa* (Washington, D.C.: Ellen G. White Estate, Inc., 1977), 53.

4. Jerry Page is General Conference Ministerial Secretary, and Janet Page is General Conference Associate Ministerial Secretary for Prayer Ministries and Pastoral Families.

Preface

1. Ellen G. White, *Counsels for the Church* (Nampa, Idaho: Pacific Press®, 1991), 319.

2. Ellen G. White, *The Ministry of Healing* (Nampa, Idaho: Pacific Press®, 1991), 509; emphasis added.

Chapter 1

1. "How Many Stars Are There in the Universe?" Universe Today, accessed December 7, 2013, http://www.universetoday.com/102630/how-many-stars-are-there-in-the-universe/.

2. "How 'Fast' Is the Speed of Light?" LTP, accessed March 14, 2014, https://www.grc.nasa.gov/www/k-12/Numbers/Math/Mathematical_Thinking/how_fast_is_the_speed.htm.

3. "Observable Universe," Wikipedia, accessed March 14, 2014, http://en.wikipedia.org/wiki/Observable_universe.

4. Ellen G. White, *Patriarchs and Prophets* (Nampa, Idaho: Pacific Press®, 2005), 116.

5. Ellen G. White, *Gospel Workers* (Washington, D.C.: Review and Herald® Publishing Association, 1915), 60.

6. White, *Gospel Workers,* 1892 edition, 52.

7. Ellen G. White, *Christian Service* (Washington, D.C.: General Conference of Seventh-day Adventists, 1947), 261; emphasis added.

8. Ellen G. White, *The Upward Look* (Washington, D.C.: Review and Herald®, 1982), 195.

9. White, *Christian Service,* 254.

10. Ellen G. White, *The Desire of Ages* (Nampa, Idaho: Pacific Press®, 2005), 672; emphasis added.

11. Ellen G. White, *The Review and Herald,* May 19, 1904.

Chapter 2

1. Ellen G. White, *Prayer* (Nampa, Idaho: Pacific Press®, 2002), 105.

2. Francis D. Nichol, ed., *The Seventh-day Adventist Bible Commentary* (Hagerstown, Md.: Review and Herald®, 1953, 1976), 2:1004.

3. Ellen G. White, *From Eternity Past* (Boise, Idaho: Pacific Press®, 1983, 1986), 361, 362.

4. Ellen G. White, *Welfare Ministry* (Washington, D.C.: Review and Herald®, 1952), 123, 124.

5. Claude Chilton Jr., quoted in E. M. Bounds, *The Complete Works of E. M. Bounds on Prayer* (Grand Rapids, Mich.: Baker Publishing Group, 2004), 7.

6. Bounds, *The Complete Works of E. M. Bounds on Prayer,* 460.

Chapter 3

1. Ellen G. White, *Steps to Christ* (Mountain View, Calif.: Pacific Press®, 1956), 93.

2. Ellen G. White, *Christ's Object Lessons* (Washington, D.C: Review and Herald®, 1941), 129, 130.

3. Paraphrase of Exodus 32:11–13.

4. White, *Patriarchs and Prophets,* 318.

5. Eric and Leslie Ludy, *Wrestling Prayer: A Passionate Communion With God* (Eugene,

Ore.: Winston and Brooks, Inc., 2009), 18, 19; emphasis in the original.

6. "Indite" is a legal term that means God is going to arrange things in such a way that the answer will be Yes.

7. Ellen G. White, *General Conference Bulletin,* April 2, 1903, para. 6.

8. *Pacific Union Recorder,* February 16, 1905, para. 4.

9. White, *Christ's Object Lessons,* 159.

10. Ibid., 159, 160.

Chapter 4

1. This is a Seventh-day Adventist Church worldwide prayer initiative that takes place every January. To learn more, visit http://www.tendaysofprayer.org.

2. Greg Budd, *Kidnapped!* (Nampa, Idaho: Pacific Press®, 2013).

3. White, *Gospel Workers,* 161.

4. White, *The Desire of Ages,* 300.

5. Quoted in V. Raymond Edman, *They Found the Secret* (Grand Rapids, Mich.: Zondervan Publishing House, 1984), 20, 21.

6. Ibid., 21.

7. Think you're too old to work for God? Dave and Beverly Waid began working in Bangladesh when Dave was already in his early seventies, and he turned eighty-six while I was there. Their unselfish work has touched the lives of the children in their orphanage, the lives of hundreds more through their efforts to feed children in schools throughout the country, and even the lives of those in the United States who have been inspired to missionary labor. For more information and how to support the Waids in this beautiful ministry, visit http://www.banglahope.org.

8. "Himself," by Dr. A. B. Simpson, in *They Found the Secret,* 13, 14.

Chapter 5

1. Captain E. G. Carré, ed., *Praying Hyde, Apostle of Prayer: The Life Story of John Hyde* (Alachua, Fla.: Bridge-Logos, 1982), 22.

2. Ibid., 23.

3. White, *Christ's Object Lessons,* 69.

4. Ibid., 146.

5. White, *Steps to Christ,* 98.

6. Ellen G. White, *The Great Controversy* (Nampa, Idaho: Pacific Press®, 2005), 209.

7. Ibid., 210.

8. Ibid.

9. Ellen G. White, *In Heavenly Places* (Washington, D.C.: Review and Herald®, 1967), 82.

10. White, *Testimonies to Southern Africa,* 67.

11. Paraphrase of Jeremiah 33:3; Isaiah 55:8, 9; Matthew 7:7, 8; James 4:2; Matthew 6:33.

Chapter 6

1. Ron E. M. Clouzet, *Adventism's Greatest Need: The Outpouring of the Holy Spirit* (Nampa, Idaho: Pacific Press®, 2011), 166.

2. White, *The Review and Herald,* March 19, 1895.

3. Clouzet, *Adventism's Greatest Need,* 168.

4. White, *Patriarchs and Prophets,* 203.

5. Ellen G. White, *Sermons and Talks* (Silver Spring, Md.: Ellen G. White Estate, Inc., 1990), 1:391.

6. Jerry Page, Revival and Reformation, Shenyang, China, http://www.revivaland reformation.org/content_series/11/entries/8#.U13z3RZq6Os.

7. J. Oswald Sanders, *Prayer Power Unlimited* (Chicago: Moody Press, 1977), 120.

8. Ellen G. White, *Selected Messages,* bk. 1 (Washington, D.C.: Review and Herald®, 1958), 124.

9. White, *Counsels for the Church,* 185, 186; emphasis added.

10. Ibid., 185.

11. Ricardo Graham, "Pray About It," *Pacific Union Recorder* 114, no. 3 (2014), http://pacificunionrecorder.org/issue/90/9/1740.

Chapter 7

1. White, *Gospel Workers,* 258.

2. Wesley L. Duewel, *Mighty Prevailing Prayer* (Grand Rapids, Mich.: Zondervan Publishing House, 1990), 157, 158.

3. White, *The Desire of Ages,* 125.

4. Ellen G. White, *Manuscript Releases* (Silver Spring, Md.: Ellen G. White Estate, Inc., 1981), 9:303; emphasis added.

5. Ellen G. White, *Evangelism* (Washington, D.C.: Review and Herald®, 1946), 414.

6. Pseudonym used for safety of individual.

7. Ibid.

8. Ibid.

9. This story is based on Hanh's experience as told in an interview with Isah Young, a pastor in the Southeastern California Conference, in the United States. It is used with permission from Adventist Southeast Asia Projects Ministries' DVD titled, *Our 10 Favorites: Mission Stories From ASAP Ministries,* vol. 2.

10. A former hip-hop artist who now loves to preach the gospel, Pastor Myers is the founder of ARME Bible Camp Ministries, which was established to train people how to study their Bibles more effectively. For more information, you can visit us online at http://www.armeministries.org.

11. The name ARME comes from two words put together, "ARM-ME." Our slogan is "Arming people with tools for biblical revival." Some team members like to say that it's an acronym that stands for "Adventist Revival Movement for the End time."

12. White, *The Review and Herald,* June 30, 1896.

Chapter 8

1. Pastor Jerry Page is currently the Ministerial Association Secretary at the General Conference of Seventh-day Adventists. Janet, also working for the Ministerial Association, is Associate Secretary for Pastoral Spouses, Families, and Prayer. Because of their leadership and powerful testimony, they are in high demand as speakers all over the world, and they travel extensively promoting revival and reformation.

2. White, *The Great Controversy,* 525.

3. White, *Christ's Object Lessons,* 331.

4. Ellen G. White, *The Acts of the Apostles* (Nampa, Idaho: Pacific Press®, 2005), 594.

5. These donation values are from a few years back. Updated values can be obtained from ASAP Ministries at http://www.asapministries.org.

6. Ibid.

7. Max Lucado, quoted in "Quotes on Prayer," K-LOVE Morning Show on Facebook, https://www.facebook.com/notes/k-love-morning-show/quotes-on-prayer/393332117479.

8. Norman Grubb, *Rees Howells: Intercessor: The Story of a Life Lived for God* (Fort Washington, Penn.: Lutterworth Press, 1952), 231.

9. Ibid., 245.

10. Ibid., 253.

11. Ibid., 257.

12. White, *Patriarchs and Prophets,* 550.

13. White, *In Heavenly Places,* 75.

14. Bounds, *The Complete Works of E. M. Bounds on Prayer,* 447.

Chapter 9

1. Author unknown. Slightly modified from a handout from Pastor Jerry Page in 2010.

2. Ellen G. White, *Testimonies for the Church* (Nampa, Idaho: Pacific Press®, 1948), 1:158.

3. Ellen G. White, *Education* (Nampa, Idaho: Pacific Press®, 1952), 260, 261; emphasis added.

4. Greg Budd, *One Miracle After Another: The Pavel Goia Story* (Hagerstown, Md.: Review and Herald®, 2009).

5. "Prayer Quotes," HopeFaithPrayer, accessed April 4, 2014, http://hopefaithprayer .com/prayernew/prayer-quotes/.

6. "Famous Prayer Quotes," Christ Bible Church, accessed April 4, 2014, http://www .christbiblechurch.org/famous_prayer_quotes.htm.

7. "Christian Prayer Quotations," Christian Prayer Quotes, accessed April 4, 2014, http:// www.christian-prayer-quotes.christian-attorney.net. Emphasis in the original.

8. White, *The Desire of Ages,* 362.

9. The QBC Daily Nugget, accessed April 4, 2014, http://www.qbchurch.org /dn/20130920-www.qbchurch.org-qbc_daily_nugget.pdf.

10. Ellen G. White, *Our High Calling* (Washington, D.C.: Review and Herald®, 1961), 44.

Chapter 10

1. Ellen G. White, *Messages to Young People* (Washington, D.C.: Review and Herald®, 1930), 96.

2. White, *Manuscript Releases,* 7:224.

3. Bounds, *The Complete Works of E. M. Bounds on Prayer,* 464.

4. "M'Cheyne Quotations," The Robert Murray M'Cheyne Resource, accessed May 22, 2014, http://www.mcheyne.info/quotes.php.

5. "In the Secret Place," Set Apart Girl, The Ministry of Leslie Ludy, accessed April 13, 2013, http://setapartgirl.com/magazine/article/09-1-10/secret-place.

6. White, *Steps to Christ,* 70.

7. Ellen G. White, *Child Guidance* (Nashville, Tenn.: Southern Publishing Association, 1954), 523.

8. To learn more and join thousands of others reading through the Bible, visit http://www.revivedbyhisword.org.

9. Ellen White (1827–1915), although receiving only a third-grade education and suffering with poor health for much of her early life, became one of the most prolific authors of all time. She wrote more than five thousand periodical articles and forty books during her lifetime. Today, more than one hundred titles are available in English alone. She is also the most translated female non-fiction writer in the history of literature. Her life-changing masterpiece on successful Christian living, *Steps to Christ,* has been published in more than 140 languages. Her writings cover a broad range of subjects, including religion, education, health, social and family relationships, prophecy, publishing, and Christian leadership.

Although Ellen White herself never claimed to be a prophet, she did see herself as a "messenger," and her writings have impacted countless millions both inside and outside the church. The more I read her works, the more I appreciate her, and also the more I'm inspired to get into the Word and learn of Christ. For more, visit http://www.whiteestate.org/about/egwbio.asp.

10. White, *Steps to Christ,* 90.

11. To access this Bible study handbook, visit http://www.revivalandreformation.org.

12. White, *Prayer,* 292.

13. White, *Steps to Christ,* 94.

14. White, *Prayer,* 10.

15. White, *Manuscript Releases,* 19:258.

Chapter 11

1. White, *Christ's Object Lessons,* 315, 316.

2. White, *Christian Service,* 41.

3. White, *Patriarchs and Prophets,* 497; emphasis added.

4. White, *Christian Service,* 227.

5. White, *Gospel Workers,* 272.

6. White, *Steps to Christ,* 47; emphasis in the original.

7. White, *The Review and Herald,* June 4, 1889.

Chapter 12

1. "Great Wall of China," Wikipedia, accessed April 13, 2013, http://en.wikipedia.org/wiki/Great_Wall_of_China.

2. Talk on fortification by Eric and Leslie Ludy, unknown date.

3. Taken from "The Sacred Shield" lecture by Leslie Ludy, given July 2010. Used with permission.

4. White, *The Ministry of Healing,* 113.

5. See Exodus 15:26; Psalms 30:2; 103:3; Jeremiah 30:17; Ezekiel 36:26; 2 Corinthians 5:17; James 5:14, 15; and 3 John 1:2.

6. White, *Christ's Object Lessons,* 205, 206.

7. Paul Washer, *The Gospel's Power and Message* (Grand Rapids, Mich.: Reformation Heritage Books, 2012), 62.

8. White, *Steps to Christ,* 52.

9. White, *The Ministry of Healing,* 470, 471.

Chapter 13

1. Inspired by "The Sacred Shield" lecture by Leslie Ludy, given July 2010. Used with permission.

2. Ellen G. White, *Counsels on Stewardship* (Washington, D.C.: Review and Herald®, 1940), 85; emphasis added.

3. White, *Prayer,* 276.

4. White, *Christ's Object Lessons,* 158.

Chapter 14

1. White, *The Desire of Ages,* 352.

2. White, *Our High Calling,* 330.

3. Quoted in Clouzet, *Adventism's Greatest Need,* 148.

4. White, *Christ's Object Lessons,* 148.

5. Ellen G. White, *Mind, Character, and Personality* (Nashville, Tenn.: Southern Publishing Association, 1977), 2:650, 651.

6. White, *Steps to Christ,* 23.

7. White, *Christ's Object Lessons,* 157.

8. White, *Counsels for the Church,* 78.

9. White, *Testimonies for the Church,* 8:21, emphasis added.

Chapter 15

1. White, *The Great Controversy,* 600.

2. Ellen G. White, *Darkness Before Dawn* (Nampa, Idaho: Pacific Press®, 1997), 12; emphasis added.

3. White, *The Desire of Ages,* 713, 714.

4. White, *Testimonies for the Church,* 5:294.

5. White, *The Great Controversy,* 621.

6. White, *Steps to Christ,* 57.

7. White, *Prayer,* 101.

8. White, *Steps to Christ,* 34.

9. White, *The Desire of Ages,* 125.

10. Ellen G. White, *Pastoral Ministry* (Washington, D.C.: Ellen G. White Estate, Inc., 1995), 25.

Chapter 16

1. Paraphrase of Numbers 13:28, 31.

2. Paraphrase of Numbers 14:7, 8; 13:30.

3. White, *Patriarchs and Prophets,* 388.

4. Paraphrase of Numbers 14:11.

5. Paraphrase of Numbers 14:23, 28, 29, 31, 34.

6. White, *Patriarchs and Prophets,* 293.

7. Ellen G. White, *Prophets and Kings* (Nampa, Idaho: Pacific Press®, 2005), 243.

8. White, *Patriarchs and Prophets,* 657.

9. White, *Education,* 253, 254; emphasis added.

10. White, *Testimonies for the Church,* 6:393.

11. White, *Christ's Object Lessons,* 147.

12. White, *Evangelism,* 633.

13. Ellen G. White, *The Bible Echo,* September 24, 1894, para. 4.

14. LeRoy Froom, *The Coming of the Comforter* (Washington, D.C.: Review and Herald®, 1928), 157, as quoted in an audio sermon by Shane Anderson, April 2010.

15. White, *Our High Calling,* 119.

16. Froom, *The Coming of the Comforter,* 156, as quoted in an audio sermon by Shane Anderson, April 2010.

17. White, *Prayer,* 268.

18. Ellen G. White, *Lift Him Up* (Washington, D.C.: Review and Herald®, 1988), 372.

19. White, *Steps to Christ,* 94, 95.

20. Quote by George Bernard Shaw, cited in a sermon by Shane Anderson.

Chapter 17

1. This story is used by permission of ASAP Ministries and comes from the recently released DVD *United in Prayer.* To read more amazing stories like this, visit www.asapministries.org.

2. "Hudson Taylor—Powerful Quotes on Prayer," SermonIndex.net, accessed May 26, 2014, http://www.sermonindex.net/modules/newbb/viewtopic.php?topic_id=36715&forum=34&5.

3. White, *The Desire of Ages,* 431; emphasis added.

4. Paraphrase of Matthew 17:21.

5. Paraphrase of Matthew 6:17, 18.

6. See Ellen G. White, *Medical Ministry* (Mountain View, Calif.: Pacific Press®, 1932, 1963), 283.

7. Albert Barnes, *Notes on the Bible,* "Isaiah Chapter 58," Sacred-texts.com, accessed May 26, 2014, http://sacred-texts.com/bib/cmt/barnes/isa058.htm.

8. White, *Christ's Object Lessons,* 59.

9. Duewel, *Mighty Prevailing Prayer,* 181.

10. James White, *The Review and Herald,* editorial, April 25, 1865; January 31, 1865; February 21, 1865.

11. Ellen G. White, *Counsels on Diet and Foods* (Washington, D.C.: Review and Herald®, 1938 1946), 187.

12. Ibid., 188.

13. White, *Selected Messages,* bk. 2, 364.

14. White, *Testimonies for the Church,* 5:134.

15. Ellen G. White, *Daughters of God* (Hagerstown Md.: Review and Herald®, 1998), 46.

16. White, *The Desire of Ages,* 431.

17. See *Adventist Review,* March 27, 1980, 8.

18. Ibid.

19. White, *Counsels on Diet and Foods,* 187, 188.

20. White, *Testimonies for the Church,* 2:202.

21. Ellen G. White, *Counsels on Health* (Nampa, Idaho: Pacific Press®, 1951), 148; White, *Counsels on Diet and Foods,* 190; and G. D. Strunk, "Fasting," *Canadian Adventist Messenger* 27, no. 24 (December 21, 1978): 5.

22. White, *Counsels on Diet and Foods,* 189.

23. White, *The Desire of Ages,* 278.

24. Elmer L. Towns, *The Daniel Fast for Spiritual Breakthrough* (Ventura, Calif.: Regal, 2010).

Chapter 18

1. White, *The Great Controversy,* 251.

2. White, *Evangelism,* 294.

3. Incidentally, after spending her early young adult years as a single woman waiting for the right man, Raluca (now in her thirties) recently married a God-fearing German man named Roman, who she met at one of the conferences where she was leading prayer. I know this is *not* what she had in mind when she prayed: "Give me Germany, Lord, or I die!" but God does have a unique sense of humor, and it's quite likely that much of Raluca's future prayers and ministry will continue to focus on the people of Germany.

4. Ellen G. White, *Christ Triumphant* (Hagerstown, Md.: Review and Herald®, 1999), 54.

5. Adapted from the sermon "Gritted Teeth," by Eric Ludy, given May 1, 2011. Used with permission.

6. White, *Education,* 256.

7. White, *Christ's Object Lessons,* 175.

8. White, *Testimonies for the Church,* 8:10, 12.

9. L. B. Cowman, *Streams in the Desert* (Grand Rapids, Mich.: Zondervan, 1996), cited in "May 12," e-Sword 10.1.0.

10. Ibid.

11. White, *The Great Controversy,* 621.

12. White, *General Conference Daily Bulletin,* April 13, 1891, para. 31.

13. A few of my favorite faith-building books are *A Thousand Shall Fall,* by Susi Hasel Mundy (Hagerstown, Md.: Review and Herald®, 2001); *One Miracle After Another: The Pavel Goia Story,* by Greg Budd (Hagerstown, Md.: Review and Herald®, 2010); *The Kneeling Christian,* by an unknown Christian (CreateSpace Independent Publishing Platform, 2009); *Ellen White: Woman of Vision,* by Arthur L. White (Hagerstown, Md.: Review and Herald®, 2000); *Mission Pilot: High Adventure in Dangerous Places,* by Eileen E. Lantry (Nampa,

Idaho: Pacific Press®, 2002); and *Lessons on Faith,* by Alonzo T. Jones and Ellet J. Waggoner (Ringgold, Ga.: TEACH Services, Inc., 1995).

Chapter 19

1. Pseudonyms used to protect the privacy of individuals.

2. Ibid.

3. L. B. Cowman, *Streams in the Desert,* cited in "February 9," e-Sword 10.1.0.

4. White, *Steps to Christ,* 97.

5. White, *The Ministry of Healing,* 474.

6. White, *Prayer,* 102.

7. "David Wilkerson Devotions: When All Means Fail," accessed May 28, 2014, http://davidwilkersontoday.blogspot.com/2011/04/when-all-means-fail.html.

8. White, *Prophets and Kings,* 174, 175; emphasis added.

Chapter 20

1. White, *The Review and Herald,* December 8, 1904, para. 8.

2. White, *Selected Messages,* bk. 1, 344.

3. White, *Steps to Christ,* 95.

4. Ivor Myers, *Operation Blueprint: Earth's Final Movie: The Ultimate Search & Rescue Mission* (Roseville, Calif.: Amazing Facts, Inc., 2013). Outline adapted and reprinted with Pastor Myers's permission.

5. Cardinal Gibbons, quoted in the *Catholic Mirror,* September 23, 1893, states, " 'The Catholic church by virtue of her divine mission changed the day [of worship] from Saturday to Sunday,' " quoted in Myers, *Operation Blueprint,* 53.

6. White, *The Great Controversy,* 595.

7. Ken McFarland, *The Called . . . the Chosen: God Has Always Had a People* (Hagerstown, Md.: Review and Herald Graphics, 2006), 76.

Chapter 21

1. Thoughts gleaned from White, *Patriarchs and Prophets,* 359.

2. White, *The Great Controversy,* 595.

3. Ellen White never claimed to be a prophet, but her life bore witness to the fact that she was. Many of her visions were accompanied by supernatural physical phenomena, such as absence of breathing for long periods of time, accurate foreknowledge of coming events, incredible strength (so that strong men could not move her), and more. Her visions all pointed to Scripture as the authoritative Word of God and never contradicted it. To learn more about her ministry, see note 9 under chapter 10. You may also visit http://www.whiteestate.org /about/egwbio.asp.

4. Ellen G. White, *Early Writings* (Washington, D.C.: Review and Herald®, 1945), 56.

5. Paraphrase of Daniel 1:8.

6. White, *The Great Controversy,* 464; emphasis added.

7. Ellen G. White, *The Faith I Live By* (Washington, D.C.: Review and Herald®, 1958), 326.

8. White, *Pastoral Ministry,* 24.

9. White, *Testimonies for the Church,* 6:426, 427.

Chapter 22

1. White, *Lift Him Up,* 213.

2. "I Will Do a New Thing," AudioVerse, accessed June 1, 2014, https://www.audioverse .org/english/sermons/recordings/5033/i-will-do-a-new-thing.html.

3. White, *The Great Controversy,* 464; emphasis added.

4. Ibid., 465; emphasis added.

5. Speaking in tongues is never incoherent babbling. According to Scripture (see Acts 2:4–12 and 1 Corinthians 14:27, 28), it is speaking another language that someone can understand. If no one can understand it, it shouldn't be spoken in the congregation.

6. White, *The Great Controversy,* 463.

7. Inspiration from White, *Last Day Events,* 159, 160.

8. Inspiration from White, *The Acts of the Apostles,* 64.

9. *Merriam-Webster's Collegiate Dictionary,* 11th ed., s.v. "emergent."

10. John MacArthur, *Reckless Faith* (Wheaton, Ill.: Crossway Books, 1994), 21.

11. Brian D. McLaren, *A Generous Orthodoxy* (Grand Rapids, Mich.: Zondervan, 2004).

12. Howard A. Peth, *The Dangers of Contemplative Prayer* (Nampa, Idaho: Pacific Press®, 2012), 58, 59.

13. Leonard Sweet, *Quantum Spirituality* (Trotwood, Ohio: United Theological Seminary, 1991), 76.

14. Dan Kimball, *The Emerging Church: Vintage Christianity for New Generations* (Grand

Rapids, Mich.: Zondervan, 2003), 60.

15. Ibid.; emphasis added.

16. Peth, *The Dangers of Contemplative Prayer,* 59.

17. As cited in an interview with Pastor Steve Wohlberg, director/speaker of White Horse Media ministry, for *Advindicate:* http://advindicate.com/articles/2013/10/25/interview -with-steve-wolhberg-on-the-emerging-church. Emphasis added.

18. White, *The Review and Herald,* March 22, 1892; emphasis added.

19. White, *The Review and Herald,* September 17, 1903; emphasis added.

Chapter 23

1. "Know Your Money," United States Secret Service, accessed April 13, 2013, http:// www.secretservice.gov/money_detect.shtml.

2. Mark Finley, "Biblical Spirituality: Rediscovering Our Biblical Roots or Embracing the East?" *Ministry* Magazine, accessed May 7, 2013, https://www.ministrymagazine.org /archive/2012/08/biblical-spirituality-rediscovering-our-biblical-roots-or-embracing -the-east. Emphasis added.

3. "Finding God in All Things," Jesuits, accessed May 7, 2013, http://www.jesuit.org /spirituality.

4. Inspiration from "Spiritual Direction Key for Discernment," thinkJESUIT.org, accessed May 7, 2013, http://www.thinkjesuit.org/spiritual-direction.

5. "The Jesuits," Jesuits, accessed May 7, 2013, http://www.jesuit.org/aboutus.

6. *Brief Bible Readings for Busy People* (Hagerstown, Md.: Review and Herald®, 1950), 19, as quoted in Myers, *Operation Blueprint,* 52.

7. "The Jesuits," Jesuits, accessed May 7, 2013, http://jesuits.org/aboutus.

8. White, *The Acts of the Apostles,* 474; emphasis added.

9. White, *Selected Messages,* bk. 1, 200.

10. Ibid.

11. White, *Testimonies for the Church,* 5:294.

12. From downloadable brochure, "Method of Centering Prayer," inspired by the book *Open Mind, Open Heart* by Thomas Keating (New York: Bloomsbury Academic, 2006), a monk and priest, known as one of the architects of centering prayer, 2. http://www .contemplativeoutreach.org/category/category/centering-prayer.

13. Thomas Merton, *Conjectures of a Guilty Bystander* (New York: Doubleday Publishers, 1989), 157, 158.

14. Paraphrase of Genesis 3:5.

15. White, *The Great Controversy,* 511–517.

16. Thanks to Mark Finley and others for their research in this area.

17. White, *The Great Controversy,* 557, 558.

18. Apostolic Letter *Rosarium Virginis Mariae* of the Supreme Pontiff John Paul II, #40, as cited in Rick Howard, *The Omega Rebellion: What Every Adventist Needs to Know . . . Now* (Coldwater, Mich.: Remnant Publications, 2010), 190; emphasis added.

19. White, *The Great Controversy,* 561, 562.

20. Howard, *The Omega Rebellion,* 17; emphasis in the original.

21. Mark Finley, *Revive Us Again* (Nampa, Idaho: Pacific Press®, 2010), 75.

22. "Our Labyrinths," Grace Cathedral, accessed April 14, 2014, http://www.gracecathedral .org/visit/labyrinth/. For more research, visit the Veriditas homepage at http://www.veriditas .org/guidelines.

23. White, *Darkness Before Dawn,* 43.

24. White, *Last Day Events,* 170.

25. White, *The Great Controversy,* 593.

26. Mark Finley, "Biblical Spirituality: Rediscovering Our Biblical Roots or Embracing the East?"

27. Thanks to Mark Finley for his research in this area.

28. White, *The Desire of Ages,* 83.

29. Ibid.

Chapter 24

1. Pseudonym used to protect the privacy of the individual.

2. Ellen G. White, *Ye Shall Receive Power* (Hagerstown, Md.: Review and Herald®, 1995), 322; emphasis added.

3. White, *Manuscript Releases,* 21:147, 148.

4. White, *Selected Messages,* bk. 1, 202.

5. Ellen G. White, *Testimony Treasures* (Mountain View, Calif.: Pacific Press®, 1949), 1:169; emphasis added.

6. Ellen G. White, *The Voice in Speech and Song* (Nampa, Idaho: Pacific Press®, 1988), 325, 326.

7. White, *The Great Controversy,* 465; emphasis added.

8. White, *Selected Messages,* bk. 1, 18.

9. Ellen G. White, *Thoughts From the Mount of Blessing* (Mountain View, Calif.: Pacific Press®, 1956), 146.

10. White, *Manuscript Releases*, 18:53.

11. White, *Testimonies for the Church*, 5:46.

12. Ellen G. White, *Spiritual Gifts* (Washington, D.C.: Review and Herald®, 1945), 3:19, 20.

13. White, *Last Day Events*, 189.

Chapter 25

1. White, *The Review and Herald*, August 22, 1899, para. 10; emphasis added.

2. White, *Spiritual Gifts*, 4b:31.

3. For more resources and ideas for prayer groups and to download the resource *Praying for Rain*, visit http://www.revivalandreformation.org/.

4. White, *Child Guidance*, 524.

5. White, *Manuscript Releases*, 10:130.

6. White, *Our High Calling*, 130.

7. White, *Testimonies for the Church*, 4:315.

8. White, *Counsels for the Church*, 292; emphasis added.

9. Ivan Charles Blake, "Pastor for Life," *Ministry* Magazine, accessed November 10, 2013, https://www.ministrymagazine.org/archive/2010/07-august/pastor-for-life.

10. White, *The Review and Herald*, November 10, 1885; emphasis added.

11. White, *Counsels for the Church*, 293.

12. White, *Selected Messages*, bk. 1, 326.

13. Ellen G. White, *Fundamentals of Christian Education* (Nashville, Tenn.: Southern Publishing Association, 1923), 239.

14. White, *The Review and Herald*, December 16, 1890.

15. Ibid.

16. White, quoted in *The Seventh-day Adventist Bible Commentary*, 2:997.

17. White, *Counsels on Health*, 373.

18. White, *Mind, Character, and Personality*, 2:456.

19. White, *Testimonies for the Church*, 5:645.

20. White, *Selected Messages*, bk. 1, 327.

21. White, *Testimonies for the Church*, 3:429.

Chapter 26

1. "Quotes, Major W. Ian Thomas," Living En the Word, accessed April 13, 2013, http://

livingentheword.wordpress.com/quotes/.

2. White, *Testimonies for the Church,* 8:104–106; emphasis in the original.

3. Andrew Murray, *Humility and Absolute Surrender* (Peabody, Mass.: Hendrickson Publishers, 2005), 25, 27.

4. "Holy Spirit Active at Pastors Retreat," Revival and Reformation, accessed November 20, 2013, http://www.revivalandreformation.org/content_series/11/entries/17 #.U1mDOxZq6Os.

5. White, *Pastoral Ministry,* 24, 25.

6. White, *Testimonies for the Church,* 5:17, 18.

7. White, *Fundamentals of Christian Education,* 511; emphasis added.

8. White, *The Review and Herald,* November 17, 1891; emphasis added.

9. Ellen G. White, *Sons and Daughters of God* (Hagerstown, Md.: Review and Herald®, 1955, 1983), 207.

10. Clouzet, *Adventism's Greatest Need,* 66..

11. Collin Hansen and John Woodbridge, *A God-Sized Vision: Revival Stories That Stretch and Stir* (Grand Rapids, Mich.: Zondervan, 2010), 102.

12. "Conviction for Sin Necessary: Conviction and a Revival of Holiness," accessed June 3, 2014, http://www.liftupusa.com/conviction.html.

13. Wesley L. Duewel, *Revival Fire* (Grand Rapids, Mich.: Zondervan Publishing House, 1995), 210.

14. Clouzet, *Adventism's Greatest Need,* 66.

15. Ibid.

16. White, *Gospel Workers,* 1892 edition, 224; emphasis added.

17. White, *Selected Messages,* bk. 1, 124.

18. White, *Christ's Object Lessons,* 59.

19. White, *Manuscript Releases,* 1:180, 181.

Chapter 27

1. Thanks to Pastor Dwight Nelson for this thought, who, among many others, has inspired me to keep daring to ask for much more!

2. See Acts 2. Looking at the context, we see this to be *other languages,* not an incoherent, chaotic babbling that many claim as "tongues" today.

3. Ellen G. White, *Signs of the Times,* March 15, 1910.

4. White, *Counsels on Health,* 580; emphasis added.

5. Quoted in Clouzet, *Adventism's Greatest Need,* 43. Originally cited in David Watson, *I*

Believe in the Church (Grand Rapids, Mich.: Eerdmans, 1978), 166.

6. White, *General Conference Bulletin,* February 4, 1893, para. 11.

7. Ellen G. White, *That I May Know Him* (Washington, D.C.: Review and Herald®, 1964), 338.

8. White, *The Desire of Ages,* 823.

9. White, *That I May Know Him,* 34.

10. White, *Christian Service,* 106.

11. White, *The Desire of Ages,* 362; emphasis added.

12. White, *Testimonies for the Church,* 1:262; emphasis added.

13. White, *Manuscript Releases,* 5:347.

14. White, *Gospel Workers,* 115.

15. "Ten Shekels and a Shirt," Paris Reidhead Bible Teaching Ministries, accessed April 28, 2014, http://www.parisreidheadbibleteachingministries.org/tenshekels.shtml.